September 1914: the whole of Europe was at ˙
Archduke Franz Ferdinand and his beloved w
Sarajevo on 28 June 1914.

In France and Belgium, the British Expeditionary Force were struggling to hold back the German hordes as their casualties began to mount. Back in Britain, the call went out for volunteers to join the 'Pals' battalions which were springing up in the northern towns of England – and one of the first to volunteer was young Jack Smallshaw of Accrington.

On 15 September 1914, Jack became an 'Accrington Pal' – a member of a battalion of men who are remembered more than any other of the 'Pals' battalions because of the appalling tragedy which befell them on the killing fields of the Somme. On that fateful day on 1 July 1916, the battalion attacked the fortified village of Serre and were virtually wiped out on the slopes in front of the village. Jack was one of the very few who survived. He continued to serve on the front throughout the remainder of 1916 and into 1917, where he took part in the battle at Oppy Wood in May of that year. Shortly afterwards, he was struck down by a second bout of trench fever and spent the rest of the year recovering in England.

By February 1918, he was back in France serving on the front line, but Jack was never the same man. He was in the thick of the action again in March when the Germans launched their spring offensive against the Allied lines. He weathered that too, and stuck it out to the bitter end.

This is the story of a quite remarkable survivor of the 'war to end all wars', whose diaries have lain unpublished – in the possession of his family – since 1919.

Steve Corbett has had a lifelong interest in military history and the collecting of artefacts from the Great War. At the age of 12, he joined the local Army Cadet unit in Hulme, Manchester and remained a member until he decided to join the Regular Army in January 1969.

After serving in Germany for two years – and completing two tours of duty in Northern Ireland – Steve finally left the army in November 1974 and transferred to the Reserves. He moved to Warrington with his wife, Pam, in 1977 and took up a career in the chemical industry. He retired in early 2001 and in 2008, decided to turn the diaries he kept while serving in Northern Ireland into a book: *Belfast Diaries: A Gunner in Northern Ireland*, which was eventually published in July 2013 by Helion. He went on to write a second book: *A Tough Nut To Crack: Andersonstown – Voices from 9 Battery Royal Artillery in Northern Ireland, November 1971-March 1972*, which was published in August 2015.

Steve still lives in Warrington with Pam, where he spends much of his free time with his two daughters and two grandchildren.

AN ACCRINGTON PAL

The Diaries of
Private Jack Smallshaw
September 1914 to March 1919

Steve Corbett

**Diary entries transcribed from the originals
by Louise Baird née Everett**

Helion & Company

Helion & Company Limited
26 Willow Road
Solihull
West Midlands
B91 1UE
England
Tel. 0121 705 3393
Fax 0121 711 4075
Email: info@helion.co.uk
Website: www.helion.co.uk
Twitter: @helionbooks
Visit our blog at http://blog.helion.co.uk/

Published by Helion & Company 2016
Designed and typeset by Mach 3 Solutions Ltd (www.mach3solutions.co.uk)
Cover designed by Paul Hewitt, Battlefield Design (www.battlefield-design.co.uk)

Printed by Henry Ling Limited, Dorchester, Dorset

Original diary entries © Louise Baird née Everett 2015,
additional text © Steve Corbett 2016
Photographs © Louise Baird née Everett unless noted otherwise
Maps © as individually credited

Front cover: An illustration of Pte Jack Smallshaw by Peter Dennis © Helion &
Company Limited 2016. Rear cover: Jack's diary entry for July 1st 1916 © Louise
Baird née Everett.

ISBN 978-1-910777-93-0

British Library Cataloguing-in-Publication Data.
A catalogue record for this book is available from the British Library.

For details of other military history titles published by Helion & Company Limited,
contact the above address, or visit our website: http://www.helion.co.uk

We always welcome receiving book proposals from prospective authors.

This book is dedicated to the memory of Pte Jack Smallshaw
and all the men of the 'Pals' battalions
of the 31st Division, 1914-1918

'The Drum'

I hate that drum's discordant sound,
Parading round, and round and round:
To thoughtless youth it pleasure yields,
And lures from cities and from fields,
To sell their liberty for charms
Of tawdry lace, and glittering arms;
And when Ambition's voice commands,
To march, and fight, and fall, in foreign lands.

I hate that drum's discordant sound,
Parading round, and round, and round:
To me it talks of ravag'd plains,
And burning towns, and ruin'd swains,
And mangled limbs, and dying groans,
And widow's tears, and orphans moans;
And all that Misery's hand bestows,
To fill the catalogue of human woes.[1]

---

1   Poem by John Scott of Amwell (1730-1783).

Contents

List of Illustrations

List of Maps

Foreword

Jack Smallshaw… Just an ordinary name when compared to his three brothers – Archibald Aloysius, Harry Ignatius and Joseph – but Jack Smallshaw was far from being an ordinary man! He went to an ordinary school and lived in an ordinary house in an ordinary street in the northern town of Accrington, Lancashire, where he worked as a grocery assistant, but it was the outbreak of the Great War which set Jack apart from many of his contemporaries. My grandfather was one of the first to answer Kitchener's call for volunteers, and he became a soldier of the most famous of all the 'Pals' battalions of the Great War: The Accrington Pals.

My grandfather's diaries, which consist of four small notebooks, were passed on to me by my mother some 25 years ago when I first became interested in genealogy. They have spent most of that time in a rusty green tin box stored in the attic – and probably the 70 years before that, in the same tin box in my grandfather's attic. It was always my intention to transcribe the diaries, and with the approaching centenary of the Great War being so much on everyone's minds, I decided that now was the time. I felt that it would be a tragedy if the diaries were just left to fade away, and so I decided to make a hard copy of all the entries and preserve this important piece of history.

The diary entries were written in (now fading) tiny spidery writing in pencil, and naming places in France I had never heard of before made it quite difficult for me to decipher. I started off with lots of question marks before I eventually discovered the Accrington Pals website, which is run by the author Andrew Jackson.[1] I then read his book – *Accrington's Pals: The Full Story – The 11th Battalion, East Lancashire Regiment (Accrington Pals) and the 158th (Accrington and Burnley) Brigade, Royal Field Artillery (Howitzers)* and after this I did some further research and came across three books written by William Turner: *Pals: The 11th (Service) Battalion (Accrington) East Lancashire Regiment – A History of the Battalion raised from Accrington, Blackburn, Burnley and Chorley in World War One*; *The Accrington Pals: A Tribute to the Men of Accrington and District, Blackburn, Burnley, Chorley and the Neighbouring Villages, who volunteered, fought and died in the Great War 1914-1918*; and *Accrington Pals Trail: Home and Overseas (Battleground Europe)*. The latter was donated by a dear friend, Jack Moran, who showed great interest and gave me enormous encouragement when I started on this arduous task.

---

1 <www.pals.org.uk>

The contents of these books proved to be a great asset – and without them I doubt whether the diaries would ever have been fully transcribed, let alone published! The more research I did, the more interested I became – especially when I was able to place, name and date several of grandfather Jack Smallshaw's photographs, as well as tracing the Pals' war by using his diaries. One particular entry, whilst he was suffering from a bad attack of trench fever, caused me a lengthy investigation… '*Wed June 20th/17. I went by motor from 'F.A.' to 42nd C.C.S. at Orbigney*'. I searched for 'Orbigney' on maps, in books, at Field Ambulance ('F.A.') and Casualty Clearing Stations ('C.C.S.') – anywhere and everywhere I could think of… but without success; then I tried a different tack and searched for '42nd C.C.S.' – and what a relief when I found Aubigney! Now feeling more confident with the transcription, I purchased a Collins' map of the Somme and was then able to pinpoint the trail of the Accrington Pals, as well as gaining a fuller picture of the battlefields.

Until reading the diaries, I knew nothing of grandfather Jack Smallshaw's time served during the Great War. Like many of his generation, it was something he never talked about, but memories he took to his grave. I am amazed how he managed to survive for three long years on the Western Front – dodging bullet and shell every single day while living in absolute squalor in the disease-ridden and rat-infested trenches of France and Belgium; then there were his two bouts of trench fever, and his gassing in 1918 – and the unimaginable feeling of grief and guilt at the loss of fellow 'Pals', and the sometimes horrific nature of their deaths.

My grandfather's account of one of their outposts being hit by a German shell was a stark reminder of the awful and random nature of life and death in the trenches. On New Year's Eve in December 1916, he wrote the following account:

Sunday Dec 31st/16: Still in the trenches up to tonight when we were unfortunate enough to have one of our outposts shelled, and eight were killed and two wounded. This happened this afternoon we were told, but of course we could not get at them on account of going over the top in the daylight. When the relief went to this post, they found the men in an awful condition and reported same. We wasted no time in hurrying to the scene, and got to work digging the poor lads out. One lad died only five minutes after we got him out.

One of my grandfather's photographs is of Pte Albert Gibson, who was killed at the Battle of the Somme, and written on the back is: '*I last saw Albert with a bag of Mills bombs! July 1916*'. This photo – and the inscription – brought home to me the sadness of the war. My grandfather had survived, but I looked down at the face of Albert Gibson – a strikingly handsome young soldier – whose short life was over, and whose family and friends, tragically, would never see again. I wept!

I secretly hoped that perhaps one day I might be able to turn my grandfather's diaries into a book for family and friends – and then in about September

2014, I was reading through the *Warrington Guardian* and noticed an appeal that had been printed on behalf of the publisher Helion & Company. The publisher's founder, Duncan Rogers, was hoping to bring out a book on the Great War which would comprise entirely of letters, diary entries and photographs from soldiers and family members – and he was requesting that anyone with such material to contact him. I got in touch with them more or less immediately – and not long afterwards, I was paid a visit by the northern representative of the company, Christian Ewen. He brought along with him his father-in-law, Steve Corbett, to evaluate the diaries – and straight away he said that the diaries should be a book in their own right and not part of something else.

After further discussions with the publisher, Steve was asked if he would like to turn the diaries into a book. Without hesitation, he agreed to take on the job and fill in the gaps between the diary entries in detail, which my grandfather had omitted. Apart from the fact that the history of the Great War – and especially the Battle of the Somme – is one of Steve's great passions, he knows first-hand what it is like to serve his country; to face danger and to be parted from family and friends; and to me he seemed the ideal person to tell my grandfather's story in detail. I am indebted to him. I think my grandfather would have wanted his diaries to be read and his story to be told. I don't think he wrote the diaries as a reminder to himself; he would not have needed any written reminder of the long and painful years of war. I am sure that his memories would have been there to haunt him forever.

Life in Accrington would never be the same for my grandfather after he was demobbed in 1919. Whilst fighting for his country, he had lost first his mother and then his brother, Joseph – and then there were all his friends… killed in battles briefly mentioned in his diaries. After leaving the army, he eventually settled down in Warrington, where he met my grandmother, Mary Alice Spence – a widow with five children. He was employed as a mental health nurse at Winwick Hospital, Warrington from 1924 until his early retirement in 1954 due to ill health – caused in part by his service on the Western Front. My grandfather never kept any diaries while working there – and one can only imagine the traumatic situations he would often have found himself in when dealing with the patients (some of whom were former soldiers of the Great War, who were so traumatised by their experiences, they just couldn't cope in the outside world).

More tragedy was to follow my grandfather when in 1942, his 19-year-old son, Signalman Jack Kenneth, was killed while serving on the light cruiser HMS *Curacoa*. His ship was sunk in a collision with the RMS *Queen Mary* while on escort duty. The sinking resulted in the loss of 338 lives and was described at the time as one of the worst naval disasters of the war.

In 1954, my grandfather and grandmother set sail for New York on board the MV *Britannic*, where they spent some time with step-daughter Minnie Norton on a three-month touring holiday. While they were in Pennsylvania, my grandfather met up with his brother Archie, whom he hadn't seen for 35 years. In a letter to my mother, he wrote:

> *But let me tell you this (the kindness of Min and Eddie), they made a detour of our route about 280 miles or more from N York thro' New York State, New Jersey, Delaware, Maryland into N.E. Pennsylvania eventually turning up along a country lane off the main road. Eddie says: "Grandpop, we had better halt for a cup of tea." He sounded his horn and out came a stout lady, followed by a fairly stout man. I did not at once recognise them but the woman's face was a bit familiar; it was Evelyn. The other was Archie. My God! Did I fall into his arms, you couldn't separate us, well after about 35 years and to beat it all you could see Min and Eddie had not told us where we had arrived at. Can you imagine what a beautiful surprise it was?*

But just three years after meeting his long-lost brother, my grandfather sadly passed away. I am very proud to say… Private Jack Smallshaw, you were an extraordinary man. I salute you, and I will always remember you.

Some of the names in the diary are not easy to decipher, and I apologise for any inaccuracies which may have occurred.

Louise Baird
2 October 2015

Author's Preface and Acknowledgements

As a child, I had an absolute passion for reading anything that I could on the Great War. Much of my free time was spent in the local library, where I would pore over the books. One book in particular stood out in my memory... I couldn't have been much more than eight or 10 at the time, but I was reading about the fighting on the Somme and I saw an aerial photograph of two of the four copses at Serre: Luke and John Copse. The picture had been taken from an aircraft shortly after the July battle in 1916 – and in-between the shattered tree stumps could be picked out the lines of trenches. That view fascinated me – and more than 50 years later, that image still remains with me... locked in my mind.

As I grew older and I read more on the subject of the Great War, I reached a better understanding of the horrors that these brave soldiers from all sides experienced when they served in the trenches. Eventually, I was to join the army myself at the age of 17 – and whilst stationed in Germany in 1969, my regiment paid a visit to the killing fields of Verdun. I recall how we were ushered together a short distance away from Fort Douaumont; everywhere the ground was cratered like the surface of the moon – and then something happened which really brought home to me how badly affected these men were by what they had been through... An elderly Frenchman – a veteran of the fighting of the 1916 battle at Verdun – stepped forward. He introduced himself, told us about his regiment and which sector of the battlefield he fought on; then, as he started to recount the battle on the very ground where we were gathered, he broke down in tears, shook his head and walked away. We all stood there in silence, watching him and not knowing what to do as he sobbed uncontrollably. There was no way we young soldiers could even begin to understand what he must have gone through. All those brave men of his generation are now gone – and all we have left to remind us of their courage, determination and sacrifice on the field of battle are their letters, diaries and photographs. We owe it to these men to keep their memory alive for future generations.

In September 2014, I was asked by my publisher – Duncan Rogers – to view a set of diaries which had been written by Pte Jack Smallshaw of the 11th (Service) Battalion, East Lancashire Regiment: The Accrington Pals. At the time, he was considering commissioning a book on the Great War – made up entirely of soldiers' letters, accounts and photographs – and he wanted me to view the diaries to see if they would be of any use. I travelled with my son-in-law – Christian Ewen of Helion & Company – to visit Jack Smallshaw's granddaughter, Louise Baird, the owner of the diaries. What she showed me that afternoon was quite astonishing… Louise passed me one of the notebooks to look at, and as I opened it, I was amazed to see that by chance I had chosen Jack's account for July 1st 1916. It started off with: *'At 7.30 a.m. the order was given to advance. Every officer and man of our battalion got over the parapet and advanced as if they were just on parade…'* On that fateful morning, the Accrington Pals had at their disposal for the assault on the village of Serre just over 700 men – and by the end of the day, 584 of them were recorded as being either dead, wounded, or missing. The slaughter was beyond belief. The final death toll was 235 officers and men – of which 135 of them have no known grave – and here I was, reading Pte Smallshaw's own words, which were written on the battlefield where so many of his friends perished.

I duly reported back to my publisher and advised him that he really should be thinking of turning Jack's diaries into a book in their own right. Not long afterwards, Duncan travelled up to meet Louise and to examine the diaries for himself. After a brief examination, he soon reached the same conclusion as I did, and he immediately asked me if I would be prepared to undertake the task of turning the diaries into a book. It was a task I could hardly refuse, but little did I realise the enormity of the job I had taken on. Jack's diaries had already been carefully transcribed by Louise – and this in itself saved me an enormous amount of time. I set out with the aim of keeping just to the facts and steering clear of going into too much detail about the individual personalities involved in the battles. This book is not intended to be yet another account of the Accrington Pals; there are several books that already tell the story quite admirably. This book is purely about Pte Jack Smallshaw and what he saw, where he was and what he went through. In places, it has been necessary to go into greater detail than I would have liked when covering some of the battles which involved the 11th East Lancashires, but there was simply no other way of explaining the part they played without first describing the actions of the 31st Division. I have made extensive use of the division, brigade and battalion war diaries held at the National Archives to piece together the progress of the 11th East Lancashires through France and Belgium.

While writing this book, I feel that I have grown to know Jack quite well. I reached the conclusion that after his two bouts of trench fever in 1916 and 1917, he never seemed to be quite the same man. The war had taken its toll on him – and after being gassed in October 1918, his health suffered even more. There were many casualties of the Great War whose names never appeared on the Roll of Honour, or on any of the many memorials dotted around every village, town and city in the country, for these men died *after* the war… through ill health caused *by* the war. Jack Smallshaw was one of those men. If, after reading Jack's account of his war, it causes you – the reader – to stop and think of their sacrifice and suffering, then I will consider that I have achieved my aim in helping to keep their memory alive.

I would like to thank Louise Baird, for making available to me her grandfather's collection of photographs, documents and diaries; Jane Brunning of the Accrington Library, for providing me with copies of the *Accrington Observer & Times* covering July 1916; Jane Davis of the Lancashire Infantry Museum at Fulwood Barracks, Preston, for the highly detailed copies of trench maps of Serre, Oppy Wood and Ploegsteert; my son-in-law, Chris Ewen, and friend, Dr Michael LoCicero, for their diligent work in proofreading the manuscript; and Kim McSweeney at Mach 3 Solutions for the superb job she has done with the typesetting.

Steve Corbett
11 November 2015

Part 1: 1914

THE OUTBREAK OF WAR

On June 28th 1914, one single act of savagery plunged the whole world into a war which would last for four long years and result in the loss of millions of lives. On that fateful day, the heir to the Austrian Empire – Archduke Franz Ferdinand – and his beloved wife, Sophie, were on their way to visit officers who had been wounded in an earlier assassination attempt on the royal couple after a bomb had been thrown at their car. The device exploded under the following vehicle – killing two of the occupants and injuring some of the bystanders who were trying to catch a glimpse of the Archduke and his wife. Apparently unperturbed by the earlier attempt on their lives, the couple made their way to visit the injured officers who had survived the explosion. As their vehicle reached the junction of Appel Quay and Franz-Josef Strasse, Serbian activist Gavrilo Princip stepped forward out of the crowd and opened fire on the Archduke and his wife with a Browning Model 1910 pistol. This act of madness set in motion a rapid chain of events which had terrifying global consequences…

Austria-Hungary held Serbia wholly responsible for this terrible act, and the following month – on July 28th – they declared war on Serbia; then the following day, Russia started a partial mobilisation of their troops against Austria in defence of their Serbian allies. Germany followed suit on August 1st and declared war on Russia in defence of their own Austrian allies. France was the next country to be sucked into this rapidly expanding war; they were allies of Russia, and Germany demanded of them that they remain neutral during the conflict. France refused to give any such undertaking and started to mobilise its own army to counter the German threat – and as a result, Germany declared war on France on August 3rd 1914.

Germany then asked neutral Belgium for the right of passage through their country to enable them to move in on the French border – promising that there would be no acts of aggression towards them if they did not interfere – but Belgium refused this request, as it would have been in breach of their stance of neutrality during time of war. On August 4th, German troops advanced over the Belgian border and started to close in on the armies of France. Britain was a signatory to a treaty with Belgium drawn up in 1839, which guaranteed that they would protect Belgium's neutrality from any hostile acts. With Germany's blatant disregard of this treaty, Britain was left with no alternative but to come to Belgium's defence, and they issued a warning to Germany that they must withdraw their troops from Belgium by midnight on

August 4th. Germany refused to give any such undertaking, and at 11:00 p.m., Britain finally declared war on Germany. On August 5th, Lord Kitchener took up the post of Secretary of State for War – and unlike many of his Cabinet colleagues, he correctly predicted that the conflict would last for several years. On August 7th, the advance party of the British Expeditionary Force (BEF) set sail for France to prepare for the arrival of the main body of the army...

The German armies were already occupying the Belgian city of Liège and had started their assault on the massive fortresses which surrounded the city, but it would be several more days before they were able to subdue the garrisons manning the defences. On August 12th, Britain and France declared war on Austria-Hungary and Kitchener had, by now, launched his recruiting drive to build up the strength of the regular forces. Shortly afterwards, posters were appearing all over the country bearing the now famous slogan: 'Your King and Country Need You'.

'Lads, you're wanted, go and help,'
On the railway carriage wall
Stuck the poster, and I thought
Of the hands that penned the call.

Fat civilians wishing they
'Could go and fight the Hun'.
Can't you see them thanking God
That they're over forty-one?

Girls with feathers, vulgar songs –
Washy verse on England's need –
God – and don't we damned well know
How the message ought to read.

'Lads, you're wanted! Over there,
Shiver in the morning dew,
More poor devils like yourselves
Waiting to be killed by you.

Go and help to swell the names
In the casualty lists.
Help to make the column's stuff
For the blasted journalists.

Help to keep them nice and safe
From the wicked German foe.

Don't let him come over here!
Lads, you're wanted – out you go.'

There's a better word than that,
Lads, and can't you hear it come
From a million men that call
You to share their martyrdom?

Leave the harlots still to sing
Comic songs about the Hun,
Leave the fat old men to say
Now we've got them on the run.

Take your risk of life and death
Underneath the open sky.
Live clean or go out quick –
Lads, you're wanted. Come and die.[1]

Even at this very early stage of the war, it was apparent that a much larger army would be needed to take on the military might of Germany. Originally, the call was for men between the ages of 19 and 30 – and by the end of August, volunteers were joining at the rate of around 30,000 every single day. The recruiting age by then had been extended to 35 – and by the middle of September, more than half a million men had volunteered. Up and down the country, men were rushing to join. The general feeling was that it would all be over by Christmas anyway, and no-one wanted to miss out; everyone wanted to do their bit.

It is claimed that on August 19th, Kaiser Wilhelm II issued a special order from his headquarters at Aix-la-Chapelle to the commander of the First German Army – General Alexander von Kluck – in which he expressed his desire for the annihilation of the British Army: 'It is my Royal and Imperial command that you concentrate your energies, for the immediate present, upon one single purpose, and that you address all your skill and all the valour of my soldiers to exterminate first the treacherous English and walk over General French's insignificant little army'.[2]

So the story goes, the word 'insignificant' was lost in the translation to English, and became 'contemptible'. The British regular soldiers took this as a compliment and adopted the name 'The Old Contemptibles' – a name which became forever associated with those brave men of the BEF who went to the aid of France and Belgium in August 1914. There was never any proof that any such order was ever

1   Passage taken from the poem 'Recruiting' by E.A. Mackintosh (1893-1917).
2   Accessed at: <www.epitaphsofthegreatwar.com/contemptible>

given by the Kaiser, and it is highly likely that it was nothing more than a piece of inspired propaganda on the part of the British.

In Belgium on August 21st, the BEF sent out small scouting patrols to try and locate the advancing German armies which were believed to be heading straight towards their lines. On Saturday, August 22nd, 'C' Squadron of the 4th Dragoon Guards sent out two patrols just north of Mons to see if they could make contact with the enemy. A troop of Uhlan Cavalry were observed just near Casteau, and the men of 1st Troop immediately gave chase. Trooper E. Thomas of 4th Troop became the first British soldier to fire a shot in anger during the Great War when he opened fire with his rifle after dismounting from his horse. He succeeded in hitting a German officer at a range of about 400 yards. Trooper Thomas said of his encounter after the war: 'Immediately I saw him I took aim, pulled the trigger and automatically, almost instantaneously, he fell to the ground'.[3]

On Sunday, August 23rd, the German hordes finally met up with the bulk of the BEF, which had taken up defensive positions along the Mons–Conde Canal. The British force of around 70,000 men were facing an enemy of at least 150,000 in strength. At around 9:00 a.m., the advancing German troops tried to cross four bridges which spanned the canal, but they were driven back by the withering fire put down by the British infantrymen armed with their Lee-Enfield rifles. The pre-war 'Tommy' was highly trained in musketry, and in an exercise known as the 'mad-minute', they were expected to be able to fire between 15 and 20 aimed shots per minute. A skilled rifleman could even manage as many as 30. The Germans who were met with this concentrated fire were convinced that the British were using machine guns against them, such was the skill of their musketry. By the following day, the BEF had been forced to retreat from their lines – but not before they had inflicted heavy losses on the Germans.

The first Victoria Crosses of the war were won by Lt Dease and Pte Godley of the Royal Fusiliers. The 4th Battalion was defending Nimy Railway Bridge, which crossed the Mons Canal, with two machine guns. During the fierce fighting, Lt Dease maintained contact with both machine guns and their crews – helping to clear stoppages whenever the guns stopped firing. Twice he was badly wounded as he dashed from gun to gun, as he strove to keep them both in action. He was shot a third time and was killed. For his courageous actions that day, he was posthumously awarded the Victoria Cross. Pte Godley took over the remaining gun and continued to hold the Germans at bay while the rest of the company withdrew. Although badly wounded, Godley's last defiant act before being captured was to dismount the gun, render it inoperable and throw it into the canal to stop it falling into enemy hands. He too was awarded the Victoria Cross. Godley survived the war and died in 1957.

---

3   Macdonald, Lyn, *1914: The Days of Hope* (Penguin Books, 1989), p.84.

'My Old Man's a Dust-Man' (song)

My old man's a dust-man
He fought at the Battle of Mons
He killed a dozen Germans
With only a couple of bombs.
One lay here, and one lay there
And one around the corner.
And another poor sod with his leg hanging off
Was crying out for water.[4]

By the end of the month, the British casualties stood at more than 14,000 dead and wounded – and by the end of September, they had lost another 15,000 men. Clearly these losses were unsustainable and gave added impetus to the recruitment drive, which by now, was well under way. It took a long time to turn a raw recruit into a soldier – and for the time being, the survivors of the BEF would have to hang on as best as they could. Up and down the country, young men were flocking to join. A popular song of the time was used to great effect by the singer Vesta Tilley in the music halls of many towns and cities. The flag-waving Vesta would leave the stage and parade up and down the aisles – inviting young men out of the audience to come out and join her; she would then lead them towards the waiting recruiting sergeants. Wives, girlfriends and parents were swept along by the heady atmosphere of patriotism and urged their men to step forward and do their bit for King and Country.

'Your King and Country Want You'

We've watched you playing cricket and every kind of game
At football, golf and polo you men have made your name
But now your country calls you to play your part in war
And no matter what befalls you, we shall love you all the more
So come and join the Forces, as your fathers did before.

(Chorus)
Oh, we don't want to lose you, but we think you ought to go
For your King and your Country both need you so
We shall want you, and miss you, but with all our might and main
We shall cheer you, thank you, kiss you, when you come back again.

We want you from all quarters, so help us South and North
We want you in your thousands, from Falmouth to the Forth

---

4   Lyrics by Anon.

You'll never find us fail you when you are in distress
So answer when we hail you and let your word be 'yes'
And so your name in years to come, each mother's son shall bless.

(Chorus)
Oh we don't want to lose you, but we think you ought to go
For your King and your Country both need you so
We shall want you, and miss you, but with all our might and main
We shall cheer you, thank you, kiss you, when you come back again.[5]

General Sir Henry Rawlinson had soon realised that even more men would be inclined to volunteer if they knew that they would be serving alongside friends, family members or work colleagues: men that they knew well. He eventually sent out an appeal to the stockbrokers in London to raise a body of men in the hope that it would set an example to the rest of the country – and as a result of this appeal, more than 1,600 men had volunteered by late August. These men were formed into the 10th (Service) Battalion, the Royal Fusiliers (the 'Stockbrokers' Battalion').

Not long after the success of Rawlinson's initiative, Lord Derby decided to follow suit and set about raising a battalion in Liverpool. Within a matter of days, there had been around 1,500 volunteers – and in an address to his men, Lord Derby told them:

I am not going to make you a speech of heroics; you have given me your answer, and I can telegraph to Lord Kitchener tonight to say that our second battalion is formed.

We have got to see this through to the bitter end, and dictate our terms of peace to Berlin, if it takes every man in the country.

This should be a battalion of pals, a battalion in which friends from the same office will fight shoulder to shoulder for the honour of Britain and the credit of Liverpool.

I do not attempt to minimise to you the hardship we will suffer, the risks you will run; I don't ask you to uphold Liverpool's honour, it would be an insult to think you could do anything but that.

But I do thank you, from the bottom of my heart, for coming here tonight and showing what is the spirit of Liverpool. A spirit that ought to spread through every city and every town in the kingdom. You have given a noble example in thus coming forward; you are certain to give a noble example on the field of battle.[6]

---

5   Music and lyrics by Paul A. Rubens (1875-1917).
6   Lord Derby, August 1914.

This rousing speech had such an effect that it wasn't long before enough men had volunteered to raise three more battalions in Liverpool. Within the space of five days, 4,000 had answered the call. Lord Kitchener was so impressed by the results that he encouraged similar recruiting drives all over the country – and so the 'Pals' battalions came into being: The Manchester Pals, the Salford Pals, the Grimsby Chums, the Birmingham Pals... Every city and town had their own – and perhaps the best remembered of them all were the 11th (Service) Battalion, East Lancashire Regiment: The Accrington Pals.

At the time, it all seemed such a good idea; the volunteers would be in the company of men they knew so well – friends they had known since their school-days, neighbours and relatives. They would be like one big happy family – all of them united in the same cause of fighting for King and Country – but there was a fatal flaw in the plan that no-one had taken into account when they formed the 'Pals' battalions... Unlike other regiments, where the men were drawn from up and down the country, the volunteers who made up the Pals came from the same towns; the same streets; the same mills; the same coal pits, where *everyone* knew each other. These brave men would live together, fight together and ultimately die together on the battlefields of France and Flanders. The men of Accrington, Blackburn, Burnley and Chorley suffered grievous losses during the Battle of the Somme on July 1st 1916 – as did other cities and towns up and down the country. Many of the close-knit communities were torn apart by the loss of life which affected so many families – and by the end of 1918, there were hardly any of the original volunteers of 1914 left to 'cheer', 'thank', or 'kiss' when they came home again; but one man *did* make it home. He was one of the lucky ones who managed to live through it all: 15148 Private Jack Smallshaw of 'W' Coy, 11th (Service) Battalion, East Lancashire Regiment: The Accrington Pals.

The Volunteers

While the storm clouds of war had been gathering over Europe, the Lancashire town of Accrington was in the grip of industrial unrest. The town's largest employer of men – the machine works of Howard & Bullough's – had refused to meet the demands of its workers for union recognition. On July 2nd, the men went on strike – and as a result, the management eventually locked out the entire workforce of 5,000 men and boys. Even after Britain declared war on Germany, both sides in the industrial dispute refused to give in.

On August 26th, British troops were engaged in the bitter Battle of Le Cateau while the workforce of Howard & Bullough's remained locked out. Amongst certain circles, there was a feeling of resentment that while soldiers were losing their lives fighting for their country, others back home in Accrington were lying idle and were seen as not wanting to do their bit.

On August 29th, an article appeared in the *Accrington Observer & Times*:

> Men of Bullough's, what are you doing in this time of stress and trial? Shall I tell you the plain and unvarnished truth? You are daily wasting bright golden hours in registering yourselves at your club house. You are sitting on your heels at the kerbstones twiddling your thumbs. You are propping up the railings of the Ambulance Hall. You are trapesing aimlessly through the already too crowded streets. You are lounging, sitting and standing near the war office in Dutton-street discussing tactics and methods of a warfare in which you will not, either with hammer or gun, play your part for the honour of your country.[7]

On August 31st – and no doubt influenced to some extent by the success of Lord Derby in Liverpool – the Mayor of Accrington, Councillor Captain John Harwood JP, contacted the War Office and offered to raise half a battalion of men; but at that time, the policy of the Army Council was that they could accept nothing less than a full battalion, and so they declined his offer. On September 6th, Harwood contacted the War Office again and promised them that he would raise a full battalion. This time his offer was accepted.

Over in France, the German advance continued – and they were (by now) just within 30 miles of Paris. On September 4th, the Germans launched a fresh assault on the capital from the east. This deviated from their original plans, as set down in the 'Schlieffen Plan', and left their right flank exposed. The following day, the British and French forces launched their counter-attack and forced the Germans to retreat. After crossing the Aisne, the Germans took the high ground at the Chemin des Dames Ridge on September 12th and started to dig in. This signalled the start of the nightmare of static warfare – and soon after, the trench systems of the Western Front stretched all the way from the Belgian coast to the Swiss border in the south.

On the same day that the Germans started setting up their defensive positions, Harwood's appeal for volunteers appeared in the *Accrington Observer & Times* – and on Monday, September 14th, the men of Accrington turned up in large numbers outside Willow Street School to enlist. Such was the enthusiasm to do their bit for King and Country, that even the small village of Rishton had raised 19 volunteers for the battalion on this first day of recruiting. The very next day, young 18-year-old Jack Smallshaw arrived and joined the queue of men waiting to enlist. He duly recorded in his diary: '*Tuesday Sept 15/14: I enlisted in the 11th East Lancashire Regiment ('W' Coy. No.15148)*'.

By September 24th, the battalion had reached full strength. Around half the number were raised in Accrington, and the rest had come from the surrounding

---

7   *Accrington Observer & Times*, August 29th 1914.

towns of Blackburn, Burnley and Chorley. For the next five months, young Jack and his fellow volunteers were subjected to the rigours of army discipline and training which all new recruits had to face. Much of the early training took place at Ellison's Tenement, where they would practise their drill. At this early stage, the men hadn't yet been issued with uniforms – and the rifles they had were the Lee-Metford rifles of Boer War vintage. The men soon learned that every drill order in the army appeared to be carried out by numbers – everything done to the count of 'two three'. Drill instructors didn't talk to the recruits – they screamed; every order was bellowed out across the parade ground – words exaggerated and drawn out. "Squad!... Squaaad... Shun!" Up two three, down two three. "This squad will move to the right, righhht-tahn." Right two three, down two three. "Stand aaaht eaase!" Down two three. "Staaand easy."

God help anyone who had forgotten their left from their right. The public humil-iation which would follow could reduce grown men to tears. The drill instructors were merciless in their quest for perfection on the parade ground. When the men gradually started to receive their blue uniforms towards the end of November, they had to learn how to apply knife-sharp creases to sleeves and trousers, as well as the art of 'bulling up' their boots to a mirror-like finish. Crowds would gather to watch the men practise their drill. There would be howls of laughter as men bumped into each other after taking a wrong turn on the command. Children followed and mimicked the marching recruits as they strode up and down to the screams of "Left-right-left-right-left-right-lerrrft!" from the drill instructors as

October 1914: Some of the Accrington volunteers – still without uniform, but now armed with rifles.

they tried to keep the men in step with each other – the parentage of the recruits always being questioned; but gradually, as the days turned into weeks, and the weeks turned into months, the men started to look and behave like soldiers. Their backs straightened and their chests puffed out as they shouldered their weapons and marched up and down and paraded through the town. They were full of pride now; there was no more laughter as they marched by. Cheers and applause greeted them everywhere they went. Besides all the foot and rifle drill, they learned the art of field craft, building trenches and redoubts, and all the other skills they would need when they eventually faced the enemy.

While Jack and his friends were still learning the basics of soldiery, the BEF were fighting for their very existence as the German onslaught continued. After the fall of Antwerp to the Germans on October 10th, the BEF withdrew towards Ypres in support of the Belgian and French troops who were defending the town. On October 19th, the Germans launched their assaults against the Allied lines. To the east of Ypres, the British 7th Division managed to drive off repeated assaults on their defences. To the north-east at Langemarck, the deadly rifle fire of the British infantry caused absolute carnage amongst the tightly-packed ranks of Germans and brought their advance to a halt. On October 29th, Turkey entered the war on the side of Germany – the very same day that the Germans renewed their assault on the besieged town of Ypres. This time they attacked from the south between Gheluvelt and Messines. On October 31st, the Germans managed to break through the British lines, but thanks to the heroic efforts of the 2nd Worcesters, the enemy were driven back and the line restored.

The last major assault on the British lines happened on November 11th at Nun's Copse, when the Prussian Guards managed to break through the British defences, but they were eventually forced back – and by November 22nd, the fighting drew to a close. Ypres had been saved, but it was now surrounded on three sides by the German Army.

'Far, far from Wipers' (song)

Far, far from Wipers I long to be.
Where German snipers can't get at me.
Dark is my dugout, cold are my feet.
Waiting for Whizzbangs[8] to send me to sleep.[9]

Back in England, the training of the new recruits continued. There was even time to spend Christmas with families before they entered the New Year and met new challenges.

---

8   'Wipers' was slang for Ypres; 'whizzbang' is a type of German artillery shell.
9   Lyrics by Anon.

Part 2: 1915

CARNARVON

Up to this point, all the individual companies which made up the battalion had been billeted in their own towns – and many of the men were still living with their families – but now there was a need to bring all of them together so that they could train together rather than as individual units, and so it was decided to send them off to Carnarvon in North Wales.

On February 21st, a farewell service was held at St John's Church for the men and their families – and on February 23rd, the volunteers marched down to the railway station. The people of the town turned out in their thousands to see their men off. Schools and factories closed for the day so that mothers, fathers, sisters, brothers, wives, sons and daughters could cheer their men on their way.

'A' Company, 3 and 4 Platoon, February 1915.

The *Accrington Observer & Times* reported the impending departure in their paper:

The 'Pals" Departure
THIS MORNING'S SEND-OFF
ACCRINGTONS "AU REVOIR."

Amid the hearty good wishes and "God-speed" of the whole community, the men of the Accrington and District "Pals" Battalion leave this (Tuesday) morning; for their new training quarters at Carnarvon.

As is stated in fuller detail in today's "Observ(er)ations" column, the first train leaves Accrington at 9-15 a. m., and the second at 10-15 a. m. the first contingent will parade at the Accrington tram shed at 9-15 a. m., and march to the station, and the second contingent will leave in ample time for the later train.

The Burnley and Chorley companies will travel by a third special train leaving Burnley at 11 a. m, and Chorley at 12. 5 p. m.

The Battalion will no doubt be given a most enthusiastic send-off. It is stated that some of the mills are to suspend work until after the departure of the "Pals," and many people will be glad to avail themselves of the opportunity to show their admiration for "Accrington's Own," and to participate in a general "au revoir."[1]

'Called Away'
(Darnley Rigg)

They're going yes, going to leave us;
God speed them on their way.
"A smarter lot of soldiers
"I've not seen for many a day."
So spoken Major General Dickson
To their Colonel on parade,
After inspection on the Tenement
Of the Accrington "Pals Brigade."

Though our hearts are aching
We must smile to hide the tear,
And send them on their journey
With a hearty ringing cheer.

---

1 · *Accrington Observer & Times*, February 23rd 1915.

Your Mayor and M. P.'s proud of you,
And the progress you have made:
Lord Kitchener's highly gratified,
With the Accrington "Pals" Brigade.

If you are called on active service,
To face the German Hun,
You'll bravely do your duty
With both bayonet and gun;
Defending your country's honour,
With courage undismayed.
Making a name on the scroll of fame,
For the Accrington "Pals" Brigade.[2]

Jack wrote of the move in his diary: '*Tuesday Feb 23rd/15: Left Accrington for Caernarvon (Big 'send-off' at Acc). (Visited Caernarvon Castle)*'.

'W' Company, Castle Square, Carnarvon.

---

2   *Accrington Observer & Times*, February 23rd 1915.

Amongst Jack's possessions, which he kept throughout the war, was a newspaper cutting taken from the *Accrington Advertiser and Northern Morning News*:

JACK O' MOLESIDE'S LETTER

"Pals" Depart.
Not since the day when John Bright passed through Accrington on his way home from Gawthorpe Hall to One Ash his Rochdale residence, have we seen the approaches to Accrington station packed as they were last Tuesday morning. The crowd were estimated at fifteen to twenty thousand.

*   *   *

Au Revoir, but-
Wives, sweethearts, fathers, mothers, sisters, brothers, uncles, aunts, cousins, grandfathers and grandmothers of the eleven hundred departing "pals" [sic] assembled along with the Mayor [Captain Harwood] and leading townspeople to give our lads a send-off. The "Pals" marched to the station smartly and looked very well. It was a great sight and yet one trembled lest some of them might be seeing Accrington for the last time. But we hope not. There were more cheers than tears on this bright February morning when our lads left for Carnarvon to the accompaniment of fog signals.

*   *   *

No Music.
There was no band to play the Pals up to the station and this caused great disappointment. But Lord Kitchener at the outbreak of the war, ordered that the troops should be moved quietly. Nover [sic] mind, we will have all our bands at the station when our lads come back after beating the Germans.

*   *   *

The "Pals" Farewell Call.
The "Pals" farewell shout as the train moved out of Accrington station was "This way to Berlin!" "Are we downhearted?" shouted the crowd. "No" shouted the Pals.

*   *   *

The Terrier.

A little terrier dog, when the Pals departed was "the cynosure of all eyes." It was dressed in the Union Jack and accompanied one of the "Pals."[3]

* * *

In Blackburn, Burnley and Chorley, the remaining companies which made up the rest of the battalion were also being waved off by family and friends as they transferred to their new training camp in North Wales. On February 24th, the battalion formed up on parade together at Castle Square, Carnarvon for the very first time. Just a few days later, Lieutenant Colonel A. Rickman took over as Battalion Commander. One of the first changes he made to the battalion was to the company structure: 'A', 'B', 'C', 'D' and 'E' Company were re-designated 'W', 'X', 'Y' 'Z' and 'R' Company. The soldiers were billeted with local families and soon settled into their new surroundings – the community making them most welcome. Evening entertainment was laid on, and at the weekend there was all manner of team sports, as well as church services for them to attend so that they could also look after not only their spiritual well-being, but also their fitness.

The training resumed as the men prepared for war. Each day, after morning parade at Castle Square, they would march off to Coed Helen Field and continue with their drills. The instructors taught them how to 'fix bayonets', although rifles were still in short supply... "When I give the order to 'Fix'... your left hand shoots behind your back and grabs the bayonet handle and swings it down, and your right hand thrusts the rifle forward from your side – and when I shout 'Bayonets'... you withdraw the bayonet from the scabbard, bring it to your front and mount it on the rifle, so remember... When I shout 'Fix'... you don't fix – and when I shout 'Bayonets'... you whip it out and whop it on." The men would then be taken forward to the straw-filled sacks suspended from frames and they would learn the fine art of driving home cold steel into the torso of a fellow human being. The art of killing is brutal and bloody. To learn how to properly use the tools of war takes time... "Think of that sack as your mum-in-law or me. Think of it as someone you hate enough to want to kill. Charge forward and scream... Thrust forward with your rifle, stick it in, give it a twist and pull it out. Shove the body to one side and advance. Kill him before he can kill you."

Physical training played a large part in their daily routine, as the men were gradually toughened up. Much of the field craft which the men practised was based on the manuals used during the Boer War. The emphasis was always on attacking the enemy and wearing them down until you were close enough to go in with the bayonet. The grim realities of trench warfare on the Western Front would prove to be somewhat different, but to his credit, Rickman did seem to

---

3   *Accrington Advertiser and Northern Morning News.*

have a grasp of the kind of tactics which they would need to use – and many an evening was spent practising night-time attacks on trenches and fortifications.

Towards the end of April, the men were issued with their khaki uniforms and equipment – and for the first time, there were enough rifles for every man in the battalion. Rumours started to circulate of an impending move to France – and on May 8th, the men were informed of their new posting: they were to be sent to Penkridge Bank Camp in Staffordshire. On May 13th, the battalion was assembled on Castle Square before heading off to the railway station. The residents turned out in their hundreds as the men marched off – singing as they went…

'Good-bye-ee'

Brother Bertie went away
To do his bit the other day
With a smile on his lips
And his Lieutenant's pips
Upon his shoulder bright and gay
As the train moved out he said,
'Remember me to all the birds.'
Then he wagged his paw
And went away to war
Shouting out these pathetic words;

Good-bye-ee, good-bye-ee,
Wipe the tear, baby dear, from your eye-ee,
Tho' it's hard to part I know,
I'll be tickled to death to go.
Don't cry-ee, don't sigh-ee,
There's a silver lining in the sky-ee,
Bonsoir, old thing, cheer-i-o, chin, chin,
Nah-poo, toodle-oo, Good-bye-ee.[4]

'Thursday May 13th/15: Left Caernarvon for Penkridge Camp (Cannock Chase, Staffs)'.

---

4   Music and lyrics by R.P. Weston (1878-1936) and Bert Lee (1880-1946).

Weapons Training

Rugeley Camp – also known as Penkridge Bank Camp – was the volunteers' first experience of life on a military base… and what a shock it turned out to be. The weather was atrocious when the battalion arrived; the surrounding area was just a sea of mud – and to their horror, many of the newly-constructed huts were not even finished (most of the buildings did not even have a roof) – but gradually, over the next few weeks, the camp was brought up to a presentable standard as the men resumed their training. By now the 11th East Lancashires had been joined by three other battalions: the 12th (Service) Battalion – Sheffield City, 13th (Service) Battalion – 1st Barnsley, and the 14th (Service) Battalion – 2nd Barnsley (all of the York & Lancaster Regiment). These four battalions became the 94th Brigade, 31st Division of the New Fourth Army.

Up on the moors, an elaborate trench system had been constructed, where the individual battalions of the brigade could practise both attack and defence of entrenchments. Each battalion would take turns to be the 'enemy', or the attacking force. Their stay at Penkridge only lasted a few months – and towards the end of July, an advance party was sent ahead to their new base at South Camp, Ripon, while the bulk of the battalion went on a recruiting drive in Lancashire: '*Friday July 30th/15: Left Penkridge for a Recruiting March around Chorley, Blackburn, Accrington and Burnley. Gave exhibition of our training at Lancashire Royal Show Blackburn (Sat). At Burnley, our Colonel, A.W. Rickman, presented a D.C.M. medal to Lance-Corporal Watson of the 2nd E. Lancs for bravery in France*'.

Rugeley Camp. Jack has written on the back: '*K of K mugs. Some of the boys of the NEW brigade. 11th Service Battalion ELR, June 1915*'.

Training at Rugeley Camp; Jack is kneeling.

L/Cpl Harry Watson was badly injured when on January 5th 1915 – and under heavy fire from the enemy – he went to the aid of a severely wounded Royal Engineer sergeant who was caught up on the German wire. As he reached the injured soldier, he was himself hit in the head by a bullet fired by a German sniper. Grievously injured, he spent the next 12 hours in no man's land before he could be rescued. He never fully recovered from his injuries and was invalided out of the army. His citation gave a brief description of the action, for which he was awarded the Distinguished Conduct Medal: 'For gallantry and devotion to duty at Neuve Chapelle in going out and rescuing a wounded man who was entangled in the barbed wire in front of our trenches'.[5]

'*Thursday Aug 5th/15: Entrained at Burnley for Ripon. 1st & 2nd Firing Courses (Visits to Fountains Abbey and Harrogate)*'. The new camp at Ripon was situated on meadow land and surrounded by orchards – a far cry from the squalid conditions of Rugeley Camp. The emphasis now was on skill at arms. New ranges had been constructed near Bishop Monkton, and it was the men of 'W' and 'X' Company who had the honour of being the first to try them out. Up to this point, they were still armed with the old Lee-Metford rifles, but even with these old guns, they were able to put on a remarkable display of musketry.

Around mid-September, the battalion was given a special four days' leave before their next move to Salisbury Plain: '*Friday Sept 24th/15: Left Ripon for Hurdcott*

---

5   Accessed at: <www.burnleygallantry.co.uk>

Camp Nr Salisbury. Inspection by Sir Arthur Paget'. Upon arrival at the camp, the men were issued with brand-new rifles – and they were perhaps the finest military bolt-action rifles ever made: The Rifle, Short, Magazine, Lee-Enfield No 1 Mk III. Affectionately known to all soldiers as the 'Smelly', the rifle was sighted up to 2,000 yards and micro-adjustments could be made to the rear sight via a worm-wheel set into the right side of the sight. On the left of the rifle was a volley sight which was ranged from 1,600 yards to 2,800 yards. There was a charger guide fitted to the top of the receiver, which held in place a clip of five rounds when loading the weapon. The magazine held 10 rounds, whereas most weapons of that period only held five. The bayonet for the weapon had a vicious-looking 17-inch-long blade. The bolt action was silky-smooth and allowed the trained rifleman to let off at least 15 to 20 aimed shots per minute.

Another addition to their armoury of weapons was the Lewis Gun – and it was truly a remarkable weapon for its time. Most machine guns of the period weighed between 32 and 50 lbs; they were water-cooled and usually mounted on a tripod which weighed as much as the gun itself, but the 47-round drum-fed Lewis Gun only weighed 27 lbs. It was air-cooled, had a small foldable bipod and fired at a very handy rate of around 550 rpm. The Germans had nothing like it – and any they managed to capture were highly prized amongst their own troops. The closest they ever came to matching the Lewis was with their MG 08/15, but that was a much more cumbersome and heavier weapon to use.

'Nov 16th/15: I underwent a Bombing Course. Left Hurdcott for Larkhill Camp for our 3rd and 4th Firing Course. (Bad Weather)'. The men chosen to be 'bombers' learned how to handle the new Mills Grenade. It was a nice, handy fist-sized weapon which was armed with a seven-second fuse. To arm the grenade, the bomber withdrew the safety pin while holding down the lever on the side of the grenade. The grenade armed itself once it was released from the thrower's grip. The lever flew off and the striker was driven down by a powerful spring and ignited the fuse. The lethal range of the grenade was far greater than it could actually be thrown, and care had to be taken by the bomber when using it.

Some of the earlier grenades were of the 'stick' type and had impact fuses rather than the later timed fuses. These early types of grenades were extremely dangerous to use within the confines of a trench. If the bomber brought his arm too far back before throwing it – and he caught the parados (rear of the trench) with the top of the grenade – the bomb would instantaneously explode (with disastrous results to anyone unfortunate enough to be in close proximity).

The remaining two firing courses gave the battalion a chance to get used to the much handier – and shorter – SMLE rifle. It was quicker to load because of the charger guide for the ammunition clip, and the modified rear sight allowed for greater adjustment and accuracy over the older Lee-Metford (although the bolt action remained largely unchanged). The instructors took them through the procedures as the men lay in the prone position at the firing point... "With the safety-catch in the 'off' position, lift the bolt with the palm of your hand and draw it to the rear. Make sure the magazine cut-off is in the 'open' position and place a clip of five rounds into the charger bridge. With the right thumb placed on the top round in the clip, press down until all the rounds are seated in the magazine. Remove the empty clip and repeat the procedure with a fresh clip. Close the bolt using the palm of your hand and with your right thumb, apply the safety-catch. When I give the command to 'fire', pull the rifle-butt tightly into the shoulder, place the safety-catch in the 'off' position, aim the weapon at the target and slowly breathe out and steady your aim before squeezing the trigger. Always squeeze the trigger – never pull it."

Jack Smallshaw.

The individual companies continued with their skill at arms training, and then on November 29th, the 31st Division was finally warned for service in France. Some of the men were still waiting to finish their musketry courses and had to be rushed back to the ranges to complete their marksmanship test before they could be pronounced as ready for active service, but a few days later, the embarkation order was cancelled and the battalion was told that their new destination was to be Egypt.

Egypt

After Turkey entered the war on the side of Germany in October 1914, they declared a Holy War against the Allied Powers. The Ottoman/Turkish Army consisted of around 600,000 men, which were formed into 38 divisions. This sizeable army was viewed as a considerable threat by the British to their own interests in the Middle East – and by January 1915, the British had amassed a force of 70,000 troops in Egypt to counter the threat. Around 30,000 of these men were used for the defence of the strategically important Suez Canal, which was a vital artery for Allied shipping.

There had been minor skirmishes back in November 1914, but on January 28th 1915, a large column of Turkish troops were observed crossing the Sinai Desert. A force of British and French ships entered the Suez Canal and opened fire on the advancing Turks and drove them back. On February 2nd, there were several more skirmishes between opposing patrols – and then on the following day, the Turks launched an assault on the canal. The Indian troops manning their machine guns on the west bank opened fire as the Turks launched their rafts onto the waters from the opposite bank. More troops were massed in the gullies as they waited to join in the assault. The assaulting forces were cut to pieces by the deadly fire from the machine guns as they frantically tried to cross the stretch of water – and then they began to retreat in disarray as panic began to set in amongst the Arab troops fighting alongside them. The following day, there were renewed attacks from the Turkish Army, with additional assaults launched near Ismailia and Kantara. By the afternoon, the Turks were forced to withdraw by the combined fire from the British and French ships, as well as the ground troops manning the defences. In total, the Turks lost around 1,500 men during their attack on the Suez Canal – and after their defeat, they withdrew their armies back across the Sinai and towards Beersheba.

As a result of these battles, the British concluded that the Turkish Army were not very good soldiers and posed little threat to their own forces, but they *had* realised their mistake in relying on the Suez Canal as their main line of defence. It would not be until the Dardanelles campaign at Gallipoli, which started on April 25th 1915, that the British opinion of 'Johnny Turk' would change – and their mistake in underestimating the opposition they faced would cost them dearly. The idea had seemed simple enough at the time: if the Royal Navy could force through the straits which gave passage from the Aegean Sea to the Black Sea, they could link up with the Russians and attack Germany via the back door, but the naval assault failed after the British and French ships ran into a Turkish minefield and three battleships were sunk. The fateful decision was taken to land troops and try and capture the Turkish positions which overlooked the straits, but by the time the expedition had reached the peninsula, the Turks had already strengthened their defences – and the resulting land campaign ended in disaster.

'Old Gallipoli's a Wonderful Place'
(sung to the tune of 'Mountains of Mourne')

Oh, old Gallipoli's a wonderful place
Where the boys in the trenches the foe have to face,
But they never grumble, they smile through it all,
Very soon they expect Achi Baba to fall.
At least when I asked them, that's what they told me
In Constantinople quite soon we would be,
But if war lasts till Doomsday I think we'll still be
Where old Gallipoli sweeps down to the sea.

> We don't grow potatoes or barley or wheat,
> So we're on the lookout for something to eat,
> We're fed up with biscuits and bully and ham
> And we're sick of the sight of yon parapet jam.
> Send out steak and onions and nice ham and eggs
> And a fine big fat chicken with five or six legs,
> And a drink of the stuff that begins with a "B"
> Where the old Gallipoli sweeps down to the sea.[6]

Throughout the summer of 1915, the British forces defending the canal were gradually reduced, as the need for further troops at Gallipoli grew – and later in the year, another force was sent to the Western Frontier to put down a rebellion by the Senussi. By now, the Turks had driven through a railway line to Beersheba – and this caused some consternation amongst the British High Command, who realised the threat that this posed to the Suez Canal. A decision was taken to dispatch the 31st Division to build up the strength of the Imperial Strategic Reserve, which was formed for the defence of Egypt and placed under the command of Lieutenant General Sir Archibald Murray. It was against this backdrop that Jack Smallshaw began to record his impending departure for war:

'*Dec 2nd/15: Went back to Hurdcott from Larkhill*'.

'*About Dec 10th or 12th/15, we were promised 48 hours' leave previous to going overseas, but failed*'.

'*Dec 16th/15: Cinematographed on the march in our Sun Helmets for use in Acc* [Accrington] *& District*'.

'*Dec 18th/15: Left Hurdcott for proceeding overseas (EGYPT)*'.

'*Dec 19th/15: Embarked at Devonport on Troopship 'Ionic.' The Regimental Band played 'Home Sweet Home' and 'Auld Lang Syne' as the ship left England*'.

The SS *Ionic* was built as a passenger liner for the White Star line in 1902 by Harland & Wolff of Belfast. At the outbreak of war in 1914, she was requisitioned for use as a troopship by the New Zealand forces. The *Ionic* survived the war and was scrapped in 1936.

A few weeks prior to the departure of the 31st Division, the second Inter-Allied Conference was held at Chantilly (near Paris) on December 6th 1915.

---

6   Lyrics by Anon.

Representatives from the Allied Powers of Britain, France, Italy, Serbia and Russia met again to discuss future plans and strategy for the coming year (1916). The meeting, which was led by the French Commander-in-Chief, Marshal Joseph Joffre – and attended by his British counterpart, General Sir John French – was an extension of the previous discussions held back in July. The talks would also cover a memorandum: 'The Plan of Action Proposed by France to the Coalition', which was circulated by Joffre the previous month. Joffre proposed in his memorandum that new offensives should be opened up on the Italian Front, the Eastern Front and on the Western Front in simultaneous actions – and as soon as conditions were favourable; the Gallipoli campaign should be brought to an end, and the troops withdrawn and sent to Egypt, where they could be reorganised and given time to recover. They could then be used to bolster the defences to the east of the Suez Canal. Joffre's plans were met with full approval from those in attendance.

As Jack and his comrades set off for Egypt, the British and Commonwealth forces on the Gallipoli Peninsula continued with their withdrawal from Suvla Bay and Anzac Cove, which had started within days of the decision being made at the Chantilly Conference. By December 20th, an estimated 105,000 men and equipment had been successfully withdrawn from Suvla Bay and Anzac Cove without a single loss of life. Oblivious to the decisions being made, which would ultimately affect the 11th East Lancashires, Jack continued to record his progress to Egypt:

'*Dec 23rd/15: Sighted Gibraltar*'.

'*Dec 24th/15: Sighted Moroccan Coast*'.

'*Dec 25th/15 (Xmas Day) Sports on-board. Escorted from Gib to Malta by two Destroyers, (02) & (Acorn 88)*'.

'*Dec 27th/15: Arrived at Malta (Saw several French battleships here)*'.

While in Malta – and much to the anger of the troops on board – the officers were allowed to go ashore. This caused considerable resentment amongst the 'other ranks' and several decided to jump ship and visit the various clubs and bars around the harbour. Upon their return, nothing was said and this breach of discipline went unpunished: '*Dec 28th/15: Some survivors from the French ship (which was sank on Christmas Eve by an Austrian Submarine) arrived at Malta (Over 100 lives lost)*'. The French ship which Jack mentions in his diary entry was the 6,431-tonne SS *Ville De La Ciotat*, which was sunk by *Kapitänleutnant* Claus Rücker of SM *U-34*, with the loss of 81 lives while she was sailing from Japan to Marseille.

The New York Times reported the sinking on December 29th 1915:

Sinking of the Ville de la Ciotat Without Warning is verified

TOKIO, Dec28. The sinking of the French steamship Ville de la Ciotat has intensified the feeling aroused in Japan by the torpedoing of the Japanese liner Yasaka Maru.

Advices received by the Japan Mail corroborate previous reports that the Yasaka Maru was sunk without warning. The company's agent at Port Said reports that three times the usual number of lookouts were on duty, and that they saw nothing before the explosion occurred.

The Ville de la Ciotat carried a large amount of medical supplies and clothing for wounded Italian soldiers, purchased with contributions by Japanese and by foreigners in this country.

The Japanese cruisers Tokiwa and Chitose are to sail tomorrow from Yokosuka on a secret mission. It is believed they will go to the South Seas.[7]

On December 29th, Rücker struck again. This time it was the turn of the SS *Kenkoku Maru* to fall victim to his torpedoes. The 3,217-tonne ship was sunk south-west of Glad Island, Crete while heading for Savona. *Kapitänleutnant* Claus Rücker was one of the top U-Boat aces of the Great War. In all, he sunk 80 ships (with a total of 174,655 GRT) and damaged a further three.

Back in France, Sir Douglas Haig had succeeded Sir John French as Commander-in-Chief of the British forces. On December 29th 1915, he had a private meeting with Joffre at Chantilly, where discussions were held on the British taking over the Lens-Arras sector from the French Tenth Army – a request which Haig agreed to.

Jack recorded in his diary the departure of the *Ionic* from Malta: '*Dec 29th/15: Left Malta without an escort. One man (Pte Wickstead [sic] of X Company) took sunstroke and was buried by our R.C. Chaplain at sea at 6.45 a.m.*'. Private Wixted had the dubious distinction of being the first casualty of the 11th East Lancashires to die while on active service. He was buried at sea – south-west of Crete – and his name appears on the Helles Memorial, Gallipoli.

The departure of the *Ionic* without an escort caused some concern amongst the men sailing on her. There was considerable submarine activity in the area – and on the day after they set sail, the SS *Persia* was torpedoed without warning while *en route* to India. At lunchtime on December 30th, the SM *U-38* – commanded by *Kapitänleutnant* Max Valentiner – launched his attack on the ship. The SS *Persia* sank off the island of Crete within minutes – taking 343 passengers and crew to their deaths. The sinking broke the Prize Rules, or the so-called 'Cruiser

---

7   *The New York Times*, December 29th 1915.

Rules', which stated that passenger ships must not be sunk. Merchant ships could be stopped and searched, but their crews had to be put in a place of safety before the ship could be sunk.

Kapitänleutnant Valentiner was credited with 143 ships sunk (with a total tonnage of 298,794 GRT), one warship of 680 tonnes sunk, one warship of 10,850 tonnes damaged, five other ships damaged and three ships captured and taken as a prize. After the war, the British Government branded Valentiner a war criminal because of his 'no warning' attacks on shipping. As a result of the sinking of the *Persia*, the passengers and crew of the *Ionic* were put on high alert. Jack commented in his diary: '*Dec 30th/15: Ordered to wear our lifebelts continuously for 48 hours*'.

Their fears were well-founded too. On the very next day, the *Ionic* was attacked by a German submarine. Rather strangely, Jack referred to the submarine as being an Austrian gunboat:

> *Fri Dec 31st/15: My Platoon was going on guard this morning when we were fired on by an Austrian Gunboat, a torpedo just missing us only by a few feet, a most exciting time, but we were all ready with our lifebelts. We were reported sunk at Alexandria. This happened off the Crete Isles. I was on guard all night (New Year's Eve).*

A picture postcard of the SS *Ionic*.

The following poem was found written in the back of Jack's diary:

THE SUBMARINE ATTACK ON THE TROOPSHIP 'SS IONIC'

'Twas Hogmanay Day and the morning bright,
No land in view, or ship in sight
Our Skipper steered over the mighty deep
Two thousand souls in his care to keep

As the sun shone from the Eastern sky
Like a bolt from the blue came the warning cry
There we stood as men, for the fatal blow
That our ship and men would end below

As we watched the streak in the ocean blue
'Twas the hidden foe beneath we knew
A submarine in the distant sea
Had done her work not well, for she
Had missed her target by some feet
Then 'neath the surface made retreat
No soldier's home was left in gloom
They failed to send us to our doom.

Then as we watched the fading streak
With rifles then, no heart was weak
The lads from Lancashire stood
As only British soldiers should

The Engineers from Renfrew, stood too,
A picture to admire

Auld Rukies lads proved their pluck
To duty and their honour stuck
The breathless moments slowly went
Each man on vengeance he was bent
To fire on the hidden hell
Each man on duty took his spell.

As the danger flag went up the mast
A warning o'er the sea was cast
Those friends in need were quickly found
But God had taken us by the hand
And brought us safely to the land

Can we forget the closing year?
When we to death were all so near
In memory lives the closing scene
The ending of the year 1915.[8]

---

8   Poem by 'One aboard her'.

Part 3: 1916

'*Jan 1st/16: New Year's Day. We landed at Alexandria (Egypt). Some survivors landed here off a Japanese ship which was sank*'. It is likely that Jack was referring to the SS *Kenkoku Maru*, which was sank on December 29th 1915. Jack also recorded the landing of more survivors in his diary. The entry is dated 'December 30th', but is actually slotted in after January 1st. There is the possibility that this is a correction of his earlier entry of New Year's Day after he had heard of the sinking of the *Persia*: '*Dec 30th/15. The mail steamer "Persia" was sank. She left London Dec 18th/15 for Marseilles, Gib., Egypt, Aden & Bombay. Four boat-loads of survivors landed at Alexandria same time as ourselves (New Year's Day)*'.

On 5th January 1916, the Australian newspaper *The Argus* reported the sinking of the *Persia*:

SINKING OF THE S.S. PERSIA
200 Persons Still Missing
WHAT WILL AMERICA DO?

LONDON, Jan. 4

Hope had been abandoned in London of any further survivors from the R.M.S. [*sic*] Persia, when, late on Monday evening, news arrived that Colonel Lord Montague of Beaulieu (the recently appointed Inspector of Mechanical transports in India), and ten other persons, had been landed at Malta by a vessel which picked them up after the liner sank.

Doubt still continues as to the exact number of people on board, but it is now certain that 200 at least are missing. Only 12 out of the 80 first class passengers are saved.

The belief prevails that the submarine which sank the Persia is Austrian.

Apparently some of the survivors saw the submarine, but the second officer of the Persia, who was saved, reports that he saw the ripple of the torpedo which struck her.[1]

---

1   *The Argus*, 5th January 1916.

The question posed by the newspaper – 'What Will America Do?' – was a reference to the earlier sinking of the RMS *Lusitania* by the German submarine SM *U-20* on May 6th 1915. Of the 1,962 men, women and children on board, 1,201 of them perished; the sinking caused outrage in the United States at the time. One-hundred and twenty-eight of those who died were US citizens – and America was a neutral country. The British Government had hoped that this incident would bring the US into the war against Germany, but President Wilson stuck to his stance of neutrality. The sinking of the SS *Persia* caused further outrage, but it would not be until April 6th 1917 that America finally declared war on Germany.

As for Jack and his comrades – after their own narrow escape with the German U-Boat on December 31st (and possibly thinking that this may be their last chance they would ever get to enjoy themselves) – a large group of those on board decided to take drastic action while the SS *Ionic* was still in port at Alexandria: *'Jan 3rd/16: About 100 men rushed the gangway guard on account of them not allowing us off board'*. After the previous incident in Malta when some of his men jumped ship, Lieutenant Colonel Rickman had issued strict orders that no-one was to be allowed ashore. This latest breakdown of discipline infuriated him – and this time he decided that he had no option but to come down hard on those involved. All the men were arrested and confined to quarters. The next day, the ship set sail…

'Jan 4th/16: Left Alexandria and had 12 hours' rough sailing'.

'Jan 5th/16: Arrived at Port Said (our temporary destination) and were under canvas'.

After disembarking from the *Ionic*, the men encamped near the railway station alongside the other battalions of the 94th Brigade. The Imperial Strategic Reserve – of which the 94th Brigade was a part – was made up of 12 divisions. The role of the reserve was quite straightforward: they had to protect shipping on the canal from attacks launched by enemy raiding parties and to keep all enemy formations outside artillery range of the canal, but the nearest Turkish troops were around 100 miles away on the east of the Sinai Desert – and they were only a single division in strength.

On January 8th, the evacuation of the remaining troops from the Gallipoli Peninsula got under way at Cape Helles – and by the following day, every man had been taken off the beaches without loss of life. The evacuations were considered to be the only real success of the whole campaign.

'Charlie Chaplin'
(sung to the tune of 'Little Red Wing')

The moon shines down
On Charlie Chaplin
He's going balmy
To join the army
But his little baggy trousers
They need a-mending
Before they send him
To the Dardanelles.

The moon shines bright
On Charlie Chaplin
But his shoes are cracking
For want of blacking
And his baggy khaki trousers
Still need mending
Before they send him
To the Dardanelles.[2]

'Jan 15th/16: A party of 11th E.Ls. picked for Guard of Honour to Admiral of the French Fleet (at the Casino Palace Hotel)'.

'Jan 22nd & 23rd/16: The 13th Division (6th E.Ls. 6th S.Ls. 6th N.Ls.) landed at our camp at Port Said from the Peninsular'.

The 6th East Lancashires, 6th South Lancashires and 6th North Lancashires were part of the 13th Division who were evacuated from Cape Helles between January 8th and January 9th 1916. Their losses in that disastrous campaign were quite considerable – and the sight of the bedraggled survivors must have come as a shock to the men of the 'Pals' battalions who had yet to experience the full horrors of war.

In France on January 20th, a further meeting was held between Haig and Joffre at the British GHQ, Montreuil, where Joffre put forward his latest idea of multiple French offensives to take place towards the end of April 1916. The British role in this ambitious plan would be to launch diversionary attacks over a seven-mile front on the German positions north of the Somme, but Haig refused to be involved in any such scheme which he believed would prove to be rather costly (although he *was* prepared to help out in a joint Anglo-French offensive,

---

2   Lyrics by Anon.

which in his view would offer a greater chance of success). Haig's preference was for a July attack on the Messines-Wytschaete Ridge and to the north of Ypres, while Joffre wanted Picardy.

On January 25th, the 11th East Lancashires were taken by rail to 94th Brigade Headquarters at El Ferdan on the west bank of the Suez. The 40-mile trip had taken over eight hours in open wagons and torrential rain: *'Jan 25th/16: Left Port Said (in cattle trucks) and landed at El Ferdan (40 miles distant)'*. By the following day, the men had set up camp next to the canal – and for the next two weeks, they were employed operating the ferry, but they were soon on the move again: *'Feb 9th/16: Left El Ferdan and marched across desert to trenches at Abu-Aruk (with N.Z. Engineers and relieved by the 8th Northumberland Fusiliers (Indians' grave) (Chapattis)'*.

On February 9th, the men of 'W' and 'Z' Companies moved out to Abu-Aruk – a small cluster of huts situated some six miles from El Ferdan. Sir Archibald Murray, the commander of the force, had decided that the defensive line around the canal should be moved further out into the desert – and so the men of 'W' and 'Z' Companies were put to work digging trenches and erecting barbed wire around the settlement.

In France, Haig and Joffre held a further meeting on February 14th and a compromise was reached on Joffre's plans. The proposed offensive would be a joint venture between the British and French forces in an area where both armies met on the Somme River. Although Haig had lost out on his preference for the Ypres sector, he did manage to secure July as the month for the attack.

On February 19th, 'W' and 'Z' Companies were relieved from their duties of strengthening the defences at Abu-Aruk and returned to base: *'Sat Feb 19th/16: Left Abu-Aruk back to El Ferdan. We bivouacked at night (Saw defaulters hand-cuffed up to poles) (from Peninsular)'*. The men which Jack saw handcuffed to the poles were being subjected to 'Field Punishment Number One'. This form of punishment was brought out after the abolition of flogging in 1881. It was given for various transgressions of military discipline, where the offender would be tied or handcuffed to a fixed object (such as a cartwheel or post) for around two hours each day. This was usually meted out by giving the offender one hour in the morning and one hour in the afternoon. One of the prevailing myths of the Great War was that some prisoners were 'crucified' while being subjected to this field punishment and placed in full view of the enemy lines. There can be no doubt that some prisoners were indeed tied up with their arms outstretched – and it is probably the sight of this which led to talk of soldiers witnessing crucifixions – but to suggest that these men would have been placed in full view of the enemy is quite ridiculous. Such an act would have been tantamount to issuing a death sentence to the soldier involved. It is likely that the men which Jack referred to were from the 13th Division, who had just recently been evacuated from Cape Helles the previous month.

On February 20th, the 11th East Lancashires were on the move again. Ahead of them lay a 14-mile march to the town of El Kantara (El Qantarah on modern maps). Upon reaching their destination, they were dismayed to find that yet again, no preparations had been made for their arrival: *'Sunday Feb 20th/16: Reveille 3.30 a.m. Marched up to Kantara (a hard march). Kantara only 12 months ago had a population of 10,000 inhabitants but is now levelled down to the earth by the Turks in the early part of the war (On this march I found a shell which was used in early 1915)'.*

In France and Belgium, sporadic fighting continued along the front as both sides strove to push their lines forward. As in all theatres of war, there were 'quiet' sectors on the front where very little fighting took place. Soldiers would grow accustomed to this and adopt a 'live and let live' system; each side would tolerate the presence of the other. The daily routine of trench life, where both sides suffered the same depravations as each other, would be allowed to continue without the distractions of constant artillery duels and small arms fire. There would, of course, have to be the occasional strafing (just to keep the generals happy), but this would usually be done at set times to allow the soldiers to have their meals in peace and then move out before the shelling started. Watering holes and streams would be shared with the enemy; after all, there was no point in depriving your enemy of water, because you would only end up depriving your own men too. Both sides adopted this practice – and it worked extremely well. Such was the system in use on the Verdun sector in France, it was believed by the French troops to be a 'safe' posting. At times, the officers became so concerned about the fraternisation of some of their men with the Germans that they had to remind them that the Germans were their enemy and not their friend. The French considered that the chances of an attack in this sector were so remote that they even started to remove many of the guns from the various forts which dotted the area for use in the forthcoming offensive planned for the Somme in July, but for the past few weeks, there had been a feeling of unease – and the French (rather hurriedly) started strengthening their defences and brought in extra troops.

At 7:15 a.m. on the morning of February 21st, the hounds of hell were unleashed on the fortress of Verdun when the Germans opened up with a nine-hour artillery barrage on the French positions around the city. Much of the shelling from the smaller-calibre weapons was put down on the east bank of the Meuse River, while the larger-calibre siege guns and howitzers turned their attention to the forts and the city of Verdun itself. It was later estimated that more than one million rounds were fired in the opening bombardment, which could be heard almost 100 miles away. The ensuing battle would become the longest – and probably the bloodiest – of the Great War. Erich von Falkenhayn, the German commander of the Fifth Army, correctly predicted that for the French, the battle would become a matter of honour.

After the war, he wrote in his memoirs that he had sent a memorandum to the Kaiser in December 1915 concerning the state of the French Army (although some sources dispute this and claim that it is doubtful that any such message was ever sent, and what Falkenhayn actually wrote was nothing more than a later reflection of his thoughts at the time):

> Within our reach behind the French sector of the Western front there are objectives for the retention of which the French General Staff would be compelled to throw in every man they have. If they do so the forces of France will bleed to death – as there can be no question of a voluntary withdrawal – whether we reach our goal or not.[3]

In Egypt, on February 22nd, the 11th East Lancashires left El Kantara and marched out to Point 108 to relieve the 18th Durham Light Infantry, who had been manning the defensive positions: '*Tuesday Feb 22nd/16: Left Kantara and marched to trenches at Point 108 near Hill 108*'.

On February 23rd, the battalion had their second fatality since leaving England. Lieutenant Harry Mitchell of 'Z' Company was hit by a railway truck on February 20th at El Ferdan. He was admitted to hospital and had his right leg amputated, but he died several days later as a result of infection and was buried in Port Said War Memorial Cemetery.

Lieutenant Mitchell was highly regarded by everyone who knew him – and his death came as a great shock. Major St George Ross, his company commander, wrote a letter to his parents:

> I have had the pleasure of being his Company Commander from the very first, and a better Lieutenant and comrade I could not possibly have wished for. His men were devoted to him and I can assure you we all feel his loss very greatly. He is the first officer in the Brigade to give his life for his country and we shall always hold his name in honour and reverence.[4]

Back in France, the Germans continued with their assault on Verdun – and on February 25th, they captured Fort Douaumont. Four small groups of pioneers from the *24th Brandenburg Infanterie Regiment* were advancing independently of each other towards the fort. *Sergeant* Kunze and his patrol were the first to arrive – and to their utter amazement, they found that they were able to enter the fort without anyone challenging them. After exploring the deserted galleries inside,

3   Horne, Alistair, *The Price of Glory: Verdun 1916* (Penguin Books, 1978), p.44.
4   Turner, William, *Pals: The 11th (Service) Battalion (Accrington) East Lancashire Regiment – A History of the Battalion raised from Accrington, Blackburn, Burnley and Chorley in World War One* (Wharncliffe Publishing Ltd., 1987), p.116.

they eventually linked up with the other three individual groups commanded by *Oberleutnant* von Brandis, *Leutnant* Radtke and *Hauptmann* Haupt. *Sergeant* Kunze had already started rounding up the French soldiers manning the complex when he was joined by Radtke and his group. For some inexplicable reason, the French had left only around 50 men to defend Daumont. It was a mistake, which in terms of lives lost trying to re-take the fortress, was to cost them dearly – and the Germans had captured it without a single shot being fired.

In Egypt, the threat of any attack on the Suez Canal from the Turkish armies had receded. The dry season wasn't far away – and it was considered unlikely that the Turks would risk launching an attack across the Sinai Desert. The decision was taken to reduce the Imperial Strategic Reserve to three divisions and to send the rest to France and Belgium, where they were sorely needed. The 31st Division was finally on the move; the 11th East Lancashires withdrew from their positions and returned to Kantara: '*Monday Feb 28th/16: Left Point 108 and marched to Kantara*'.

Within a few days of their return to Kantara, the battalion was leaving Egypt for France, but one of the men had to be left behind. A volunteer from Rishton, 15478 Private William Baron was seriously ill in hospital. He died on March 25th 1916 and was buried close to Lieutenant Mitchell at Port Said War Memorial Cemetery: '*Thursday March 2nd/16: Left Kantara at 7.30 a.m. by rail. As we were waiting at the station the Durham Light Infantries band played 'Where are the boys [sic] of the village tonight?' as the Battalion moved out of Kantara. Embarked at Port Said on the Union Castle Liner 'Llandovery Castle' at 4.30 p.m. Sailed at 9 p.m. bound for France'.*

'Where Are the Lads of the Village Tonight?'

The West End's not the same tonight
The lights aren't shining quite so bright
That's what I hear the little ladies say
To give a glad eye is a crime, for it's a sad eye all the time
The dear lads of the village are away
The barmaid at you tries to wink
But with a tear-drop has to blink
And won't be ashamed to tell you why
Tho' the mob their flags are waving
Singing jingo songs and bragging
All the girls will ask each other with a sigh

(Chorus)
Where are the lads of the village tonight?
Where are the nuts we knew?
In Piccadilly? In Leicester Square? No, not there
No, not there. They're taking a trip on the Continong
With their rifles and bayonettes bright
Facing danger gladly where they're needed badly
That's where they are tonight.

No, Algie isn't on the moors
And bringing pheasants down by scores
He's shooting quite a different kind of bird
And Gussie isn't with the hounds
He's now on foreign hunting grounds
He's hunting German foxes so I've heard
And Percy tho' at sea a lot
Is not at Cowes upon his yacht
When last our Percy boy was seen
He was back as master gunner on a twenty thousand tonner
Dropping shells on a German submarine

(Chorus)
Where are the lads of the village tonight?
Where are the nuts we knew?
In Piccadilly? In Leicester Square? No, not there
No, not there. They're taking a trip on the Continong
With their rifles and bayonettes bright
Gone to teach the vulture murder is not a culture
That's where they are tonight.

We miss those gay dare-devil boys
The student lads, all fun and noise
But Guys and St Bartholomew's knew well
That in the trenches kneeling low
They tend the wounded though they know
The Red Cross Flag's a mark for German shell
But all the boys are doing grand
For King and Home and Motherland
And when at last they've turned the tide
Tho' Berlin's the place they'll rush for
They'll do nothing we need blush for
No, they'll play the game, and we shall say with pride

(Chorus)
Where are the lads of the village tonight?
Where are the nuts we knew?
In Piccadilly? In Leicester Square? No, not there
No, not there. They're taking a trip on the Continong
With their rifles and bayonettes bright
Where the Kaiser humbled, knows his power has crumbled
That's where they are tonight.[5]

Serre

The voyage of the *Llandovery Castle* from Port Said to France passed without incident – and within days, the 11th East Lancashires had reached their destination:

'*Monday March 6th/16: Sighted Sicilian Isles*'.

'*Wednesday March 8th/16: Entered Marseilles (France) Harbour at 7 a.m. (the V111 Army Corps – 4th Army)*'.

'*Thursday March 9th/16: Disembarked from the 'Llandovery Castle' 7 a.m. at Marseilles. At 2 p.m. we entrained at Marseilles. At 9 p.m. stopped at Orange for Rum and Tea Rations. Passed through Amiens. Arrived at Pont Remy*'.

'*Detrained at a small village and marched to our destination eight miles away, a village called Huppy and about 35 miles in the rear of the firing line. At this time the French were fighting heavily around Verdun*'.

The French were indeed fighting heavily at Verdun – and they were fighting for their very existence. The German onslaught on their positions continued day and night without respite. On the same day that Jack and the rest of the battalion was landing at Marseilles, the Germans were trying to capture the strategically important high ground of the Morte Homme, Côte 265 and Côte 304, but still the French held on. The sheer scale of the horrific slaughter caused by the artillery duels between the French and the Germans earned the Verdun battlefields the grim title of 'The Mincing Machine'.

After a few days' rest at Huppy, the 11th East Lancashires set off on a four-day march to the front line. This was to be their first taste of the realities of trench warfare on the Western Front, where the enemy would not be hundreds of miles from their trenches, as they were in Egypt; the distance was measured in just a few yards in places. Life in the trenches was a grim and deadly business, where death

5   Music and lyrics by R.P. Weston (1878-1936) and Herman Darewski (1883-1947).

was never far away, and where the unwary could easily fall victim to the sniper's bullet. The casual lifting of one's head to sneak a quick look over the parapet, or failing to stoop down at a low spot in the trench, had cost many a man his life.

'I Tracked a Dead Man Down a Trench'

I tracked a dead man down a trench,
I knew not he was dead.
They told me he had gone that way,
And there his foot-marks led.

The trench was long and close and curved,
It seemed without an end;
And as I threaded each new bay
I thought to see my friend.

I went there stooping to the ground,
For should I raise my head,
Death watched to spring; and how should then
A dead man find the dead?

At last I saw his back. He crouched
As still as still could be,
And when I called his name aloud
He did not answer me.

The floor-way of the trench was wet
Where he was crouching dead:
The water of the pool was brown,
And round him it was red.

I stole up softly where he stayed
With head hung down all slack,
And on his shoulders laid my hands
And drew him gently back.

And then, as I had guessed, I saw
His head, and how the crown –
I saw then why he crouched so still,
And why his head hung down.[6]

---

6   Poem by W.S.S. Lyon (1886-1915).

Jack Smallshaw continued with his diary account of his journey to the front line:

'Sun March 26th/16: Set out on a four days' march to the firing line, full marching order (on 12 hrs guard previous night) Raining heavily at 8 a.m. We landed at Longpre about 13 or 14 miles distant. Bivouacked here for the night in a barn'.

'Monday March 27th/16: Set out again at 8 a.m. and arrived at Vignacourt about 10 or 12 miles. Bivouacked in a barn for the night'.

'Tues March 28th/16: Left Vignacourt about 7 a.m. and marched to Beauval about 10 miles away'.

'Wed 29th March/16: Left Beauval at 8 a.m. and landed at Bertrancourt about three miles in rear of firing line (Somme District) Billeted in huts. As soon as we landed here we witnessed a German artillery attack on a British aeroplane. Several shells were fired and some of them fell among the Durham Light Infantry who were marching on the road in rear of firing line. One man was killed and several wounded'.

'Friday March 31st/16: The Germans shelled the next village to where we were billeted and our Battalion had to hurry away to fresh billets to make room for another Battalion who had been resting in this shelled village'.

After this diary entry, Jack wrote no more for the next 28 days, but the 94th Brigade war diaries and the battalion war diaries give an insight into what was happening at the time.

On April 3rd, the brigade was on the move again. The 12th and 14th Battalions, the York & Lancaster Regiment, took over the stretch of trenches which ran from Beaumont Hamel to the northern edge of Luke Copse opposite the village of Serre. This part of the front ran past the formidable German strongpoint known as the *'Heidenkopf'*, and then towards the so-called 'Gospel' copses of Matthew, Mark, Luke and John. The four copses were situated at the lower end of the gently-sloping ground which rose up to the village of Serre some 800 yards away. The German defences could be seen as four jagged white scars cutting through the chalky soil of the slope opposite the copses – the closest trench being roughly 150 yards in front of the British line. They were deep and well-constructed from various materials such as stout timber, steel girders and concrete, with many of the dugouts sunk to a depth of 20 feet or more below ground; they were impervious to anything but a direct hit from the heaviest calibre of guns. Just behind Walter and Serre Trench – and on the left of the village – the Germans had fortified the farm buildings which were visible through the gaps in trees at the top of the rise. To the right of the village and down the slope ran Munich Trench towards the *Heidenkopf.*

Thick belts of barbed wire ran across in front. Elaborate traps were constructed, with gaps in the wire deliberately left to draw attacking troops into 'killing-grounds', where they would be at the mercy of machine guns positioned to cover the breaks in the wire. At the northern extremity of the line – and just outside the 31st Division boundary – the British and German lines made a slight turn to the left before continuing north past Hebuterne and Gommecourt. From this point – and from the *Heidenkopf* in the south – the Germans were able to use their Maxim machine guns to fire across the full length of the 94th Brigade lines (in enfilade). They had held these positions since late 1914 – and since then, their time had been spent constructing and strengthening the defences. Their philosophy was totally different to that of the British: they were determined to hang on to the ground they had captured, and went to a great deal of effort with the construction of their lines to make sure that they were impregnable; any attacking force would pay a very heavy price. The British and French, however, viewed things differently: they were there to try and drive the Germans out of the occupied lands, and so there was no point in building permanent trench systems when their strategy was one of attack rather than defence.

While the York & Lancasters manned the front line trenches, the 11th East Lancashires were ordered to vacate their billets at Bertrancourt and move to Courcelles au Bois, where they would come under the command of the General Officer Commanding, the 144th Infantry Brigade. Later that evening (April 3rd), they received fresh orders to move to Colincamps and act as Brigade Reserve. At 9:50 p.m. on April 4th, the Germans mounted a small raid on the line held by the 14th York & Lancasters. The enemy six-man patrol entered the lines between Flag Avenue and Bleneau Trench, which ran approximately 400 yards south of Matthew Copse. In the ensuing struggle, the second-in-command of the 14th York & Lancasters – Major Sanford – was bayoneted and wounded by one of the enemy patrol.

Shortly after 9:00 p.m. on the evening of April 6th, the Germans opened up with a ferocious artillery barrage on a 1,200-yard stretch of the British front line, which ran from Bess Street Trench (just north of the *Heidenkopf*) to the point where the front line crossed the road out of Beaumont Hamel (known to the British troops as 'Watling Street'); the barrage also targeted the support and reserve lines in the surrounding area. Some 15 minutes later, the British responded and put down a counter-barrage on the *Heidenkopf.* At 9:25 p.m., the 11th East Lancashires were ordered forward to occupy the reserve lines, as at that stage it still wasn't clear what the intentions of the enemy were. The 12th East Yorkshires were then brought forward into Colincamps to fill the gap left by the advance of the 11th East Lancashires. At 10:25 p.m. a large fire and white flares were observed at the *Heidenkopf* – and by 10:50 p.m. the bombardment from

'Somewhere in France'.

both sides started to die down. A short while later, the 11th East Lancashires were stood down and returned to Colincamps.

On April 12th, the brigade was relieved by the 92nd Brigade and moved back to Bertrancourt – and from April 13th to the 27th, they were put to work repairing the reserve lines. Back in 1915, these trenches had originally been the front line and the scene of bitter fighting between the French and German armies. In June 1915, French troops under the command of General de Castenau tried to recapture the ground previously taken by the Germans in 1914. The fortified positions at Touvent Farm were attacked – and although the French made some initial gains, they came at a very high cost. The fighting dragged on for over a week, but no further progress was made. Eventually, the Germans reorganised their front line and made a tactical withdrawal to the higher ground in front of the village of Serre.

Jack's battalion – the 11th East Lancashires – was given the task of deepening and widening the reserve trenches. While the battalion was carrying out this work, they started to unearth the remains of French soldiers killed in the battles of 1914 and 1915. For many of the men, this was the first time they had been so close to the gruesome consequences of mechanised warfare – and perhaps it served as a stark and sobering reminder of what might lie in store for them.

On April 28th, the 94th Brigade took over from the 93rd Brigade on a stretch of line which ran from Nairne Street Trench (just north of John Copse) to Ludgate Circus/Watling Street opposite Beaumont Hamel. The 14th York &

Lancasters occupied the line from Nairne Street to Board Street, while the 11th East Lancashires occupied from Board Street to Ludgate Circus/Watling Street in the south. The left flank was occupied by 'Z' Company, with 'W' Company (Jack's company) on the right and 'Y' Company in the centre. The 12th York & Lancasters provided a company of men to occupy the reserve trenches for the first four days – and they in turn were relieved by a company from the 14th York & Lancasters for the remaining four days' occupation of the front line: *Friday April 28th/16: Our Battalion except X Coy moved into the front line trenches starting from Bertrancourt about 5 p.m. and arrived in trenches at 'Stand To' (We relieved the 'West Yorks)'*.

At 11:00 p.m. on April 29th, a bombardment opened up on the enemy trenches to the right of Jack's position in support of a raid being carried out by units from the 29th Division. The Germans retaliated with small arms fire and rifle grenades along the 11th Battalion lines – and one of Jack's comrades was gravely injured by one of the grenades which landed on their position:

> *Sat April 29th/16: About 11 or 11.30 p.m. our Artillery and etc. started 'strafing' the Germans. About 12.15 midnight, three of our section (of six men and one N.C.O.) got wounded by a rifle grenade. Pte A Riley who was wounded in the small of the back died in hospital next day at Beauval where he was buried. Our Pioneers made a fine cross for his grave. Pte Roger Singleton and Jim Renton were wounded at the same time and taken out of the trenches.*

> *Between 12-15 and 12-30 p.m. the bombardment ceased a great deal. Directly after the bombardment was over the Germans were very active with their machine guns and rifle-fire, and so were we, our lads let a good few rounds go over to 'Fritz' (Our three lads were wounded at a place called TOM FOYS CAMP).*

The fatalities which Jack mentions in his diary were L/Cpl 15718 Joseph G. Hartley and Pte 16033 Jack Clark. Both men were killed in action on April 29th and were interred at Sucrerie Military Cemetery, Colincamps. Pte 20972 Arthur Riley died the following day of the wounds sustained in the grenade attack and was interred at Beauval Cemetery.

'Hush! Here Comes a Whizz-Bang' (song)

Hush! Here comes a whizz-bang
Hush! Here comes a whizz-bang
Now you soldier boys
Run down those stairs

Down in the dugout and say your prayers.
Hush! Here comes a whizz-bang
And it's heading straight for you.
And you'll see all the wonders of no-man's land
If a whizz-bang hits you.[7]

During their eight-day tour in the front line, the battalion was put to work digging out new communication trenches and improving the saps which went out to the advanced listening posts in no man's land. An old trench which ran between Bess Street and Board Street Trenches was also repaired, with the intention of this becoming the new front line trench: *Saturday May 6th/16: Our Battalion were relieved by the 13th East Yorks in the afternoon. The casualties for the eight days and nights we were in action were about two killed, one died of wounds and about 12 or 15 wounded. We marched from the trenches to our encampment in a wood two miles from Bus (Warnimont Wood, Bus-les-Artois)'.* While at Warnimont Wood – and supposedly on rest – Jack's battalion was put to use on general fatigues, going out on working parties and ferrying supplies to the front.

On May 15th, the 12th York & Lancasters moved back into the front line while the 11th East Lancashires moved into billets at Courcelles au Bois. The 31st Division lines had been reorganised by this time and the 94th Brigade took over the stretch of line running from Number Four Trench – approximately 200 yards south-east of Matthew Copse – to Number One Trench on the northern edge of John Copse. On May 20th, the 11th East Lancashires relieved the 12th York & Lancasters in the front line: *'Sat May 20th/16: Our Battalion went into the trenches for ten days and our casualties were from 15 to 20'.*

During their occupation of the lines, the battalion was put to work repairing the barbed wire defences in front of their trenches. These duties were an extremely hazardous and nerve-racking experience, which all soldiers from both sides dreaded having to do. It could only be carried out at night (when darkness offered some protection from the prying eyes of the enemy), but at the slightest hint of wiring parties at work in no man's land, the Germans would launch their flares into the sky. They streaked upwards with a loud hiss – leaving a trail of sparks in their wake; their progress was followed by the eyes of the men huddled below. The flares would then explode into a ball of brilliant shimmering light – turning night into day. They hung aloft for several seconds – creating shadows which appeared to be dancing around, as the glare illuminated and played across the battle-scarred ground below. The soldiers stood motionless, with nerves on edge – hoping and praying that they had not been seen. The slightest movement or sound from them would result in the enemy opening up with their machine guns

---

7   Lyrics by Anon.

and rifle grenades; then the light would burn out and everything would once again disappear into the inky blackness of the night...

Back in the support lines, the 12th York & Lancasters were put to work repairing Rob Roy Trench and strengthening the mortar battery emplacements. Further back, just north of La Signy Farm (and on the road to Hebuterne), stretches of the reserve line were converted into fire trenches; wire barricades were erected in front. Between his diary entries for May 20th and June 16th, Jack made a reference to his appointment as batman to Lieutenant Gorst, although he did not give an actual date for this. Lt Gorst had originally served with the 2nd Battalion, the East Lancashires and was wounded in May 1915 at the Battle of Aubers. After he had recovered from his injuries, he was sent back to the front and attached to the 11th East Lancashires: '*May,16: I was appointed batman to Lt Gorst*'.

On May 30th, Jack and his battalion came out of the trenches after being relieved by the 14th York & Lancasters. They returned to Courcelles au Bois and went into Brigade Reserve. At Verdun, the bitter struggle on the left bank of the Meuse River continued as the Germans tried to take the high ground at Côte 304. On May 3rd, more than 500 guns opened fire on a one-mile front and pulverised the French positions on the summit of the ridge. For almost three days, the French defenders were subjected to unimaginable horrors as the German guns pounded away at the ridge – and eventually their assault troops managed to gain a small foothold, but it would be another three days of close-quarter combat before the French were completely driven off the summit. It was later estimated that the French losses alone were around 10,000 men.

General Nivelle, the newly-appointed commander of the French Second Army, was determined to bring a halt to the German advances – and one of his first orders since taking over from General Petain at the beginning of May was for the reoccupation of Fort Douaumont on the right bank of the river. Since the Germans had captured it in February, they had turned it into a much more formidable fortress, with the addition of extra trenches and thick belts of barbed wire protecting its boundaries. Being situated on high ground, the fortress was of hugely strategic importance. A French machine gunner, Robert Desaubliaux, said of the Germans holding Douaumont: 'They dominate us from Fort Douaumont; we cannot now take anything without their knowing it, nor dig any trench without their artillery spotting it and immediately bombarding it'.[8] Any attempt to recapture the fort would come at a very heavy cost. The commander of the French 5th Division, General Mangin, approached Neville with proposals for an attack to re-take the fortress using two regiments of troops on a front of just 1,100 yards – but within two days of Neville accepting the plan and issuing the first orders, the Germans became fully aware of the proposed assault and started strengthening Douaumont's defences.

---

8   Horne, *The Price of Glory*, p.232.

On May 17th, the French artillery opened up on the German defences with their heavy siege guns. For five days they pounded away at the fortress – and the surrounding area – with an estimated 1,000 tonnes of shells until finally, on May 22nd, the assault troops went in. After some initial success in retaking parts of Douaumont, they were eventually driven back – and in three days of heavy fighting, the French had suffered almost 6,000 casualties and failed in their bid to recapture the fort. The bloodshed of 'The Mincing Machine' was destined to continue into December before it finally came to an end.

The plans drawn up for the impending Somme offensive envisaged an assault over a 60-mile front, but this was later reduced to a mere 23 miles after the 40 divisions committed to the battle by the French had been cut to just 11 divisions of the Sixth Army because of the situation at Verdun. The British were, by now, the largest contributor to the forthcoming battle – and on June 3rd, the start date for the offensive was set for June 28th.

Back in the 94th Brigade area at Serre, a large-scale trench raid on the German lines was carried out on the night of June 3rd/4th. The raiding party, which consisted of 70 men and 11 NCOs, was led by three officers: Captain A. Wood, Lieutenant H. Quest and 2nd/Lieutenant G.H.T. Best – all of the 14th York & Lancasters. Artillery support was supplied by the 29th and 48th Divisions on the right and left flanks, with the 94th Brigade's own divisional artillery covering the centre. At midnight, the 29th and 48th Division's artillery opened up with a heavy bombardment of 18 pdr field guns and 4.5 inch howitzers on the German first and second lines – stretching from the *Heidenkopf* in the south, to a bend in the German line known as 'The Point' at the top end of the Serheb Road (to the north of John Copse). Directly in front of the four copses, the larger-calibre weapons were brought to bear on the German communication trenches leading down from the village to the third and second lines. At 1:10 a.m., the bombardment on the front line lifted and moved onto the second line, as the raiding party moved out of a forward sap in front of Matthew Copse. They approached the German wire – and using a Bangalore torpedo, a route was blasted through. Two teams of men dropped into the trench, while the wire-cutting party guarded the point of entry. They traversed left and right along the trench and attacked two dugouts with Mills bombs – killing three other Germans who were manning the trench. After a few minutes, they withdrew and returned to their own lines. Lieutenant Quest was injured, and one other member of the patrol was killed. Lieutenant Quest was later awarded the Military Cross and two other men the Military Medal for their bravery that night.

On June 14th, the 11th East Lancashires moved from Gezaincourt to Warnimont Wood after completing training for the forthcoming offensive. Working parties were provided by the battalion for ferrying munitions to the front. A few days later, Jack Smallshaw received a package from home – just in time to celebrate his birthday: '*Sat June 17th/16: My 20th Birthday. I received a fine Birthday cake from*

Jack with one of his comrades.

Mother and Mona[9] along with some other lovely eatables. Had a tuck in'.

On June 19th, Jack's battalion was back in the front line after relieving the 12th York & Lancasters. This would be their last tour in the firing line before going 'over the top' on July 1st – and casualties were quite high. The battalion war diaries recorded that 12 men were killed and a further 24 wounded during their five days in the trenches. Jack erroneously recorded the date that the battalion went in the line as 'June 24th' – and he also recorded their casualties as much higher during this particular spell in the trenches: *'Sat June 24/16: Went into trenches and during our four days we had over 40 casualties. Four of our Company were buried and killed by high explosive shells in Rob-Roy Trench'.*[10]

Lieutenant Gorst, to whom Jack was batman, mentioned the same incident in a letter he wrote home to his sister:

> We are in the line at the moment but our time is very nearly over now; it's been rather beastly this time. We had four men buried by a shell this afternoon and I helped to dig them out, with the result that I've been feeling rather sick ever since; they were all dead poor chaps; and one of my best sergeants wounded too.[11]

---

9 The actual name is unclear in the diary.
10 The actual date was June 19th.
11 Jackson, Andrew, *Accrington's Pals: The Full Story: The 11th Battalion, East Lancashire Regiment (Accrington Pals) and the 158th (Accrington and Burnley) Brigade, Royal Field Artillery (Howitzers)* (Pen & Sword Books Ltd., 2013), p.95.

On June 23rd, Operation Order No.45 was issued by the 94th Brigade: the countdown to the assault had begun.

The very next day, June 24th – 'U' Day – the British guns opened up on the German wire. This preliminary artillery bombardment was intended to cut lanes through the enemy wire in preparation for the advance by the 94th Brigade. Operation Order No.46 stated that:

1. The Artillery commence cutting the German wire to-day.
2. 11th East Lancs. Regt. and 12th York and Lancs. Regt. will send out patrols to examine the enemy's wire on the night of June 25 and June 26. There will be no Artillery fire on the enemy's front line between 11 p.m. and 12 midnight on June 25, and between 10.30 p.m. on June 26.
3. 92nd Infantry Brigade are carrying out a raid on the German trenches at 12 midnight on June 27. Point of entry – K 29 b 3535.[12]
4. (a) Gas will be discharged on night of June 25 if wind is favourable; if not, on nights of June 26th or 27th.
    (b) There will be 10 minutes' discharge of smoke along our whole front, on the following days.
    June 26th – 10.15 a.m. to 10.25 a.m.
    27th – 5.45 a.m. to 5.55 a.m.
    6.55 p.m. to 7.5 p.m.
    28th – 7.15 a.m. to 7.25 a.m.
    5.15 p.m. to 5.25 p.m.[13]

The 11th East Lancashires were relieved by the 10th East Yorkshires from the 92nd Infantry Brigade after completion of their four days in the line; they returned to Warnimont Wood. Up to this date, Jack's diary accounts have always proven to be extremely accurate when checked against battalion records, although he appears to have written some of his entries several days after the actual event. It is possible that Jack was involved in the patrols which were sent out to inspect the German wire on the night of June 25th/26th and that he wrote up his diary account after completing his tour in the trenches, as well as the patrols. Jack duly recorded: *June 27th/16: our battalion came out of the trenches*.

On June 24th, the British artillery had opened up with their barrage on the German front line – held by the *169th Infanterie Regiment* – as they strove to demolish the wire, deep underground shelters, strongpoints and communication trenches. The patrols that ventured out to inspect the damage brought back varying tales of success: in some areas, the gaps in the wire were minimal; in others, there had been a complete failure to cut through. Right up to the eve of the assault, the

---

12 Located opposite the southern end of Mark Copse.
13 The National Archives (TNA) WO 95/2363/1: 94th Infantry Brigade Operation Order No.46.

31st Divisional HQ were aware of this, but there was little which could be done at such a late stage of the operation. Orders were issued to the patrols going out at night to try and cut through with Bangalore torpedoes and wire cutters as best as they could. Since June 23rd, there had been rain every single day – and by June 27th, low cloud (combined with heavier rain) was severely hampering the work of the RFC, who were out spotting for the artillery. The following day, the weather was no better – and finally a decision was taken to postpone the assault for 48 hours in the hope of some improvement in the weather. At 12:15 p.m. on June 28th, a telephone message was received by Brigade Headquarters from Divisional HQ – postponing all movements within the brigade area until Saturday, July 1st due to the adverse weather conditions. It gave the artillery a vital extra 48 hours to pound away at the wire and the defences, but it made little difference to the outcome other than to offer a brief respite from the slaughter which was about to happen. The message was quickly relayed to the battalions in the field and reserve: 'B.M. 971. 28th June, 1916. Zero has been postponed 48 hours aaa June 29 will become Y1 day, and June 30 'Y2' day. aaa July 1 will be 'Z' day. aaa Acknowledge. – From 94th Inf Bde, 9.30pm'.[14]

That same day, Brigadier General H.C. Rees – commanding the 94th Infantry Brigade – issued his 'Special Order of the Day' to the brigade:

> SPECIAL ORDER OF THE DAY: by Brig.-General H.C.REES, D.S.O., Commanding 94th Infantry Brigade.
> Bde. H.Q. 28.6.16
>
> You are about to attack the enemy with far greater numbers than he can oppose to you, supported by a huge number of guns.
>
> Englishmen have always proved better than the Germans were when the odds were heavily against them. It is now our opportunity.
>
> You are about to fight in one of the greatest battles in the world, and the most just cause.
>
> Remember that the British Empire will anxiously watch your every move, and that the honour of the North Country rests in your hands.
>
> Keep your heads, do your duty, and you will utterly defeat the enemy.
> Sd. F. S. G. PIGGOT, Captain,
> Bde. Major, 94th Inf. Bde.[15]

The role of the 94th Infantry Brigade was to capture the fortified village of Serre and secure the left (northern) flank of the 18-mile line of attack being undertaken by General Rawlinson's Fourth Army. The new line was intended to run from

---

14 TNA WO 95/2363/1: 94th Infantry Brigade war diary.
15 TNA WO 95/2363/1: 94th Infantry Brigade war diary.

John Copse at the northern end of the divisional boundary and across the Serheb Road – passing through the northern edge of the village and through the Serre–Puisieux Road to a point to the eastern side of the village (a distance of some 1,500 yards). The left assaulting battalion, the 12th York & Lancasters (Sheffield City Battalion), occupied the front line from John Copse to the southern tip of Mark Copse. The 14th York & Lancasters (2nd Barnsley Pals) acted as reserve, with one company occupying Nairne Street Trench on the left of John Copse and the remaining three companies occupying the assembly trenches to the rear of John and Luke Copse. The right assaulting battalion, the 11th East Lancashires (Accrington Pals), covered the remainder of the line from Mark Copse down to Matthew Copse. The right reserve battalion, the 13th York & Lancasters (1st Barnsley Pals), occupied the assembly trenches immediately behind the assaulting companies in the line. The plan of attack was laid down according to a rigid timetable of events which appeared to make little allowance for delays or failures which usually occur during an advance.

At 7:20 a.m., two platoons from 'W' and 'X' Companies of the 11th East Lancashires move out into no man's land and position themselves as close to the German wire as their own artillery barrage will allow. The remaining platoons of 'W' and 'X' Companies follow five minutes later and position themselves 50 yards further back. At 7:30 a.m., the barrage lifts and targets the German fourth line, while the first and second waves of the 11th East Lancashires advance to the German third line and consolidate their positions. At 7:35 a.m., the third and fourth waves of 'Y' and 'Z' Companies leave Campion and Monk Trench, and advance to the German third and second line: 'Where they will lie down until 0.28;[16] & at this hour they will again advance, and pass through the leading line in the fourth German trench, approaching as near to the village of SERRE as the fire of our own guns will permit'.[17] While the third and fourth waves were advancing upon the final objective of the first 'bound', the 13th York & Lancasters (1st Barnsley Pals) supply two platoons to carry out the 'mopping-up' operations on the German second and third lines, as well as the communication trenches which ran up to the fourth line.

The next objective for the 11th East Lancashires was the village of Serre, where they were to sweep through and capture the German lines running along the flank and the southern and eastern boundaries of the village. The detailed plans continued to list the objectives of these 'bounds':

---

16 7:58 a.m.
17 TNA WO 95/2363/1: 94th Infantry Brigade Operation Order No.45.

0.40.[18] Second "bound"

The Artillery barrage lifts from the western edge of SERRE village, and the third and fourth waves, who have previously passed through the leading Companies now holding the fourth German trench, advance to secure the second objective.

The attack on the village will be directed with the object of securing as quickly as possible the main trenches on the flanks and at the Eastern end of the village, and holding these trenches in sufficient strength to enable attacks to be made inwards against any small parties of Germans in the village who may still be holding out, should the parties detailed to deal with the Germans here be unable to complete their task.

Only small parties of men should be detailed to work through the village itself, but each party will be given a definite objective. All attacking parties will closely follow our Artillery barrage.

This barrage will move slowly up the village at a rate of four minutes for the first 200 yards, afterwards lifting at the rate of four minutes for each 100 yards. This barrage finally lifts from the North-East edge of SERRE at 1.20;[19] two 18pdr. Batteries and two 4.5 inch Howitzers continue firing on the Orchard near L25 a 16[20] and neighbouring trenches until 1.40.[21]

The 12th York & Lancs. Regt. will occupy and consolidate that portion of the trench selected as a defensive flank as shown on the map already issued.

One Company of the 13th York & Lancs. Regt. from front line will proceed to fourth German line, replacing the Companies of 11th East Lancs. Regt.

Two Platoons of the 13th York & Lancs. Regt. from COPSE to front line.

1.20.

The consolidation of the north-eastern corner of SERRE village immediately it has been seized at 1.20, is of vital importance. Strong bombing parties from both 11th East Lancs. Regt. and 12th York & Lancs Regt. will immediately proceed along the communication trenches towards the Orchard near L25 a 16.

1.40. Third "bound"

The Artillery barrage lifts from the Orchard near L25 a 16.

11th East Lancs. Regt. will capture the Orchard, having gone up to it as our Artillery barrage will permit previous to the hour of 1.40, connecting

---

18 8:10 a.m.
19 8:50 a.m.
20 The eastern edge of the village.
21 9:10 a.m.

with the 12th York & Lancs. Regt. at K30 b 68[22] and with the 93rd Brigade on their right.

The 12th York & Lancs. Regt., in addition to their Bombing Party, will detail one Platoon to take part in the attack, supported by such troops as the officer on the spot considers necessary.[23]

Several Russian saps (shallow tunnels) had been dug across no man's land towards the German first line – three of which were situated in the 94th Brigade area. According to the brigade plans, these three saps ('C', 'D' and 'E') were only to be used for communications during the assault, but they were eventually used by Stokes mortar teams to put down a barrage from close range on the German lines; there was also a fourth sap ('F') mentioned within the original brigade plans. This was driven out from the northern side of John Copse in addition to sap 'E', which already ran out from the southern edge of the copse: 'A Russian sap, numbered F, is being constructed from JOHN COPSE towards German C. T [sic],[24] K 23 d 81.[25] It will be cleared and converted to an open trench on day of attack, and will form a fire trench of portion of the defensive of the 94th Brigade'.[26] Both saps 'E' and 'F' were listed as terminating at the same point on the German line. One platoon from the pioneer battalion of the King's Own Yorkshire Light Infantry (KOYLI) and two platoons from the second company of the 14th York & Lancasters were given the task of converting sap 'F' into a fire trench to secure the left flank (facing north) and link up with the 12th York & Lancasters at the point where the fourth German line turned towards the Serheb Road.

Back at Warnimont Wood, the 11th East Lancashires rested as they waited to start their long journey to the front line. It was now Friday, June 30th: 'Y2' Day. Amongst the assembled men, there was a feeling of great optimism for the forthcoming battle. They had witnessed and heard the terrific bombardment on the German lines for the past few days; nothing could possibly have survived all that. It was going to be a stroll in the park… the Germans were all going to be dead – their guns smashed and useless – but there were those who harboured doubts: the men who had been out at night on patrols inspecting the wire… they knew the true state of the German defences. They had seen the uncut wire and the trenches full of enemy troops armed to the teeth – and they were full of dread for what lay in store for them when they went over the top the following morning.

As Jack Smallshaw and his friends in 'W' Company waited to make their way to the front, there were last letters to write home before they left – just in case

---

22 Approximately 300 yards to the left of the orchard.
23 TNA WO 95/2363/1: 94th Infantry Brigade Operation Order No.45.
24 Communication Trench.
25 'K 23 d 81' is a map reference for a Russian sap.
26 TNA WO 95/2363/1: 94th Infantry Brigade document ('Instructions to Commanding Officers in relation to the forthcoming advance').

they did not make it. Of course, most of them thought and hoped the same: it would not happen to them; it was always someone else who got the chop; but deep down, they wondered whether 'maybe this time'... How do you put into words your fears for what lay ahead? How do you tell your wife, your children, that if they are reading this – your last letter – it means that you did not make it through?

'To My Daughter Betty,
The Gift of God'

In wiser days, my darling rosebud, blown
To beauty proud as was your mother's prime,
In that desired, delayed, incredible time,
You'll ask why I abandoned you, my own,
And the dear heart that was your baby throne,
To dice with death. And oh! they'll give you rhyme
And reason: some will call the thing sublime,
And some decry it in knowing tone.
So here, while the mad guns curse overhead,
And tired men sigh with mud for couch and floor,
Know that we fools, now with the foolish dead,
Died not for flag, nor King, nor Emperor, –
But for a dream born in a herdsman's shed,
And for the secret Scripture of the poor.[27]

Jack didn't have much to say in his diary about the forthcoming assault. He didn't reveal his thoughts on what might happen to him, but he must have harboured the same fears that all men have on the eve of battle. No-one wanted to die – not even for King and Country – but if they *were* to die, they hoped it would be quick and painless: *'Friday June 30th/16: The eve of the Great Push of July 1st 1916'*.

That evening, Jack and the rest of the battalion left Warnimont Wood on the seven-mile march to the front line trenches. Every man carried two days' rations of food and water, 120 rounds of ammunition in pouches and 50 rounds in a bandolier, four Mills bombs, a pick or shovel, four sandbags tied to his pack, a gas helmet and a steel helmet; every man wore a metallic identification triangle fixed to his pack. They were carrying almost half their own body weight in equipment – and while wearing this, they were expected to climb out of the trenches and go into battle the following morning. Onwards they marched towards Courcelles – the skyline ahead brilliantly lit by flashes as the artillery barrage continued to pulverise the German lines in the distance. Lieutenant Colonel Rickman duly

---

27 Poem by T.M. Kettle (1880-1916).

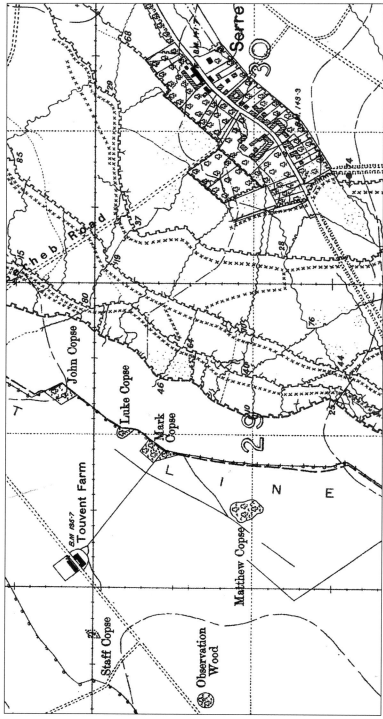

Map 1 – A trench map of the fortified village of Serre; the German trench systems can be seen to the right of the four copses. (Map used with kind permission of the Lancashire Infantry Museum, Preston)

noted in his 'Report on Operations': 'After synchronising watches at 9.30pm, the head of the column left Courcelles at 9.45pm., and marched as directed to Central Avenue. The trench was in a very bad state and over knee deep in mud which had become glutinous'.[28] Such was the state of the trenches that Rickman ordered his men to climb out and to continue over the top in an effort to make up for lost time, but they didn't get far before they were forced to re-enter the trenches to escape the shockwaves from the gun batteries who were in action close by – furiously firing away at the German front line.

By now, the German artillery was starting to answer back – the occasional shells reaching as far back as Colincamps. The column eventually reached Observation Wood after suffering a nightmare journey through damaged and waterlogged trenches, which had made their progress almost impossible – the men sinking up to their knees in the thick glutinous mud under the sheer weight of their equipment. Hereafter, the ground sloped downwards towards the four copses – and just 1,000 yards lay between them and the German first line. At 2:40 a.m. – four hours later than planned – Jack Smallshaw and his 'Pals' finally reached the front line.

'We went over the top this morning'

4:00 a.m. – Saturday, July 1st: the 11th East Lancashires finally reached their positions in the assembly trenches after struggling through the congestion and mud caused by the recent bad weather. The platoons of 'W' and 'X' Companies in the first wave of the assault moved into the already shell-damaged and waterlogged front line trench and traffic trench. The remainder of the companies (which made up the second wave) occupied Copse Trench, while the third and fourth waves from 'Y' and 'Z' Companies were 500 yards further back in Campion and Monk Trench. To their left, the assaulting platoons of the 12th and 14th York & Lancasters took up their positions and waited. Ahead in no man's land, the white marker tape – which had been carefully laid out to guide the assaulting platoons to the gaps in the German wire – also indicated to the enemy the exact spot where the 'Pals' battalions intended to break through the line.

At 5:00 a.m., the British guns gradually started to increase their bombardment on the German lines, but the reply from the enemy artillery was swift – and for the next few hours, the brigade front came under an increasingly heavy counter-barrage. Shrapnel and high-explosive shells were finding their mark amongst the tightly-packed trenches in front of the four copses – and already, the casualties were starting to mount amongst the waiting troops. The wounded began to make their way back to the Regimental Aid Post at Excema Trench, but these were the

---

28 TNA WO 95/2366/1: 11th East Lancashire Regiment war diary.

'lucky' ones – their injuries saving them from the slaughter which was about to take place in just a few hours' time.

The 94th Infantry Brigade's 'Report of Operations' for 5:00 a.m. that morning said:

> All units had reported they were in position of assembly, in accordance with Operation Orders.
>
> The German reply to our six days' bombardment had caused considerable damage to our fire-bays, traffic trench, and to Rob Roy, especially the latter; this trench, however, was not used at all in the operations.
>
> Our artillery maintained a heavy bombardment on the enemy's trenches from 5. a.m. to 7. 30 a.m., the last hour being intense.
>
> The German artillery replied to this with shrapnel and heavy M.G on our front line, particular attention being paid to junction of communicators [sic] with front line, especially the junction of NAIRNE and front line.[29]

The 14th York & Lancasters (2nd Barnsley Pals) suffered heavy casualties during this barrage on Nairne Trench; an estimated 30 percent of their men were either killed or wounded. At 6:25 a.m., the British 'heavies' – the 60 pdrs and the large-calibre howitzers – joined in as the shelling of the enemy lines intensified. Everywhere on the slope in front of Serre, the ground erupted in huge geysers of earth – the men watching in awe at the destructive power of their own artillery. The first wave of the 11th East Lancashires and the 12th York & Lancasters fixed bayonets and waited – and all around them was a scene straight from hell. Shells screaming through the sky... explosions, smoke and dust... and the distinct crack of small arms ammunition whizzing overhead as the men crouched low in their trenches to escape the inferno above.

The minutes ticked by – and then at 7:20 a.m. (and some 3,000 yards to the right of the line), the massive mine underneath the German redoubt at Hawthorn Ridge – the first of 19 mines placed along the whole front – was detonated. With a thunderous roar, 40,000 lbs of ammonal went up. The very earth seemed to shake and shudder, as if trying to contain the mighty force of the explosion, before finally breaking open – and then a huge mountain of earth shot skywards for hundreds of feet like an enormous volcanic eruption. Where once there had been men, there was just a smouldering crater some 60 feet deep and almost 200 feet across.

At that very instant, the barrage from the British heavy siege guns lifted along a four-mile stretch of the front line – and a noticeable silence descended upon the battlefield... a silence which was so sudden after the incessant artillery barrage of

---

29   TNA WO 95/2363/2: 94th Infantry Brigade document ('Operations of 94th Infantry Brigade, on July 1st, 1916').

the past week, that the assembled troops at Beaumont Hamel commented upon it – as did the 'Pals' battalions of the 94th Infantry Brigade further north:

> Across the Redan Ridge the Pals of the 31st Division, crawling out to wait in front of the wire for the signal to go for Serre, remarked on it too. The bombardment which, more than two miles away had had to cease to allow two companies of troops to attack four hundred yards of the enemy's defences on the Hawthorn Ridge, had by some error of judgement or misinterpretation of orders, stopped along the four-mile length of the 8th Corps Front. For the next ten minutes, not a single shot would be fired.[30]

At Serre, the Stokes mortar batteries positioned in the Russian saps immediately opened up with a hurricane bombardment on the German line, while the lighter field guns intensified their barrage with a mixture of high-explosives and shrapnel. The first wave of the assault climbed out of their trenches, moved forward into no man's land and took up their positions as close as they could get to the enemy wire, where they lay down and waited; but the Germans, alerted by the detonation of the mine at Hawthorn Ridge and the lifting of the barrage by the siege guns, had already started scrambling out of their deep underground bunkers and were manning their trenches. The Maxim machine guns (the 'Devil's Paintbrush') were hurriedly set up on pre-determined interlocking lines of fire and brought into action – and then the slaughter began as they opened up with everything they had on the British front line and reserve trenches.

At 7:25 a.m., the second wave moved up to take their positions just 50 yards behind the first wave in readiness for the assault. The 'Pals' hugged the ground – trying desperately to protect themselves from the onslaught during the final few minutes before the attack, but already they were taking casualties. The men knew that they stood little or no chance of survival – and in a few short moments, they would step out into the firestorm raging just above where they lay, but this didn't deter these incredibly brave men from doing their duty; and then perhaps a brief exchange of 'good luck' messages between friends, a shake of hands, as the final seconds ticked by.

At 7:30 a.m., the British guns started targeting the German fourth line in accordance with the set plan. In the front line, the shrill sound of whistles filled the air as the company commanders gave the signal for the attack to go in. All along the front, the 'Pals' rose up from their positions and walked straight into a hailstorm of bullets and volleys of grenades from the German defenders as they struggled to reach the enemy wire – the air alive with the crack and hiss of small arms fire, the dull 'smack' of bullets finding their target and the unmistakable

---

30 Macdonald, Lyn, *Somme* (PAPERMAC, 1986), p.58.

'crump' of exploding grenades. Men collapsed as they were cut down by the intense fire from the German machine guns – and as the survivors struggled forward, they walked straight into a ferocious barrage of shells from the enemy artillery and simply disappeared from view in the explosions and huge geysers of earth rising upwards. Red-hot shards of metal whirred through the air and tore through the lines of men – causing horrific injuries and death. Of those who survived the dreadful onslaught, a mere handful managed to reach the German first line. To the left of the 11th East Lancashires, the men of the 12th York & Lancasters (Sheffield City Battalion) advanced towards their first objective – but in the face of such an intense barrage of enemy fire, it was an impossible task. The sheer scale of their casualties was truly horrific: half of 'C' Company was cut down as soon as they went over the top. They had already suffered losses earlier in the morning, when their own guns started dropping short of their intended target and hit their front line trench. On the right of their line, there was some limited success when a few men from both 'C' and 'A' Companies managed to break through and enter the German lines.

On the extreme left of the line, the 14th York & Lancasters (2nd Barnsley Pals) made their way along the Russian sap (sap 'F') and reached the German line, but their advance ground to a halt in front of the uncut enemy wire; they just could not find a way through. Further back, the third and fourth waves started climbing out of Campion and Monk Trench and began walking across open ground towards their front line trench. The enemy artillery continued pounding away at the reserve lines and the advancing soldiers with a mixture of shrapnel and high-explosive shells. All around, men were cut down by the shrapnel shells bursting high above in a cloud of smoke – scattering a lethal hail of balls of lead in every direction. The machine guns positioned on the slopes in front of Serre; at the 'The Point' (some 1,500 yards to the left of the line); and at Rossignol Wood further north all opened up and caught the advancing men in a vicious crossfire as they struggled to reach the shattered trees of the four gospel copses of Matthew, Mark, Luke and John. With 200 yards still to go, the enemy artillery barrage increased in ferocity – and a hailstorm of bullets (from which there was no escape) cut swathes through the advancing men. Belt after belt of ammunition was eaten up by the Maxim machine guns at the rate of around 400 rounds per minute; thumbs locked down on triggers, the enemy machine gunners kept their weapons firing in a non-stop barrage of bullets. The men of the 'Pals' battalions were cut down in swathes – the fields around the four copses becoming a scene of absolute slaughter. Half of their number lay dead or wounded before they had even reached their own front line.

By 8:00 a.m., there were reports that some of the men from the first wave had made it into the German second line. At 8:10 a.m., the 13th York & Lancasters in Copse Trench went over the top and walked straight into a barrage of

A German MG 08 machine gun of the type used to such devastating effect against the Accrington Pals at Serre. (Private collection)

high-explosive shells of such ferocity that hardly anyone made it across – and at 8:35 a.m., the Germans started shelling their own trenches to drive out the survivors of the first two waves of the attack, who had somehow managed to make it through the enemy wire and reach their first objective.

At 8:45 a.m., on the right of the line: 'Having received a message from 11. E. Lanc. R. asking for reinforcements, the Brigade commander ordered two companies of the 13th York & Lanc.R. [*sic*] to advance, and hold German second and first lines'.[31] Although this request for reinforcements is clearly mentioned in the 94th Brigade narrative account, according to Lieutenant Colonel Rickman's account, the first time he asked for reinforcements was some three hours later at 11:50 a.m. – but regardless of who actually asked for reinforcements, the 13th York & Lancasters were sent forward. The men of 'C' and 'D' Companies advanced in two waves from Campion and Monk Trench, but again the enemy

---

31 TNA WO 95/2363/2: 94th Infantry Brigade document ('Operations of 94th Infantry Brigade, on July 1st, 1916').

shelling was of such ferocity that both companies suffered very heavy casualties and never managed to get much further than their own front line trench; the few survivors were ordered to pull back to Monk Trench and regroup.

By 10:45 a.m., it was all but over. The fighting continued for much of the day, but such was the scale of the losses to the 11th East Lancashires that Rickman became increasingly concerned about his own ability to defend his front line should the Germans choose to mount a counter-attack.

The German artillery continued to shell the British front line throughout much of the day – and at 3:50 p.m., Rickman reported:

> 3.50, R. 18. Very intense bombardment of my front line. All posts driven in by artillery fire. Men accommodated in Excema.
>
> Urgently require more men.
>
> Bombardment still intense especially from Rossignol.
>
> Lt. Ryden severely wounded.

> R. 19, I have 55 men in all, some of whom are wounded. 2 Lewis Guns – only two men to work them one of them wounded, pans[32] filled by officer's servants.

> R. 20, 9.20pm. I beg to report that at 9.20pm. [sic] I saw 2 Germans removing our wounded back to their lines from No-Mans-Land. As regards numbers I have at present 50 men including Stokes mortars & HQ HLR, I have also 1 officer & 25 men 18th West Yorks holding 3 posts in 93 area, 1 & 2 posts opposite Warley Ave. Then there is a gap until you come to Capt. Gurney who holds 4 posts immediately s. [south] of Sap C. I have one post between Sap C and Mark Copse.
>
> There are no Lewis or MG in line.
>
> I am getting the wounded evacuated as soon as possible but there are a good number yet to be attended to.
>
> I have 5 Red Rockets at Sap C & 12th Y&L have their Rockets but I have no rockets at Warley or any Very Lights or pistols.
>
> The men are a good deal rattled and have very few NCOs.
>
> Just completed inspection, SOS Rockets in position.
>
> 9.40pm. here I was knocked out by Shell.[33]

The Germans did not launch a counter-attack, for they were quite content to stay where they were, but as the dead and the wounded lay there on the slopes in front of Serre, some of the German soldiers continued with the slaughter. They

---

32   The Lewis Light Machine Gun had a 47-round drum magazine often referred to as a 'pan' because of its shape.

33   TNA WO 95/2366/1: 11th East Lancashire Regiment war diary.

climbed out of their trenches, with some lying on the parados[34] and others even standing to get a better aim. They kept their guns firing and targeted the dead and the wounded, as well as those struggling to find cover in the shell holes. All along the line, there were men stuck fast upon the German wire – having become snared as they tried to find a way through the thick belts – trapped like flies in a giant spider's web and desperately trying to free themselves. They too were shown no mercy.

The fields in front of the village were like a charnel house – the ground littered with khaki-clad mounds of mangled bodies stretching back beyond the four copses and towards Monk Trench (in front of Observation Wood). The metal identification triangles fixed on their backpacks glistened in the sun – and now marked the spot where they fell; and all around came the sound of wailing and calls for stretcher-bearers from those who lay grievously wounded – sounds which would fill the air for several days to come… sounds which would gradually grow weaker as the men finally succumbed to their injuries, or were picked off by the enemy snipers and machine gunners.

A few weeks after the battle, reports of the deliberate shooting of the wounded by some of the German defenders started to appear in the *Accrington Observer & Times* in the form of letters (reputedly sent home from soldiers serving on the front line). It was often the case that such letters were fabricated and published in the newspapers to stoke up the anti-German feelings of the general public.

Within the pages of the 94th Infantry Brigade's 'Report of Operations' concerning the battle on July 1st, there is a short paragraph which describes the actions of some of the German soldiers of *169th Infanterie Regiment* on that terrible day:

10.45 a.m. 'At odd intervals, and for the rest of the day, small groups of Germans were seen in their first line, standing up on fire step sniping at any of our men in No-Man's-Land who showed any sign of life, and making target practice of dead bodies. Our machine guns were turned on these groups, apparently with some effect'.[35]

---

34 The 'parados' is the rear of the trench, with the 'parapet' being the front.
35 TNA WO 95/2363/2: 94th Infantry Brigade document ('Operations of 94th Infantry Brigade, on July 1st, 1916').

'The Boys who Fought and Fell'
(By T. Clayton)

"What was the battle like, governor?"
Well, it's a jolly long yarn to tell.
But briefly put, what you see and hear
Make a scene that would outdo hell.
For the thundering guns make you jumpy, like,
And your nerves dwindle down to a shread [*sic*],
And it makes you think of your former life,
As the shells scream over your head.

But you ain't got time to funk out there,
Nor trouble about your skin,
Though a chap's no worse for a little prayer,
When he thinks of the game he's in;
When he thinks of the mother he's left behind,
Or the wife with the tear-dimmed lids;
He's to do and dare come ill or well,
For war's not a game for kids.

No doubt you thought us a pale-faced lot,
When you saw us forming fours;
And perhaps you sneered when you saw us pass
From the Tenement ground to the moors.
Well, we might seem to you but an awkward squad,
Who scarce knew the left from the right,
But I think we proved in the recent "push,"
That the "Pals" have the pluck to fight.

I don't want to brag of what we did,
For fighting's a soldier's game,
But 'twas "up to us" as the Yankee's say,
To earn for the "Pals" a name;
And I think you'll admit when you read the Press,
That the boys who fought and fell,
All gained a niche on the scroll of fame,
When they charged through the fields of hell.

Perhaps you thought like me, ere the war began,
That a soldier's life was grand-
Just a "swank" with a cane and a cigarette,
And a march or two with a band.

But it isn't like that in France to-day,
Nor it wasn't at the Dardanelles;
You've to shoulder a kit, you've to prove your grit,
To the tune of the bursting shells.

You ain't got time to mash with a girl,
Nor sigh for the picturedrome;
You've to crowd in a day more bustle and strife
Than you saw in a year at home;
You've to steel your heart to meet grim death,
Be it yours or that of the foe,
You've to win your way through a hail of lead,
When you hear the command to "go."

You've to kill or be killed, to maim or be maimed,
And it may be the foe or you,
But you take your chance as a Britisher should,
With the hope of muddling through.
Yes, it's hard on the lads in a wild mad charge,
When a life-long pal cries "Done,"
But you set your teeth and you rush pell mell
Till the trenches in front are won.

There are tear-dimmed eyes in the town to-day,
There are lips to be no more kissed,
There are bosoms that swell with an aching heart,
When they think of a dear one missed.
But time will assuage their heartfelt grief,
Of their sons they will proudly tell,
How in gallant charge in world-wide war
As "Pals" they fought and fell.[36]

The 11th East Lancashires had just over 700 men at their disposal on the morning of the attack – and by the end of the day, 584 of them were either dead, wounded, or missing; there were reports that some of the men actually succeeded in reaching and entering the village of Serre. How on earth they managed to do so, despite such unsurmountable odds, is difficult to understand, but they *did* make it – and that is a testament to their determination to get the job done. In the end, it was the failure of the artillery to remove the German wire and destroy the deep underground shelters which sealed the fate of the 'Pals' battalions. Of those who

---

36 *Accrington Observer & Times*, July 22nd 1916. (With kind permission of Accrington Library)

managed to reach the village, none of them ever returned to tell the tale. After the war, Jack Smallshaw never talked much about what happened on that dreadful day – and it is not even known if he went over the top with his friends in 'W' Company.

Lieutenant Gorst – the second-in-command of 'W' Company – took no part in the attack due to an army order which stated that the second-in-command of a company was to be held in reserve. This order undoubtedly saved Gorst's life – and that of Jack Smallshaw too. It is likely that Jack was by Gorst's side, carrying out his duties as his batman – a duty which would have saved Jack from the slaughter which claimed the lives of so many of his comrades – but he was there on the battlefield, and he must have seen terrible things that day… images which would haunt him for the rest of his life. All around him, men were being killed or maimed – and yet he managed to survive. Later that day, he wrote just a single line entry: *'July 1st/16: We went over the top this morning'.*

Jack eventually wrote a little more in his diary about the events of July 1st – and although it bore the date of the battle, the probability is that both entries were written several days later. Maybe he had needed time to collect his thoughts after witnessing such horrific scenes of slaughter on the slopes in front of Serre:

Sat July 1st/16: At 7.30 a.m. the order was given to advance. Every Officer and man of our Battalion got over the parapet and advanced as if they were just on parade. We were placed on the left side facing Serre and Beaumont. On our left were the 48th Division and on our right were the 4th Div. and the 29th Div. (of Gallipoli fame). In this advance our Battalion lost heavily, between 500 and 600 killed and wounded.

Our Company Commander Captain Livesey was killed in the German trenches. About 20 Officers were killed and wounded. The same night and for two or three following nights, men were crawling back off 'no man's land' either wounded or half dead with exhaustion to our trenches. There were hundreds of casualties and consequently all could not receive immediate attention. The 13th Yorkshire and Lancs Regt did splendid work in Stretcher Bearing and First Aid for all they came in contact with.

The slaughter of the Accrington Pals at Serre was on an unimaginable scale. Of the 235 officers and men from the 11th East Lancashire Regiment who were killed on that July morning, 135 of them have no known grave…

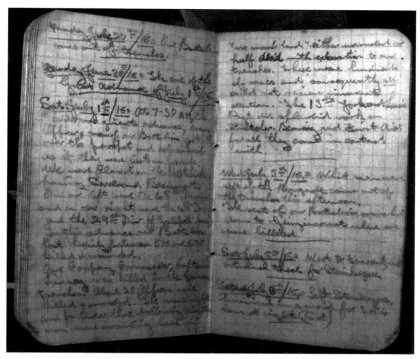

Jack's diary entry for July 1st 1916.

Roll of Honour

The officers and men of the 11th East Lancashire Regiment, who were killed in action on July 1st 1916, or who died of wounds (DOW) sustained between July 1st and July 5th 1916:

The Officers
Capt Livesey, Harry (35)
Capt Riley, Henry D. (35)
Capt Tough, Arnold B. (26)
Lt Hitchon, James F. (22)
Lt Stonehouse, Charles (34)
2/Lt Beacall, Arthur (21)
2/Lt Davies, Harry N. (21)
2/Lt Kohn, Wilfred A. (22)
2/Lt Thompson, Herbert W. (21)

Other Ranks

15361 Sgt Breckell, George E. (27)

15005 Sgt Chapman, Harry (35)

15082 Sgt Edge, Israel (23)

15071 Sgt Fletcher, Peter – **DOW, 21/7/16**

16011 Sgt Grimshaw, Thomas (36)

15486 Sgt Hersey, Harold (26)

27311 Sgt Hewitt, Edwin R. (36) **DOW, 11/7/16**

15303 Sgt Howley, Herbert (35)

15368 Sgt Ingham, Ben (24)

15657 Sgt Lang, Austin (31)

15027 Sgt Lyon, James A. (36) **DOW, 18/2/19**

15938 Sgt Marsden, Frank (33)

15259 Sgt Todd, Walter C. (21)

27274 Cpl Billington, Walter C. (22)

15956 Cpl Clarkson, William (22)

15715 Cpl Davies, John H. (44)

15872 Cpl Denney, John (28)

27295 Cpl Gibbens, Sydney –

21878 Cpl Hart, Alfred, (19)

15283 Cpl Haydock, Edgar B. (24)

15124 Cpl Hindle, John (25)

15989 Cpl Holden, Ernest (35)

22191 Cpl Lord, Alfred (22)

15173 Cpl Ormerod, Richard (22)

15397 Cpl Rimmer, Oliver (36)

27294 Cpl Rodwell, Harry (24)

17980 Cpl Rogers, Albert E. (34)

15254 Cpl Smith, Sam (25)

15755 Cpl Thompson, Jerry (22)

15635 Cpl Tomlinson, William (35)

18003 L/Cpl Allen, William (32)

15433 L/Cpl Astley, Robert (31)

15479 L/Cpl Barnes, George (23)

16057 L/Cpl Blackstone, John (23)

15223 L/Cpl Briggs, Walter (20)

15224 L/Cpl Bury, Percy (22)

27255 L/Cpl Chapman, William –

17862 L/Cpl Charnley, Robert (30)

15007 L/Cpl Cunliffe, John (26)

16589 L/Cpl Dixon, Harry (24)
15556 L/Cpl Dust, Thomas F. (24)
15437 L/Cpl Entwistle, Carswell (25)
24225 L/Cpl Heys, James (23) **DOW, 6/7/16**
15593 L/Cpl Holden, Joseph T. (26)
15026 L/Cpl Lightfoot, Norman (21)
15574 L/Cpl Lockett, John (28)
15025 L/Cpl Lund, Giles (29)
15028 L/Cpl MacKenna, William (26)
15085 L/Cpl Mercer, Albert (20)
27277 L/Cpl Moore, Arthur (21)
15334 L/Cpl Nickson, Edward –
15388 L/Cpl Ormerod, William A. (22)
15539 L/Cpl Parry, Thomas O. (24)
15594 L/Cpl Pickup, Frederick (25)
27254 L/Cpl Sanders, George (28)
15966 L/Cpl Sanders, Leonard (27)
15429 L/Cpl Thornley, Ralph H. (28)

15179 Pte Ashworth, Fred (21)
22178 Pte Aspin, Herbert (19)
15399 Pte Atkinson, Thomas (20)
15107 Pte Baines, John W. (22) **DOW, 7/7/16**
15216 Pte Banks, Roland (22)
15217 Pte Barnes, George W. (26)
15788 Pte Barnes, James (23)
15769 Pte Barnes, Joseph (30)
15560 Pte Baxter, Richard (23)
15316 Pte Beaghan, David (22)
17882 Pte Bell, Joseph (34)
15526 Pte Berry, Thomas (27)
21811 Pte Blakey, Fred (21)
15641 Pte Bolton, William (25)
24430 Pte Bowers, Walter (25)
15790 Pte Bowers, William (19)
16070 Pte Bretherton, William (31)
24417 Pte Briggs, Robert (25)
15159 Pte Brindle, Francis (20)
17839 Pte Broadley, Fred (18)
27264 Pte Brookes, John –
15738 Pte Brunskill, Arthur (22)
15708 Pte Bullen, Robert (24) **DOW, 13/7/16**

15493 Pte Bury, Albert –
15886 Pte Calvert, Jack (20)
15739 Pte Camm, Fred (19)
15494 Pte Carey, Thomas (32)
16006 Pte Carr, William (20)
15794 Pte Chadwick, Edward –
18031 Pte Clark, Charles –
15077 Pte Clayton, George (21)
15711 Pte Clayton, Herbert (22)
17983 Pte Clegg, William (19)
24176 Pte Clinton, Harry (23)
18011 Pte Coady, Tom (33)
24152 Pte Coates, James (23)
15194 Pte Conway, Arthur P. (20)
15915 Pte Cook, Thomas –
24924 Pte Cook, William (21)
15644 Pte Cowell, Will (25)
15927 Pte Cox, Charles (23)
18973 Pte Cross, Arthur (28)
18966 Pte Cullen, Michael (22)
17987 Pte Davis, John T. –
15362 Pte Dent, Arthur (19)
13744 Pte Delaney, Thomas (24)
15957 Pte Dickenson, James (18)
18017 Pte Dix, Alfred B. (39)
16035 Pte Dougherty, William (26)
17870 Pte Duerden, Orrel T. (21)
18969 Pte Edwards, Alfred –
21987 Pte Emmett, James H. (21)
15646 Pte Enderby, Joseph (23)
17989 Pte Finney, William (30)
15476 Pte Francis, Thomas E. (21)
15438 Pte Gaskell, Thomas (26) **DOW, 18/7/16**
15501 Pte Gibson, Albert –
15164 Pte Green, William (25)
24523 Pte Greenwood, Fred (25)
17920 Pte Grimshaw, Joseph (29)
17834 Pte Grimshaw, William (33)
18041 Pte Haigh, Reginald –
15690 Pte Halewood, George L. (21)
15567 Pte Halstead, Albert (22)
15855 Pte Hardman, Harry (39)

15504 Pte Hardman, Samuel D. (26)
15412 Pte Hargreaves, Albert (21)
27286 Pte Harrison, Henry B. –
15238 Pte Harling, Charles (28) **DOW, 14/7/16**
24154 Pte Heys, Walter B. (22)
21809 Pte Hirst, Adam (19) **DOW, 13/7/16**
15809 Pte Hodson, William A. (28)
18072 Pte Hogan, Peter (24)
24485 Pte Holden, Fred (19)
24209 Pte Holden, Joseph (23)
17830 Pte Holden, Richard –
17957 Pte Holding, James (34) **DOW, 7/7/16**
15328 Pte Holland, Harold (21)
24844 Pte Holmes, Frederick (20)
17943 Pte Houlker, Albert (21)
15857 Pte Hull, Jack (20)
16059 Pte Iddon, Richard (28)
15811 Pte Iley, James (25)
15465 Pte Ingham, Harry (28)
17901 Pte Ingham, Richard (24)
17963 Pte Irvine, Andrew (22)
22126 Pte Jackson, Arthur (30)
15304 Pte Jackson, James (21)
17972 Pte Jackson, Robert (26)
15747 Pte Jolly, David (22) **DOW, 9/7/16**
20931 Pte Jones, Norman (20)
15199 Pte Kennedy, Thomas (21)
27314 Pte Kenworthy, Albert W. (28)
22088 Pte Laffy, John (32)
17998 Pte Lambert, Thomas (22)
15658 Pte Lawrenson, John (30) **DOW, 4/7/16**
17898 Pte Laycock, Benjamin F. (24) **DOW, 22/6/17**
22138 Pte Leaver, James M. (19)
27315 Pte Lee, Clifford (28)
16015 Pte Lord, Alfred H. (21)
17860 Pte Lord, Samuel (22)
20989 Pte Lord, Willie (19)
15960 Pte Makinson, James (19) **DOW, 9/7/16**
15597 Pte Marsland, Edmund (32)
17949 Pte Mawdsley, James H. (34)
17851 Pte Metcalf, John (17)
20943 Pte Milton, William (39)

15941 Pte Molloy, John (26)
15818 Pte Mulhall, Albert (23)
17838 Pte Mulhall, James (42)
15817 Pte Mulhall, Tom (21)
17868 Pte Mundy, Richard H. (21)
15902 Pte Murphy, John (24)
17926 Pte Myerscough, William (33)
15371 Pte Noble, John W. (23)
15920 Pte Nutter, Harry (19)
18035 Pte O'Connor, John (26)
15134 Pte O'Hare, William (24)
15822 Pte Parkington, Fred (26)
15421 Pte Parkinson, Edward (21)
15925 Pte Parkinson, William H. (30)
20990 Pte Peel, Herbert S. (32)
15861 Pte Pendlebury, James (28)
15448 Pte Pendlebury, Richard (21)
16027 Pte Pickering, William J. (24)
15552 Pte Pickup, George (26)
15036 Pte Place, Ernest (20)
15824 Pte Pollard, John (22)
15067 Pte Pollitt, James H. (40) **DOW, 1/11/16**
15469 Pte Proctor, Harry (26)
15730 Pte Radcliffe, Fred W. (32) **DOW, 6/7/16**
15540 Pte Ratcliffe, William (22)
17936 Pte Rawcliffe, Herbert C. (23)
17966 Pte Rayton, Henry (26)
15038 Pte Rigg, Albert (20)
15586 Pte Riley, Ernest (24)
15731 Pte Riley, Willie (21)
15449 Pte Robinson, Thomas (28)
15103 Pte Robinson, Willie (21)
15964 Pte Rollins, Seth (21)
15088 Pte Russel, John (24)
15908 Pte Sharpe, William (20)
15559 Pte Shaw, Crowther (30)
15632 Pte Shuttleworth, Edward (23)
24141 Pte Simpson, Harry (20)
22108 Pte Singleton, William (18)
15425 Pte Smith, John (26)
15311 Pte Smithies, Robert (23)
15673 Pte Speakman, James (29)

15757 Pte Spedding, Thomas (20)
18060 Pte Squires, James (23)
15582 Pte Stott, Frederick (25)
15427 Pte Stuttard, George (20)
27298 Pte Sunley, Walter (20)
24074 Pte Sutcliffe, Walter (23)
24076 Pte Talbot, Joseph T. (24)
24787 Pte Taylor, Thomas (29)
15878 Pte Taylor, William A. (28)
22146 Pte Thompson, James F. –
24570 Pte Thompson, John (21)
15676 Pte Tootell, William (20)
15946 Pte Topping, John W. (18)
15734 Pte Tuhey, James –
27300 Pte Tuton, John Henry –
16055 Pte Tyson, Arthur (22)
15866 Pte Unsworth, Herbert (34)
15832 Pte Uttley, Richard (22)
27302 Pte Wade, Fred –
15151 Pte Walsh, James (29)
16001 Pte Ward, James (24) **DOW, 24/7/16**
15351 Pte Ward, John E. (22)
24887 Pte Watson, Harry (19)
24797 Pte Watson, James A. (28)
24153 Pte Webb, Frederick (23)
18062 Pte Webster, Harry (28)
15488 Pte Whalley, Joseph (18)
15834 Pte Whewell, Herbert (21)
15453 Pte Widdop, Clarence –
18496 Pte Wilkinson, Albert (19)
20946 Pte Wilkinson, Fred –
24514 Pte Winter, John (21)
15778 Pte Wixted, John (19)
17917 Pte Wood, Herbert –
24903 Pte Wray, William (31)
17863 Pte Yates, Thomas H. –
17884 Pte Young, John (25)

'Who made the Law?'

Who made the Law that men should die in meadows?
Who spake the word that blood should splash in lanes?
Who gave it forth that gardens should be bone-yards?
Who spread the hills with flesh, and blood, and brains?
Who made the Law?

Who made the Law that Death should stalk the village?
Who spake the word to kill among the sheaves,
Who gave it forth that death should lurk in hedgerows,
Who flung the dead among the fallen leaves?
Who made the Law?[37]

On July 2nd, Brigadier General G.T.C. Carter Campbell resumed command of the 94th Infantry Brigade from Brigadier General H.C. Rees. Upon his departure, Brigadier General Rees issued his 'Special Order of the Day' to the brigade:

On giving up command of the 94th Inf. Bde. To Brig.-Gen. Carter Campbell, whose place I have temporarily taken during this great battle, I wish to express to all ranks my admiration of their behaviour.

I have been through many battles in this war, and nothing more magnificent has come under my notice. The waves went forward as if on a drill parade, and I saw no man turn back or falter.

I bid good-bye to the remnants of as fine a brigade as has ever gone into action.
Sd. H. C. REES,
B. H. Q. 1-7-16. Brig. Gen. Commdg. 94th Inf. Bde.[38]

By July 3rd, the evacuation of the dead and the wounded from no man's land was well under way. The trenches were being repaired – and the following day, arrangements were made for the 6th Gloucesters to take over the front line from the battered survivors of the 'Pals' battalions. The 94th Infantry Brigade's war diary entry for July 4th recorded the casualty figures for the whole brigade as:

CASUALTIES during the period July 1 to July 4 inclusive were as follows:
KILLED –   17 officers, 131 other ranks.
WOUNDED –   36 officers, 596 ... ...
MISSING –   11 ... 872 ... ...
TOTAL –   64 ... 1599 ... ...[39]

---

37 Poem by Leslie Coulson (1889-1916).
38 TNA WO 95/2363/2: 94th Infantry Brigade war diary.
39 TNA WO 95/2363/2: 94th Infantry Brigade war diary.

The first reports of the battle at Serre gradually started to appear in the *Accrington Observer & Times* – and day after day, the casualty lists grew longer; and the pictures of the dead and the wounded became more frequent on the front pages of the local newspapers. As the days turned into weeks, the sheer scale of the disaster began to hit home, as more reports of the losses were published. Whole streets were in mourning for their dead sons, brothers and husbands. The tightly-knit communities of Accrington and the surrounding towns and villages had paid a very heavy price with their menfolk on the killing fields in front of Serre. In an attempt to keep up morale, the newspapers gave glowing and patriotic accounts of the courage shown by the 'Pals' battalions:

The "Pals" [sic] great Charge.
Heroic Advance Against Machine Gun Fire.

In its issue of Thursday the "Daily Mail" paid a great tribute to the gallant work of the Accrington "Pals" Battalion in the big offensive. The writer of the article stated:

Among the gallant regiments which took part in the offensive on Saturday and Sunday mention has been made of the Lancashires, Royal Scots, and Royal Irish Rifles. Officers and men from these forces have arrived in England, and yesterday, they fought over the battles of the week; and among the officers the dominant feeling was clearly pride in their men which consoled them even when considering the price that was paid in the loss of comrades.

For the Lancashires "comrades" meant more than the casual meeting of men in barracks and camps, for these men of whom I write (states a visitor who has talked with some-of [*sic*] them) were of the "Pals" Battalions, of Accrington, Blackburn, Chorley, and Burnley. The eyes of their surviving officers glow with enthusiasm when they speak of the deeds of the doughty sons of those towns. "Proudly they maintained the fighting traditions of their country," said one.

"We were in the fourth wave," he continued. "The third and fourth waves were to take a village. At half-past seven on Saturday after a beautiful sunrise we started, but the Germans knew we were coming over. Clearly they had concealed their machine-guns in their deep dug-outs during the artillery bombardment, and when we topped the parapet we were played upon by scores of them.

"I have heard it stated, though I cannot vouch for it myself, that in some places they had made a sort of hoist which could lower or lift the machine as required. In spite of this rain of missiles those Lancashire lads went over smoking and joking. They did not expect that hot opposition at that stage. But they were never the least shaken and went forward as though nothing unusual was going on. They had artillery fire on them as well as machine-guns, and the Germans at ...... [name censored by the newspaper] were able to enfilade them.

"Nevertheless, those who did not fall went on steadily. I was among those who fell early, I regret to say, so for a while I saw little of what followed. I slid into a shell-hole, and then with some others I managed to reach a copse. From there we could see our wounded coming away.

"From eight-o-clock till twelve we watched from there. By that time our men had taken the first two lines with tremendous dash and remarkable bravery, considering the hail of lead that was showering on them. *Incidentally let me confirm the stories that the Germans shot at the wounded. They even let the stretcher-bearers get between the lines, and then their snipers picked them off* [author's italics].

"On our right our people had gained the second line, and, I am told, in one section of the trench the Germans threw their bombs at the attacking party, then threw off their equipment and held up their hands in surrender. Never shall I forget the scene I witnessed from the copse; and I feel real pride in the men of the north who strode forward in the face of those spitting machine-guns and lines of German rifles as calmly as though going to their dinner without rushing or any charging, just heading for the objective and caring for nothing except "getting there."[40]

'Wed July 5th/16: What men were left of the Brigade came out of the trenches this afternoon. The rest of our Battalion marched down to Gezaincourt where we were billeted'.

Shortly after the move, Lieutenant General Aylmer Hunter-Weston (GOC VIII Corps) issued the following message to the brigade:

To All OFFICERS, N. C. O.'s [*sic*] and MEN of the VIII. Army Corps

In so big a command as an Army Corps of four Divisions (about eighty thousand men) it is impossible for me to come round all front line trenches and all billets to see every man as I wish to do. You must take the will for the deed, and accept this printed message in place of the spoken word.

It is difficult for me to express my admiration for the splendid courage, determination and discipline displayed by every Officer, N. C. O. and man of the Battalions that took part in the great attack on the BEAUMONT HAMEL – SERRE position on the 1st July. All observers agree in stating

---

40 *Accrington Observer & Times*, July 8th 1916. (With kind permission of Accrington Library)

that the various waves of men issued from their trenches and moved forward at the appointed time in perfect order, undismayed by the heavy artillery fire and deadly machine gun fire. There were no cowards nor waverers, and not a man fell out. It was a magnificent display of disciplined courage worthy of the best traditions of the British race.

Very few are left of my old comrades, the original 'Contemptibles,' but their successors in the 4th Division have shewn that they are worthy to bear the honours gained by the 4th Division at their first great fight at Fontaine – au – Pire and Ligny, during the great Retreat and greater Advance across the Marne and Aisne, and in all the hard fighting at Ploegsteert and Ypres.

Though but few of my old comrades, the heroes of the historic landings at Cape Helles, are still with us, the 29th Division of today has shown itself capable of maintaining its high traditions, and has proved itself worthy of its hard earned title of "The incomparable 29th."

The 31st New Army Divisions, and the 48th Territorial Divisions, by the heroism and discipline of the units engaged in this their first big battle, have proved themselves worthy to fight by the side of such magnificent regular Divisions as the 4th and 29th. There can be no higher praise.

We had the most difficult part in the line to attack. The Germans had fortified it with skill and immense labour for many months, they had kept their best troops here, and had assembled North-East, and South-East of it a formidable collection of artillery and many machine guns.

By your splendid attack you held these enemy forces here in the North and so enabled our friends in the South, both British and French, to achieve the brilliant success that they have. Therefore, though we did not do all we hoped to do you have more than pulled your weight, and you and our even more glorious comrades who have preceded us across the Great Divide have nobly done your Duty.

We have got to stick it out and go on hammering. Next time we attack, if it please God, we will not only pull our weight but will pull off a big thing. With such troops as you, who are determined to stick it out and to do your duty, we are certain of winning through to a glorious victory.

I salute each Officer, N. C. O. and man of the 4th, 29th, 31st, and 48th Divisions as a comrade-in-arms and I rejoice to have the privilege of commanding such a band of heroes as the VIII Corps have proved themselves to be.

H. Q., VIII. Corps AYLMER HUNTER-WESTON,

4th July 1916. Lieut, – General[41]

---

41 TNA WO 95/2363/2: 94th Infantry Brigade war diary.

Several days after the battalion came out of the line, an unnamed soldier wrote home to his wife – and his letter was published in the *Accrington Observer & Times*:

"COULD WRITE A BOOK"
"Pals" Having a Rest.

A member of the Accrington "Pals" Battalion who has been fortunate enough to come through the brilliant offensive movement without injury has sent an interesting letter to his wife, who resides in Lodge-street, Accrington. Previous to the war the soldier was employed at Broad Oak. After stating that he is in the best of health he writes:

"I have not really had the time to write, before, because I have been in the trenches. I think you will have heard by now that a lot of our poor lads have gone under. I think we have done as well as any who have done any fighting in France. But it is hard lines to see your pals go under. We have lost a lot I can tell you... We have come out of the trenches now and another lot have taken our places. We are moving a good way back from the trenches, and thank God for that, for it has been like hell... The 'Pals' have done splendidly and it has been a great day for them. But however great the victory is, it can't bring our poor lads back to life again. We are proud of ourselves. We have come out at the top as good as any battalion who has ever been in France. It will go down in history. I wish I could tell you in my letter how the brave lads faced death at the front of the German machine guns. Not a lad looked round, but walked straight on. Never has any battalion done better. God bless the poor lads who are dead, and may those who are left behind be able to tell the tale. God bless the mothers and wives of those poor lads. One cannot write without even thinking about it. I could write a book on the work they have done... *The Germans even shot our wounded as the poor lads were creeping back* [author's italics]. May it soon be over. ---- [name censored by newspaper] has been wounded in the neck, but I don't think it is very bad. I want a bit of a rest, but don't think I am not well myself, because I am. I cannot write any more to-night, so God bless you and the children and also the widows and mothers of Accrington. The day will come when there will be a reckoning and the war god will have to face God and answer for the work that is being done now."[42]

The Battle of the Somme was the biggest single military disaster ever to befall the British Army. By the end of the first day, they had suffered more than 57,000 casualties – of whom more than 19,000 were dead – and the fighting was destined

---

42 *Accrington Observer & Times*, July 18th 1916. (With kind permission of Accrington Library)

Accrington Observer & (

ESTABLISHED.—"TIMES" 1866. } AMALGAMATED   "OBSERVER." 1887. }   1893.   TUESDAY, JULY 25, 1916.

KILLED IN ACTION.

Among the "Pals" who have fallen in action is Private W. A. Hodson, son of Mrs. Hodson, of 151, Wellington-street, Accring-

PTE. W. A. HODSON (Accrington).

ton. Aged 28, he had been married only two years, and leaves a young widow and child. He formerly worked at Howard and Bullough's and was a member of the Church of the Sacred Heart.

SIGNALLER J. W. BAINES

(Died of Wounds.)

News has been received that Signaller J. W. Baines, of the "Pals" Battalion, has died of wounds. The only son of Mr. and

SIGNALLER J. W. BAINES.

Mrs. A. Baines, late of Ormerod-street, Accrington, and now of Blackpool, he was 22 years of age and enlisted in the "Pals" when they were formed. He worked as a decorator with his uncle, Mr. Clark, of Blackburn-road, Accrington. Wounded on July 1st, Signaller Baines died in hospital in France on July 7th, and was buried there. He was a regular attender at St. Peter's Church.

CHURCH SERGEANT'S DEATH.

Another "Pal" Gone.

Amongst those who were wounded in the thrilling attack by the Accrington "Pals" on Serres on Saturday, was Sergeant

Pte. Tom Coady.

AN APPRECIATION.

[By one who knew him in Carnarvon.]

The loyal, merry Lancashire Irishman, who made happy the hearts of his comrades wherever he was. He paid the great price, in France, July, 1916.

This morning I have a letter from Accrington saying that Private Thomas Coady, of the 11th East Lancashire "Pals" Regiment, died in France last week, and I feel very sad and also very glad.

Do you remember Coady and his stay in Carnarvon from December, 1914, to April, 1915, during the period of the training of the 11th East Lancashires under Colonel Rickman? I well recall the day the Battalion arrived. Our "Specials" had been directing the men to their billets, and in the evening I turned in to the Y.M.C.A. to give our visitors a welcome. There was a group seated in the coffee-room, just sizing up their surroundings, and, addressing them all I said "Carnarvon gives you a merry welcome, boys. What shall we do for you and what are you prepared to do for us?" A short, thin, clear-featured young man with an accent that was not Welsh, said, "That's all right, boss, sure it's we are the boys for you and you are the man for us"; and straight away we entered on a partnership arrangement for entertaining the inen in the rooms, which partnership lasted during their entire stay here.

This young man was Thomas Coady, one who had a merry jest for everyone, and whose smile infected the whole company with joy. From that day forward there was not one meeting held in the buildings that he omitted to attend except for one week when he was badly hit with vaccination, and at all our gatherings his singing, reciting and general demeanour made him "hail fellow well met" everywhere.

But it is not of Coady in Carnarvon that I would write to you, however proud we may be of the part he played here, but of Coady after he left the town and as he revealed himself to me by the letters that came to me from him about once a fortnight regularly. I have under my hand at this moment a pile of communications that arrived from various places and through them all there runs the sincere strain of the man who felt the position he was in and throughout realised the possibility of the end which has overtaken him. Space will not permit of full quotations, but you may be interested in the following:—

In April last he writes—"Feel a bit tired this morning, as I have just been helping to carry a poor chap to his last resting-place to-day, Easter Sunday. It's an awful thing, this war. Anyway, I am pleased to know we are fighting for right and you will find that God will always be on the side of them that fight for right."

Writing on May 3rd—"I am sorry to say that we have lost three of our boys killed and eleven wounded. . . . You would be surprised to hear the skylarks singing here in the morning just as the day is breaking and you are leaving the trenches. The birds sing so beautifully."

Writing on the 7th of May after an illness—"I am now all right and out of hospital. . . . I believe we have lost a few men while I was in hospital—I don't know how many—but in a war like this you cannot tell whose turn it is next. Anyway it cannot be helped; it's got to be done and I find the best thing to do is to keep on smiling."

Writing on the 23rd of May he says:— "You would be surprised to see what war is really like; out here sometimes at night everything will be very quiet then all of a sudden the big guns will start a bombardment. It is just like the sky ripping—my word, they don't half rip. I told you in my last letter that we had lost some killed and had several wounded. Of course it can not be helped, but do not forget this, Mr. E., if I am to be hit I will still think about you people in Carnarvon for all your great kindness to me. Of course I do not want to get hit, but you never can tell out here, and I wanted you to know my mind, but I hope God will let me see you all again. Dear Mr. E., never think I am downhearted, because I am not, I am looking after my soul as well as my body."

On the 18th June—"I received your most kind and welcome letter and feel pleased to hear that you often think about me and pray for me. . . . I can tell you that I

WOUNDED   "

WOUNDED   "

SERGT. J. PILKINGTON, (Accrington), suffering from wounds in the back and in the right arm, is now in hospital in France. He lives at 22, Booth-street, Accrington. His father is serving in France.

LANCE-CORPL. F. W. SECKER (Accrington has been wounded in the right leg and is now at Bristol. His home is at 48, Marlborough street. He was formerly employed at Messrs Broughton and Broughton, solicitors.

PTE. JOHN SEDGWICK, Oswaldtwistle, of the Accrington "Pals" who was wounded in the great attack. His injuries were attended to at the base. His parents reside at 280, Union-road, Oswaldtwistle.

PRIVATE JAMES KENNY (Accrington wounded, as he describes, in a "little hell," is now in hospital at Newport (M suffering from shrapnel wounds. His family live at 45, Elizabeth-street.

LOCAL SOLDIER KILLED.

Pte. J. E. Mather, Clayton-le-Moors.

Pte. Joseph Edward Mather, of 6, Oswald-street, Clayton-le-Moors, a member of the

CLAYTON SOLDIER KILLED.

Mrs. Addison, of 17, Mill Street, Clayton-le-Moors, has received the sad news of her husband, Pte. J. Addison, of the 7th Lancashire Regiment (Grenade Company),

The front page of the *Accrington Observer & Times*, July 25th 1916.
(With kind permission of Accrington Library)

'Somme lads?' Jack is in the centre of the photograph.

to drag on for several more months to come. On November 13th, another attempt was made to capture Serre, but that too ended in failure. Five days later – on November 18th – the Battle of the Somme was brought to an end, with Serre still firmly in the grip of the German defenders.

On February 24th 1917, the Germans finally decided to vacate the village and withdrew to their new defensive positions on the formidable Hindenburg Line. The day after they left, the 22nd Manchesters advanced over the now deserted trenches and entered the shattered remains of the village. The German barbed wire was still littered with the rotting corpses of the 11th East Lancashires and the men of the York & Lancasters. The sacrifice made by the 'Pals' battalions on the slopes in front of the village, where so many lives had been lost on that July morning, had been for nothing…

'Hanging on the Old Barbed Wire' (song)

If you want the old battalion
We know where they are, we know where they are,
We know where they are.
If you want the old battalion, we know where they are,
They're hanging on the old barbed wire.
We've seen them, we've seen them,
Hanging on the old barbed wire,
We've seen them, we've seen them,
Hanging on the old barbed wire.[43]

Richebourg

On July 8th, the 11th East Lancashires set off for the village of Calonne-sur-la-Lys, where they were to be reorganised, re-equipped and brought back up to strength after their crippling losses suffered during the Battle of the Somme. The 31st Division now came under XI Corps, First Army, which was commanded by General Sir Charles Munro.

The photograph sent to Jack by his friend, Albert Gibson: *'With best wishes, 14/5/1915'*. Jack added his own comment to the picture: *'I last saw Albert with a bag of Mills bombs! July 1916'*.

---

43 Lyrics by Anon.

Jack recorded the moves in his diary:

> '*Sat July 8th/16: Went to Frevent and entrained there for Steenbecque. Left Steenbecque, bivouacked in a wood for 3 or 4 hours at night (Sat)*'.

> '*Sunday July 9th/16: Left the wood and marched to Calonne* [Calonne-sur-la-Lys]. *Landed there about 9.30 a.m. (Sunday morning) Calonne is a nice little village and quite near to the town of Merville)*'.

Their brief rest would only last a few days – and after re-equipping and reorganisation, the 11th Battalion was once again heading back to the trenches: '*Sat July 15th/16: Departed from Calonne and marched through Vieille-Chapelle to a small village just in rear of firing line between La Bassee and Neuve-Chapelle (Nr Richebourg)*'.

The following poem was written anonymously – and was originally published in the soldiers' newspaper, *The Wipers Times*:

No more we'll share the same old barn,
The same old dugout, same old yarn,
No more a tin of bully share,
Nor split our rum by a star-shell's flare,
So long old lad.

Just one more cross by a strafed roadside,
With its GRC,[44] and a name for a guide,
But it's only myself who has lost a friend,
And though I may fight through to the end,
No dugout or billet will be the same,
All pals can only be pals in name,
But we'll all carry on till the end of the game
Because you lie there.

On July 24th, the battalion moved back in the line. A composite company made up from the men of 'Y' and 'Z' Companies relieved the 11th Royal Sussex and the 14th Hampshire Regiments between Oxford Street and Vine Street Trenches, while the men of 'W' and 'X' Companies relieved the 17th Notts & Derby Regiment. Two platoons took over the St Vaast post, while the remainder took over the Grotto, Angle, Rags and Bones Outposts – each position being manned with one NCO and five men. There is an undated entry in Jack's diary

---

44 Graves Registration Cross.

which refers to these strongpoints: '*W and X Coys occupied several strongholds on Richebourg, where there had been some heavy house-to-house fighting*'.

On the evening of July 26th, the enemy opened up on the front line with a barrage of mortar shells which lasted for almost four hours – causing considerable damage to the trenches and outposts. Six men were killed and five were injured during the barrage. According to Jack's diaries, the battalion came out of the line on July 26th, but the brigade war diaries state that the relief took place the following day when the 93rd Infantry Brigade took over the sector: '*Wed July 26th/16: Left village and landed six miles in rear of firing line at village of Les Lobes*'.

The fighting at Richebourg to which Jack was referring in his earlier diary entry could have been the Battle of Festubert, which took place in May 1915, but Richebourg was also the scene of another major battle in 1916 when an attack was launched on a German strongpoint known as 'The Boar's Head'. The battle for 'The Boar's Head' took place on June 30th and was conceived as a diversionary assault to try and fool the Germans into thinking that the main offensive, which they knew was coming, would take place there and not on the Somme 30 miles to the south.

On that fateful morning, the 12th and 13th Battalions of the Royal Sussex Regiment (the 2nd and 3rd South Downs) – with the 11th Battalion in support – went over the top at 3:05 a.m. after a short 15-minute bombardment on the German lines. The slaughter which followed was similar in pattern to the fate which befell the 11th East Lancashires on the following day at Serre. On the right of the line, two companies reached their objective and actually managed to hold on to the German front line for several hours. While on the left of the line, there were considerable casualties caused by very heavy machine gun fire and the inability of the attacking battalions to find a way through the thick belts of German wire. The German second line was also breached – and the Royal Sussex Regiment even managed to hold on for some 30 minutes in the face of a ferocious onslaught from the German defenders – but with casualties mounting through the incessant machine gun fire and heavy bombardment from the German artillery, they were eventually forced to pull back to their own front line. The Germans then turned their attention to the British front line and subjected the survivors of the assault to a brutal bombardment which went on for several hours. In the five hours of intense fighting, the three battalions of the Royal Sussex Regiment suffered appalling casualties on a day which to become known as 'The Day Sussex Died': 'The total casualties for the mornings fighting were 15 officers and 364 Other Ranks killed or died of wounds, and 21 officers and 728 other Ranks wounded; nearly 1,100 South Downers'.[45]

---

45 Reproduced with the kind permission of Paul Reed: <www.battlefields1418.com>

'From an Outpost'

I've tramped South England up and down
Down Dorset way, down Devon way,
Through every little ancient town
Down Dorset way, down Devon way.
I mind the old stone churches there,
The taverns around the old market square,
The cobbled streets, the garden flowers,
The sundials telling peaceful hours
Down Dorset way, down Devon way.

The Meadowlands are green and fair
Down Somerset and Sussex way,
The clover scent is in the air
Down Somerset and Sussex way.
I mind the deep-thatched homesteads there
The noble downlands, clean and bare.
The sheepfolds and the cattle byres,
The blue wood-smoke from shepherds' fires
Down Dorset way, down Devon way.

Mayhap I shall not walk again
Down Dorset way, down Devon way,
Nor pick a posy in a lane
Down Somerset and Sussex way.
But though my bones, unshriven, rot
In some far distant alien spot,
What soul I have shall rest from care
To know that meadows still are fair
Down Dorset way, down Devon way.[46]

On August 4th, the 94th Infantry Brigade went back in the line, but because of the disastrous losses on the Somme, it was still found necessary to form composite battalions to man the trenches with sufficient troops – and as a result, the 11th East Lancashires merged with the 12th York & Lancasters and one company from the 13th York & Lancasters. This composite battalion took over the right sector of the line from the 18th West Yorkshires between the Oxford Street and Vine Street Trenches. Jack commented on the shortage of manpower: *Friday Aug 4th/16: Left Les Lobes and took over trenches near Neuve-Chapelle (with only a few men)*. The composite battalion was responsible for manning five defensive posts

---

46 Poem by Leslie Coulson (1889-1916).

with just eight NCOs and 55 other ranks. Three of the posts – Port Arthur, Copse and Lansdowne – had two NCOs and 15 men each, but the Hens and Edward Posts had just one NCO and five men each. Perhaps it was one of these two posts to which Jack was sent...

On August 9th, the 13th York & Lancasters were withdrawn from the composite battalion and took over part of the line held between Oxford Street and Pioneer Trench after the 11th East Lancashires finally received their badly-needed reinforcements. For the next few days, the front remained rather quiet – and then on August 14th, Jack was wounded: '*Mon Aug 14th/16: I was wounded in leg*'. On that day, the brigade diaries reported the situation as 'normal', with one officer and eight other ranks wounded. Jack's injury could only have been slight, as it appears from his diary entry that he wasn't even taken out of the line. Jack also commented in his diary on the promotion of Lieutenant Gorst: '*Early in Aug /16: Lt Gorst promoted to Captain (O.C. 'W' Coy)*'.

On August 16th, there was considerable activity on the 94th Brigade front when a hurricane bombardment of trench mortars and 18 pdr field guns opened up on the German front line. It was reported in the brigade war diary that there was: 'Great damage done to enemy front line'.[47] Two days later – on August 18th – the 94th Infantry Brigade was relieved by the 183rd Infantry Brigade (61st Division) and went into divisional reserve. During their stay in the trenches, Jack's battalion had two officers killed and two wounded, and eight other ranks killed and 61 wounded:

'*Friday Aug 18th/16: After 14 days in front line we were relieved by the 2/7th Worcesters about dinner time and marched down to our billets in Les Lobes*'.

Sat Aug 26th/16: Left Les Lobes and went in Reserve to 12th & 13th Yorks at Croix Barbee.[48] *Between the 4th and 18th Aug /16, a message came to us in the trenches from the King to say three of our men had been awarded the Distinguished Conduct Medal for bravery on July 1st on the Somme. One was Sgt Kay, now Sgt Major. Lance Cpl Nowell of our Signalling Section and Pte Warburton all of "Y" Company. Nowell is now attached to the Manchesters and Warburton got his leg broken just recently and was sent to hospital. A Military Medal has recently been won by Pte Speak.*

L/Cpl Esmond Nowell was awarded the Distinguished Conduct Medal (DCM) for his actions on July 1st '... for conspicuous gallantry in attack. Being sent by his Company Commander to deliver a message he performed this duty, although wounded, under heavy shell fire, after returning to his

---

47 TNA WO 95/2363/2: 94th Infantry Brigade war diary.
48 Croix Barbee was a defensive strongpoint.

company'.[49] Pte W. Warburton received his DCM for his actions on July 1st '... for conspicuous courage and gallantry in attacking single handed an enemy bombing party. He killed the officer, wounded others and caused the remainder to retire'.[50]

The award of the Military Medal to Pte Holford Speak of Burnley was reported in the *Burnley News* and the *Burnley Express* in September 1916:

> The Military Medal has been won by Private Holford Speak, son of Mr. H. Speak, the licensee of the Victoria Inn, Colne Road, Burnley, who is now in hospital in Derby. *"Private Speak sought the shelter of a shell hole from heavy fire during the attack on the German lines at Serre. Shortly after reaching cover, he heard a comrade over the top crying for help. Though he himself was suffering from a bullet wound to the hand, he returned to the open field to the assistance of his comrade, there to sustain another knockout blow, this time from shrapnel. Speak received dangerous wounds to the left side of his body."* He was taken to Boulogne and afterwards transferred to England. Happily he is said to be progressing favourably.[51]

On August 17th 1916, the Romanians finally entered the war on the side of the Allies after being given assurances of support from them for their territorial claims over Transylvania at the war's end. As a result, on August 27th the Romanians launched an attack on Transylvania. Jack commented in his diary: *'Monday Aug 28th/16: Rumania joins with Allies'*.

While on divisional reserve, Jack found time to have a look around Richebourg with his friend, Starkie. He commented in his diary on the damage inflicted to the church by the German artillery:

> *Friday Sept 1st/16: This evening Starkie and I visited Richebourg Church to look at the ruins of it and also the Church yard where almost every vault was smashed by the Germans who bombarded it very heavily in the early part of the war. There are lovely vaults and statues smashed into bits and one or two have been so shelled that you can see the skeletons in their coffins. One strange thing there is, there is a large Crucifix which is among shelled tombs and etc and has never been hit but remains standing. The Church bell is among the ruins too. It makes one's heart ache to see this place.*

---

49 Accessed at: <www.chorleypalsmemorial.org.uk>
50 *London Gazette*, 22nd September 1916.
51 The *Burnley News*, September 13th 1916 and the *Burnley Express*, September 19th 1916.

On September 2nd, Jack's battalion relieved the 13th York & Lancasters and took over the outposts of Grotto, Angle, St Vaast, Loretto, Euston, Rue Du Puits and Croix Barbee – all of which formed part of the brigade reserve line. Jack was sent to the Croix Barbee Outpost, which was usually manned with just one NCO and three men: *'Saturday Sep 2nd/16: Our Battalion took over the strongholds'*.

On the night of September 9th/10th, the 12th York & Lancasters launched an attack on the enemy trenches in front of their positions. The raiding party went in at 1:30 a.m. under cover of an artillery bombardment, but apparently the Germans had anticipated an attack and had erected defensive barricades on their flanks and communication trench. As soon as the raiders had gained entry to the enemy front line trench, they were met with a fusillade of grenades from the German troops who were situated some 15 yards to the rear of the trench, but the men of the York & Lancasters fought back and killed and injured many of the defenders before withdrawing back to their own lines. The following day, the 94th Infantry Brigade was relieved by the 93rd Infantry Brigade and went in army reserve. The 11th East Lancashires were relieved by the 18th West Yorkshire Regiment and moved back into army reserve at Vieille Chapelle: *'Monday Sept 11th/16: Left Croix Barbee, went to Vieille Chapelle'*.

Festubert

On September 16th – a day earlier than originally planned – the 94th Infantry Brigade relieved the 90th Infantry Brigade in the Festubert sector. The 11th East Lancashires took over from the 16th Battalion, the Manchester Regiment (90th Brigade) on the right of the line between Grenadier Trench and Lothian Trench. Three companies manned the front line and support line – and the remaining company, with one attached from the 13th York & Lancasters. was placed in reserve. Jack commented on the state of the trenches in his diary: *'Sat Sep 16th/16: Went into trenches at Festubert (very bad trenches too)'*. Much of the land in the Festubert sector had a very high clay content and was very prone to flooding – and because of this, the usual method of 'digging in' when constructing trenches was totally out of the question. Any trenches constructed in this manner would have rapidly filled with water. Many of the trench systems were above-ground breastworks with isolated 'islands' garrisoned with just a few soldiers. Such was the nature of the defences that all reliefs of the outposts could only be carried out at night when the men were offered some protection by the dark from the prying eyes of the enemy. The wet and muddy living conditions were also an ideal breeding ground for lice and vermin, which plagued soldiers of all armies who served in the trenches. Within days of taking over from the Manchesters, Jack had taken ill: *'Tues Sept 19th/16: I was taken bad with Trench Fever and sent to the 94th Field Ambulance Hospital'*.

Body lice were the scourge of every soldier – and nobody was immune from being infected. Lice were also known as 'chats' – and one of the regular pastimes of the soldiers was 'chatting'. The men would strip off and seek out the lice and squeeze them between finger and thumb, or burn along the seams of their clothing with a lighted candle. Trench fever (also known as 'five-day fever') was transmitted by the excreta, or bites, of the lice. The symptoms were very similar to typhoid and flu – the victim suffering from skin rashes, headaches, inflammation of the eyes and leg pains. Usually, the infected person would recover in around five days; in Jack's case, his condition must have been quite severe, as he was eventually sent to Merville to complete his recovery: *'Fri Sept 22nd/16: Moved to Camps [sic] Rest Station (Merville)'.*

Jack's next diary entry is actually dated for 'October', when he set off to rejoin his unit. He then comments on his battalion being relieved on 'September 24th'. It is likely that he was just keeping a record of the battalion movements during his absence:

'Sunday Oct 1st/16: Went from rest camp and re-joined my unit'.

'Sunday Sept 24th/16: Battalion relieved from trenches'.

During the eight days in the trenches, the battalion casualties were: one officer died of wounds, four other ranks killed and one injured. On October 1st, the battalion was back in the line again. The 11th East Lancashires relieved the 13th York & Lancasters on the right sector between Barnton Road and Fife Road and occupied the 'islands'. Jack puts the date of relief as 'September 30th', but both the brigade and battalion war diaries state that it was October 1st. The confusion may have arisen because of Jack being sent to Prince's Island straight from the rest camp: *'Sat Sept 30th/16: Took over trenches at Prince's Island'.*

On October 4th, the 94th Infantry Brigade was relieved by the 13th Infantry Brigade in preparation for their move back to the Somme sector. Jack's battalion handed over their positions to the 15th Battalion, the Royal Warwicks and withdrew to the village line posts at Festubert.

On October 5th, the battalion handed over the line to the 14th Battalion, Royal Warwicks and moved to Les Choquaux, where they stayed in billets until October 6th. Three other ranks were wounded during the occupation of the islands:

'Wed Oct 4th/16: Relieved from Trenches. Billeted at a village near Festubert for a couple of days and then moved to Robecq'.

'Sunday Oct 8th/16: Left Robecq and marched to Berguette where we entrained. We detrained at Doullens and marched on to Sarton'.

Back to the Somme

According to the 11th East Lancashires' war diary for October, the battalion spent the next 10 days training in attack at brigade and battalion level with the Royal Flying Corps – supplying a 'Control Patrol Aeroplane'. The war diary went on to record that signalling between ground and air was practised on two occasions 'with success'.[52] While in reserve, the battalion received a further intake of 158 men to replace the losses they had suffered since July 1st.

Jack commented in his diary about a visit to a nearby aerodrome:

'Thursday Oct 12th/16: Visited an Aerodrome and had an interesting afternoon'.

'Fri Oct 13th/16: Had a stroll and watched some German prisoners at work'.

'A Poor Aviator Lay Dying'
(sung to the tune of 'My Bonnie Lies Over the Ocean')

A poor aviator lay dying
At the end of a bright summer's day
His comrades had gathered about him
To carry his fragments away

The airplane was piled on his wishbone
His Hotchkiss was wrapped round his head
He wore a spark-plug on each elbow
'Twas plain he would shortly be dead

He spit out a valve and a gasket
And stirred in the sump where he lay
And then to his wondering comrades
These brave parting words he did say

"Take the magneto out of my stomach,
And the butterfly valve off my neck
Extract from my liver the crankshaft,
There are lots of good parts in this wreck."

"Take the manifold out of my larynx,
And the cylinders out of my brain,
Take the piston rods out of my kidneys,
And assemble the engine again."

---

52 TNA WO 95/2366/1: 11th East Lancashire Regiment war diary.

> "Pull the longeron out of my backbone,
> The turnbuckle out of my ear (my ear).
> From the small of my back take the rudder-
> There's all of your aeroplane here."
>
> "I'll be riding a cloud in the morning,
> With no rotary before me to cuss (to cuss).
> Take the lead from your feet and get busy,
> Here's another lad needing the bus!"[53]

On October 19th, the battalion marched to Warnimont Wood and resumed their training. Over the next few days, the officers and NCOs were sent to the trench systems between Hebuterne and Colincamps to reconnoitre the communication trenches in readiness for their move to that area. The remainder of the battalion provided carrying parties to take up supplies to the forward dumps near the front line. It was around this period that Jack's time as batman to Captain Gorst came to an end: '*Wed Oct 19th/16: Left Sarton and marched to Warnimont Wood. Capt. Gorst leaves us.*'

The division continued with their training at battalion level, and also supplied working parties for the Royal Engineers. On October 30th, the 11th East Lancashires took over the front line from the 15th West Yorkshires. To Jack and the other survivors of the July 1st battle, it was very familiar territory: they were barely 500 yards away from where the 'Pals' battalions had lost so many men on the slopes in front of Serre on that dreadful day just four months previously. Their stretch of line ran for approximately 1,500 yards – extending from John Copse to the Hebuterne-Serre Road – just beyond the bulge in the German line known as 'The Point'. Two companies took over the front and support line, with the remaining two companies held in reserve. On their left flank were the 12th York & Lancasters, and on their right the 1st Battalion, the Royal Scots Fusiliers: '*Oct 30th: Went into the trenches for five days on the Hebuterne Front where I became batman for Capt. Lewis*'.

On the morning of November 1st, the enemy started shelling the reserve lines just to the west of Touvent Farm. The British guns opened up in retaliation and concentrated on the German wire along the front line. The trenches held by the 11th East Lancashires just north of John Copse came under sporadic fire from German trench mortars for much of the day, while the British guns continued with their bombardment of the German wire.

The following day – November 2nd – the German artillery started shelling the British first line trenches held by the 11th East Lancashires near Chasseurs Hedge. A little further along the line, Knox Trench – situated close to 'The Point'

---

53 Lyrics by Anon.

Sarton, October 1916: a photograph of the battalion officers.

– came under a particularly heavy bombardment from German 77 mm guns. Further back in the reserve lines, Vercingetorix Trench also attracted the attention of the German guns. That evening, the enemy lines to the right of the Serheb Road came under fire from trench mortar positions in the 11th East Lancashires' area. The following day followed the same pattern of sporadic shellfire: according to the 94th Brigade war diaries, the situation for the five days in the line was described as 'normal'; casualties for the period in the trenches were one killed and two wounded.

Jack made no mention of the enemy shelling in his diary; maybe he too viewed the situation as being 'normal':

'Nov 4th/16: Came out of the trenches and arrived in bivouacs in the Dell at Sailly [Sailly au Bois]'.

'Nov 7th/16: Moved to a wood at Coigneux'.

For the next few days, the battalion supplied men for working parties – and then on November 9th, the bulk of the battalion moved back to Warnimont Wood. Two platoons remained at Coigneux and were put to work ferrying supplies to the front line: *'Nov 9th/16: Marched to Warnimont Wood'*.

There was considerable activity in the area at that time, with several raids on the German lines planned for the early hours of November 7th. At 1:00 a.m., the 13th York & Lancasters broke through a stretch of enemy line in front of Frappier Trench – and at the same time, the 14th York & Lancasters carried out two raids on the enemy line further to the north in front of the Revel and Sonis Trenches; only the raid carried out by the 13th York & Lancasters managed to break through into the enemy lines. The detailed brigade summary of the raid carried out by the 13th York & Lancasters said: 'It is estimated that in this raid at least 30 Germans were killed in addition to any casualties inflicted by the bombing of dugouts. 4 prisoners were brought back, 2 of whom are wounded, our total casualties being 4 other ranks slightly wounded'.[54]

To the right of the 94th Infantry Brigade area, another attempt was made to capture the fortified village of Serre: at 5:45 a.m. on Monday, November 13th, the 3rd Division launched an attack on the village. To the right of the line were the 6th and 5th Brigades of the 2nd Division – and covering the left flank were the 92nd and 93rd Brigades of the 31st Division. The assault resulted in another costly failure, with many more lives lost and the village still firmly in German hands. With all the activity which had taken place over the past two weeks, the Germans were on a heightened state of alert for any further attacks on their lines. The following day – on November 14th – the 11th East Lancashires took over the right sub-sector of the front line (Hebuterne) from the 13th York & Lancasters and the 16th West Yorkshires: 'Nov 14th/16: Took over the trenches (Hebuterne)'.

On November 15th, the 94th Infantry Brigade issued Order No.89, which contained detailed plans for a raid to be carried out by the 11th East Lancashires on the German front line on the night of November 16th, but the very next day, Order No.90 was issued, which cancelled the previous Order and put the proposed raid back until the night of November 17th/18th:

1. Brigade Order No 89 is hereby cancelled, and order No 90 is substituted.

2. The 11th Bn., East Lancashire R. will carry out a raid on the night of 17th/18th November, 1916, for the purpose of securing identification, point of entry will be K.23.b.6.0.[55]

3. The raiding party will consist of 1 officer, 55 other ranks. Each flank will be protected by covering parties of at least 20 other ranks and one Lewis Gun, with an officer to command the two flanking parties.[56]

The plan for the attack was for three short bursts of artillery fire to be put down on a 1,700-yard stretch of the German line running from the right of the 'Sunken Road' (opposite Hebuterne) in the north, to John Copse in the south. The three 45-second bursts were timed to take place at 6:30 p.m., 8:00 p.m. and 9:00 p.m. The raiding party would then gain entry to the German front line at 'Point 60'

---

54 TNA WO 95/2341/6: 31st Division document ('Report of Raids Carried Out by Troops of the 94th Infantry Brigade on the Night of 6th/7th November, 1916').
55 Midway between 'The Point' and John Copse.
56 TNA WO 95/2363/3: 94th Infantry Brigade Order No.90.

(close to the Serheb crossroads). While the attack was in progress, the artillery was to fire a protective barrage around the point of entry and maintain it for 30 minutes – by which time the patrol should have started to withdraw back to their own lines. It is debatable whether the raid actually took place at all; the 31st Division war diaries only briefly mention the raid: 'A party of the 11th E. Lancs Regt., 94 Inf Bde endeavoured to enter the enemy trenches near point 60 at 9pm but failed'.[57]

The 11th East Lancashires' war diaries make no mention of the raid; the war diary entries for November 14th and November 18th state that:

'November 14th… Battalion moved into the trenches, taking over from the 13th York & Lancaster Regt. – the 16th West Yorks Regt. 12th York & Lancaster Regt. on the left and 3rd Division on the right'.

'November 18th… relieved in the line by the 13th York & Lancaster Regt. Casualties while in the trenches 6 killed, 14 wounded & 2 missing'.[58]

The 94th Infantry Brigade war diaries only report the situation as being 'normal' for the five days that the 11th East Lancashires were in the line. The 94th Infantry Brigade Situation Report for November 17th recorded the following:

Nov. 17. Morning.
Enemy artillery inactive, our artillery active to right of section. Enemy's T.M.s[59] quiet. M.G.s[60] slightly active on left. Our T.M.s and M.G.s quiet. Wind, N. E., mild. Addsd. 31st Divn. Reptd. 76th and 120th Inf. Bdes.

Nov. 17. Evening.
Enemy artillery shelled area in K.13 and K.14[61] with 77mm. and 10cm. H.E. and gas shells in early morning. JONES and the junction in K.23.c.[62] shelled with 5.9". Our artillery quiet. M.G.s and T.M.s quiet on both sides. Considerable aeroplane activity during the morning. At 10.am. one of our planes engaged a hostile one and both planes were seen to fall N. E. of HEBUTERNE. At 10.15.am. one of our planes hit by shell-fire and fell about K.17.b.65.13.[63] wind S. E. Addsd. 31st Divn. Reptd. 76th and 120th Inf. Bdes.

---

57 TNA WO 95/2341/6: 31st Division war diary.
58 TNA WO 95/2366/1: 11th East Lancashire Regiment war diary.
59 Trench Mortars.
60 Machine Guns.
61 Grid reference K.13 and K.14: reserve lines between Sailly au Bois and Hebuterne.
62 Grid reference K.23.c: Touvent Farm area.
63 Grid reference K.17.b.65.13: German lines west of La Louviere Farm.

<u>Nov. 18. Morning. And Afternoon.</u>
Situation quiet. Addsd. 31st Divn. Reptd. 76th and 120th Inf. Bdes.[64]

There is no mention in the report of any extra activity on the evening of the 17th – and Jack's diary entries for the five days in the line reveal nothing untoward either: '*Nov 18th/16: Came out of the trenches and got billeted at Sailly*'.

The following day, Jack parted company with Captain Lewis MC – to whom he had been batman since the end of October: '*Nov 19th/16: Captain Lewis. MC., left us at Sailly for the base. He shook hands with me this morning before he went. I helped him on his horse and away he went to the station. He wished me: "Good Luck" and I returned the compliment. I was very sorry indeed to lose him*'.

After just a few days' rest, the battalion moved back into the trenches on November 22nd – taking over the right sub-section of the line from the 13th York & Lancasters. The brigade war diary reported that the day was quiet, although there had been several encounters with enemy aircraft in the area. Jack recorded the move back into the line, but this was to be his last diary entry for the next month: '*Wed Nov22nd/16: Went into trenches*'.

On November 23rd, the British guns fired several salvos at the German lines. The response was immediate – and for a short while, the sector held by Jack's battalion was subjected to a heavy bombardment from the enemy artillery. The following day remained quiet due to poor weather, but on November 25th, there were reports of increased activity on both sides of the line. The 11th East Lancashires should have come out of the trenches on the 27th, but this was postponed until the following day. It is possible that this was because of the increased activity in the area, which would have made any changeover rather costly in casualties suffered. It was also common practice (by all sides) to subject the trenches to shell-fire when it was known that a changeover of troops was taking place. On November 28th, the battalion returned to their billets at Sailly au Bois and remained in brigade support until December 2nd; their casualties for the period in the front line were four killed and 11 wounded.

On December 3rd, the battalion relieved the 13th York & Lancasters – taking over the line stretching from John Copse to Jena Trench (just beyond 'The Point' in the northern sector). They remained in the line until December 7th, where they were relieved by the 13th York & Lancasters, and returned to their billets at Sailly au Bois. During their stay in the line, there was considerable artillery activity from both sides; during their four days in the trenches, the battalion casualties were five other ranks wounded.

On December 9th, two companies from the battalion were attached to the 14th York & Lancasters and sent to the front line; on December 13th, the remainder of

---

64 TNA WO 95/2363/3: 94th Infantry Brigade Situation Report (morning and evening, November 1916; Appendix A).

the battalion also moved to the front. The battalion war diary records the move: 'Battalion less two companies relieved two companies 14th Bt York & Lancaster Regt in the front trench. Line held by the battalion plus two companies 14th Bt York & Lancaster Regiment. Right boundary K.23.a.85.55.[65] Left boundary Warrior Street (inclusive). The 3rd Division held the line on the right and the 93rd Brigade the line on the left'.[66]

On December 17th, the battalion and two companies of the 14th York & Lancasters were relieved by the 12th York & Lancasters – plus two companies from the 13th York & Lancasters – and moved to Rossignal Farm, Coigneux; the casualties for the battalion during the period in the trenches were three other ranks wounded. According to the battalion diaries, the time spent at Rossignal Farm was devoted to training – and it was around this time that Jack returned to writing his diaries: '*Sunday Dec 24th/16: Had a quiet Xmas Eve at Rossignal Farm*'. While the battalion was at the farm on Christmas Eve, an incident occurred in the early hours of the morning when two German soldiers from the *8th Bavarian Infanterie Regiment* approached one of the outposts in the brigade line. They were challenged, but failed to stop – and as a result, they were fired upon, which led to one of them being killed and the other wounded and taken prisoner. On Christmas Day, two companies moved into brigade reserve at Sailly au Bois, with the other two companies moving into the line with the 14th York & Lancasters. It is possible that Jack was attached to the 14th York & Lancasters in the front line: '*Mon Dec 25th/16: Proceeded into trenches*'.

'Christmas Day in the Cookhouse' (song)

It was Christmas Day in the cookhouse,
The happiest day of the year,
Men's hearts were full of gladness
And their bellies full of beer
When up spoke Private Shortarse
His face as bold as brass
Saying: "You can keep your Christmas pudden;
You can stick it up your...

(All)
Tidings of comfort and joy, comfort and joy,
Oh, tidings of comfort and joy!

It was Christmas Day in the harem,
The eunuchs were standing around

---

65 Grid reference K.23.a.85.55: opposite 'The Point'.
66 TNA WO 95/2366/1: 11th East Lancashire Regiment war diary.

And hundreds of beautiful women
Was stretched out on the ground,
When in walked the bold bad sultan
Through his marble halls
Asking "What do you want for Christmas boys?"
And the eunuchs answered...

(All)
Tidings of comfort and joy, comfort and joy,
Oh, tidings of comfort and joy![67]

On December 29th, the two companies from the 11th East Lancashires which had gone into brigade reserve on Christmas Day were moved to the line alongside two companies from the 14th York & Lancasters, where they occupied the trenches they had previously held between December 13th and December 17th.

On New Year's Eve, Jack recorded an incident when one of their outposts was hit by a shell from a German trench mortar: the much-dreaded '*Minenwerfer*':

Sunday Dec 31st/16: Still in the trenches up to tonight when we were unfortunate enough to have one of our outposts shelled and eight were killed and two wounded. This happened this afternoon we were told, but of course we could not get at them on account of going over the top in the daylight. When the relief went to this post they found the men in an awful condition and reported same. We wasted no time in hurrying to the scene and got to work digging the poor lads out. One lad died only five minutes after we got him out.

What Jack saw that day would have been a scene of absolute carnage – and not something that would have been forgotten by him for a very long time. Such memories often stayed with you for life and came back to haunt you in later years.

This incident was also recorded in the 94th Brigade war diary entry of Monday, January 1st 1917:

Situation:- Artillery on both sides has been active. Our trenches and rear lines have been freely shelled; our battery positions were shelled during the night. Our Artillery shelled enemy's front line and communications trenches.

---

67 Lyrics by Anon.

Enemy dropped a heavy trench mortar bomb into one of our advanced posts, wrecking it and wounding or killing all the garrison.

Casualties to noon:- Killed 7 O. R

Wounded 3 O. R Total 10.[68]

A graphic account of the destructive powers of the *'Minenwerfer'* was given by Captain Sidney Rogerson of the 2nd West Yorkshire Regiment in his book *Twelve Days on the Somme*:

Standing over 3 feet 6 inches in height and filled with nearly two hundred pounds of high explosive, they had a more demoralising effect than any other single form of enemy action. There was no sound of distant discharge to give warning of their coming. Ears had to be sharp indeed to hear the warning whistle blown by the German gunners before they fired their mortars. Eyes had to be fixed in the air to watch for the shape which would soar ponderously upward, turn slowly over and over in its downward flight like a tumbler pigeon, and with a woof! woof! woof! burst with a shattering crash, sending long jagged strips of metal whirring savagely for yards and rendering into fragments anything around. The very leisureliness of their descent was demoralising. The uncertainty as to where they would pitch was demoralising. The immense clamour of their explosion was demoralising. But most demoralising was the damage they could do. Men do not easily or soon throw off the shock of seeing all that could be found of four of their comrades carried down for burial in one ground sheet.[69]

---

68 TNA WO 95/2363/4: 94th Infantry Brigade war diary.
69 Rogerson, Sidney, *Twelve Days on the Somme* (Greenhill Books, 2006), pp.6-7.

Part 4: 1917

The shelling from the German artillery heralded the start of the New Year for Jack's battalion and continued throughout much of the evening of January 1st, with particular attention being paid to the British front line trenches and Hebuterne. On January 2nd, as the artillery duels raged, Jack and his comrades finally came out of the line after being relieved by the 12th York & Lancasters and two companies from the 13th York & Lancasters. The battalion moved out of the line and took over the accommodation at 'The Dell' at Sailly au Bois; they then went into brigade support, where they provided work parties for the brigade: *We were relieved from the trenches after experiencing some very bad weather whilst in the trenches*.

'Tommy's Dwelling'

I come from trenches deep in slime,
Soft slime so sweet and yellow,
And rumble down the steps in time
To souse 'some shivering fellow'.

I trickle in and trickle out
Of every nook and corner,
And rushing like some waterspout,
Make many a rat a mourner.

I gather in from near and far
A thousand brooklets swelling,
And laugh aloud a great 'Ha, ha!'
To flood poor Tommy's dwelling.[1]

Between January 2nd and January 11th, the enemy artillery became increasingly active around Hebuterne, with both the front line trenches and the reserve areas falling victim to the German guns – and while in 'The Dell' in reserve, Jack's battalion also fell victim to the shelling: *Went to the Dell in billet and were shelled one night. I took over Batman for Lt Jones (Transport Officer) temporarily*.

---

1 Poem by Harold Parry (1896-1917).

On January 11th, the 94th Infantry Brigade moved into General Headquarters (GHQ) reserve after being relieved by the 58th Infantry Brigade of the 19th Division. Jack's battalion was relieved at 'The Dell' by the 9th Cheshires – and at 2:30 p.m., they set off by motor bus to their new billets at Beauval, where they were to undertake training and provide working parties: *'Jan 11th/17: Moved from Coigneux Woods to Beauval where we had a splendid billet'.*

On January 22nd, the battalion left Beauval and marched to Fienvillers – and while at their new billets, they had a visit from Lieutenant General W.N. Congreve VC CB MVO, commanding XIII Corps. On January 29th, the battalion proceeded to Fieffes, where they continued to supply working parties: *'Mon Jan 22nd/17: Shifted again from Beauval to Fienvillers. Batman for Chaplain the Rev Meskel. His Batman having gone on leave. Moved from Fienvillers to Fieffes'.* While at Fieffes, the battalion continued with their training, where they practised assaulting trench systems at both brigade and battalion level. The art of 'open warfare' – and village fighting and attack – was also covered. The Allies were constantly striving to make that vital breakthrough which would free their armies from the stalemate of trench warfare on the Western Front. With the introduction of the tank in 1916, the art of killing was gradually becoming more mechanised, but to use these new machines to their best advantage, they required ground which was free from the effects of years of constant shelling. For Jack, there was to be some good news: he received word that he had been granted leave – and for a short while, he would be out of the trenches and back with his family for the first time since leaving England back in 1915. *'Wed Feb 7th/17: I went home on leave'.*

'I Want to Go Home' (song)

I want to go home, I want to go home.
I don't want to go in the trenches no more,
Where whizzbangs and shrapnel they whistle and roar.
Take me over the sea, where the Alleyman[2] can't get at me.
Oh my, I don't want to die, I want to go home.

I want to go home, I want to go home.
I don't want to visit la Belle France no more,
For oh the Jack Johnsons[3] they make such a roar.
Take me over the sea, where the snipers they can't get at me.
Oh my, I don't want to die, I want to go home.

---

2   'Alleyman' is slang for the French word for Germany ('Allemagne').
3   A 'Jack Johnson' is a type of German artillery shell which gave off a black cloud when it exploded; it was nicknamed after the American boxer Jack Johnson.

'Thurs Feb 8th/17: Left Boulogne Port 11 a.m. and came across in a little over an hour to Folkestone. Caught the train for London (Victoria) and then on to Preston. Good connection from Preston to Accrington. 11 p.m. The journey from Boulogne to home only being about 12 hours'.

Soldiers often found it hard to readjust while at home on leave. Many of them were of the same opinion: their relatives just had no idea what they had to endure in the trenches. All their families knew of the war and what was happening on the battlefields, but what they read in the newspaper reports usually gave a romanticised version of life in the trenches. The transition from constantly being in danger to one of being back in the bosom of their families was difficult for many soldiers to adjust to in the short time that they had at home – and some soldiers even claimed that they were glad when their leave was over so that they could return to the front and back to their 'other family', their friends, with whom a very strong bond had been formed through the shared harsh realities of life in the trenches where death was never far away: *'Sat Feb 17th/17: Departed from home for France once more. Delayed through fog'.*

On February 20th – and while Jack was still trying to rejoin his battalion – the 11th East Lancashires and the 14th York & Lancasters moved to Terramesnil. The following day, three companies from the 11th East Lancashires moved to Coigneux. The remaining company from the battalion moved to Couin with the 14th York & Lancasters and the 94th Machine Gun Company

On February 22nd, Jack finally managed to board a ship bound for France: *'Thurs Feb 22nd/17: Folkestone to Boulogne'.*

Upon their return to the front, many soldiers, although glad to be back with their comrades (their 'other family'), had a feeling of despair. In the short time that they had been away, many familiar faces were missing – yet more victims of the constant shelling on the front line; the daily ritual of slaughter. They felt trapped in a horror from which there was only one way to escape: everyone prayed for a 'Blighty wound' – an injury of such severity which would result in their transfer away from the front – but others were convinced that they had just seen their families back in England for the last time…

> I have a rendezvous with Death
> At some disputed barricade,
> When Spring comes back with rustling shade
> And apple-blossoms fill the air –
> I have a rendezvous with Death
> When Spring brings back blue days and fair.
>
> It may be he shall take my hand
> And lead me into his dark land

And close my eyes and quench my breath –
It may be I shall pass him still.
I have a rendezvous with Death
On some scarred slope of battered hill,
When Spring comes round again this year
And the first meadow-flower appear.[4]

'*Sat Feb 24th/17: Arrived at Corbie*'.

'*Sun Feb 25th/17: landed at batt* [battalion]'.

On February 26th, the battalion war diary recorded that 400 men were sent on working parties in the back areas of Gezaincourt, Bois d'Epécamps, Doullens, Montrelet and Authieule:

'*Mon Feb 26th/17: Our Platoon went on Hospital work at Gezaincourt. I was Batman to R.T.O.*'.[5]

'*Wed Feb 28th/17: Lt Lonsdale joined us here and I became his Batman*'.

On March 1st, the three companies from the 11th East Lancashires departed from Coigneux and the remaining company (which had been with the 14th York & Lancasters at Couin) rejoined the battalion at their new billets at Thievres. The following day, they set off for Sailly Dell, where they provided working parties at battalion level.

Jack's platoon returned to their unit in readiness for the relief of the 93rd Infantry Brigade in the line:

'*Fri March 2nd/17: Gezaincourt to Thievres*'.

'*Sat March 3rd/17: Thievres to Sailly*'.

On March 4th, the German artillery was very active in the area and numerous fires were reported burning along the front line. British patrols were constantly probing the enemy defences – trying to find evidence of any withdrawal of their troops to their new line of defence. The German High Command had previously drawn up contingency plans for a much stronger line to which they could make a strategic withdrawal in the event of the earlier Allied attacks succeeding

---

4   Passage taken from the poem 'I Have a Rendezvous with Death' by Alan Seegar (1888-1916).
5   Railway Transport Officer.

in breaking through their lines, but once the construction of the new line was finished, they decided to withdraw to it anyway.

Towards the end of February, Operation 'Alberich' got under way, as the Germans started to pull back to the new 'Hindenburg Line'. As they withdrew, they began a 'scorched earth' policy of destroying everything which could be of use to the Allies. Orchards were cut down, road junctions blown up, houses and whole villages flattened, and wells filled in or poisoned. On March 5th, the new British front line to the east of Puisieux was heavily shelled by the German artillery. That afternoon, the 11th East Lancashires moved back into the line and took over the trenches from the 2nd Gordon Highlanders to the east of Puisieux. The left of the line was held by the 14th York & Lancasters, with the 2/4th Battalion, York & Lancasters on their right: *'Mon March 5th/17: Sailly to line at Courcelles'*.

The front had changed considerably since the 94th Brigade had left the area back in early January – and when the 11th East Lancashires moved back into the line, their Battalion HQ occupied the once formidable German strongpoint known as the *'Wundt-Werk'*. The frontage the battalion was defending comprised of two lines of isolated posts, with support and reserve lines at Orchard and Gudgeon Trench. That evening, patrols were sent out by the brigade to reconnoitre the enemy trenches – and all were found to have heavy belts of barbed wire defences and substantial garrisons of troops. On March 6th, the British artillery started to target the German trenches in front of Bucquoy. Patrols had been sent out again during the night to inspect the wire and to assess the strength of the enemy in the area, but they were all subjected to heavy machine gun fire; but despite this, the brigade still succeeded in establishing new outposts some 200 yards further forward.

On March 7th, the British and German artillery continued with the shelling of the front line positions – and then that evening, the Germans launched an attack on one of the new British advance posts. According to the brigade war diary, however, the raid 'was easily driven off'.[6] The British continued to send out their own patrols to probe the German lines – and at around midnight, 2/Lt Wild of the 11th East Lancashires took out a patrol of 20 men towards the enemy trenches. The battalion war diary recorded that the patrol had gone out to 'examine a suspected enemy machine gun emplacement and ascertain whether the enemy were holding Bucquoy trench in strength'.[7]

However, the 94th Brigade war diary said of the raid:

> Our artillery engaged the enemy's front system of defence and continued wire cutting. Our patrols were very active along our whole front; one of them consisting of 2/Lt. F. J. Wild and 20 o. r. failed to return, 17 subsequently

---

6   TNA WO 95/2363/4: 94th Infantry Brigade war diary.
7   TNA WO 95/2366/1: 11th East Lancashire Regiment war diary.

came in on the next and following days, and reported 2/Lt. Wild to be wounded. Search was made on the following nights but no trace of the missing men could be found.[8]

2/Lt Wild and L/Cpl Kewley were subsequently captured by the Germans on the following morning; the two other missing men were never found.

'The Night Patrol'

Over the top! The wire's thin here, unbarbed
Plain rusty coils, not staked, and low enough;
Full of old tins, though – 'When you're through, all three,
Aim quarter left for fifty yards or so,
For sounds of working; don't run any risks;
About an hour; now, over!'
And we placed
Our hands on the topmost sand-bags, leapt, and stood
A second with curved backs, then crept to the wire,
Wormed ourselves tinkling through, glanced back, and dropped.
The sodden ground was splashed with shallow pools,
And tufts of crackling cornstalks, two years old,
No man has reaped, and patches of spring grass,
Half-seen, as rose and sank the flares, were strewn
The wrecks of our attack: the bandoliers,
Packs, rifles, bayonets, belts, and haversacks,
Shell fragments, and huge whole forms of shells
Shot fruitlessly – and everywhere the dead.
Only the dead were always present – present
As a vile sickly smell of rottenness;
The rustling stubble and early grass,
The slimy pools – the dead men stank through all,
Pungent and sharp; as bodies loomed before,
And as we passed, they stank: then dulled away
To that vague fœtor, all encompassing,
Infecting earth and air. They lay, all clothed,
Each in some new and piteous attitude
That we well marked to guide us back: as he,
Outside our wire, that lay on his back and crossed
His legs Crusader-wise; I smiled at that,
And thought on Elia and his temple Church.

---

8   TNA WO 95/2363/4: 94th Infantry Brigade war diary.

From him, at quarter left, lay a small corpse,
Down in a hollow, huddled in a bed,
That one of us put his hand on unawares.
Next was a bunch of half a dozen men
All blown to bits, an archipelago
Of corrupt fragments, vexing to us three,
Who had no light to see by, save the flares.
On such a trail, so lit, for ninety yards
We crawled on belly and elbows, till we saw,
Instead of lumpish dead before our eyes,
The stakes and crosslines of the German wire.
We lay in shelter of the last dead man,
Ourselves as dead, and heard their shovels ring
Turning the earth, then talk and cough at times.
A sentry fired and a machine-gun spat;
They shot a glare above us, when it fell
And spluttered out in the pools of No Man's Land,
We turned and crawled past the remembered dead:
Past him and him, and them and him, until,
For he lay some way apart, we caught the scent
Of the Crusader and slid past his legs,
And through the wire, and home, and got our rum.[9]

On March 8th, 'Y' Company HQ of the 11th East Lancashires received a direct hit from a German shell; one officer was killed and another two were severely wounded. The following day, the battalion came out of the line after being relieved by the 13th York & Lancasters and returned to Courcelles: *'Fri March 9th/17: Relieved. Back to Courcelles'*. Jack's time out of the trenches was very short-lived, for the very next day, his company was sent back in the line close to the Battalion HQ of the 13th York & Lancasters for a further 24 hours: *'Sat March 10th/17: "W" Coy goes into the trenches again for 24 hours'*. On March 11th, 'W' Company returned to the battalion at Courcelles and were stood down, while the remaining three companies were employed on working parties.

On March 13th, the battalion was put to work constructing a light railway near Serre, but for Jack, there was to be a short break from the back-breaking work:

'Lt Lonsdale and myself, go on a course to Friecourt'.

'Sat March 17th/17: We left the Instruction School and re-joined unit at Courcelles'.

---

9   Poem by Arthur Graeme West (1891-1917).

On March 18th, the 94th Brigade moved north into the First Army area by march-route. Jack recorded each move that the battalion made:

'*Sun March 18th/17: Left Courcelles for Authie*'.

'*Mon March 19th/17: Authie to Beauval*'.

'*Tue March 20th/17: Beauval through Doullens, Frevent and stayed at Ligny*'. [Less two companies at Béthonval]

'*Wed March 21st/17: Left Ligny marched through St. Pol on to (Belval) Hernicourt*'.

'*Thu March 22nd/17: Hernicourt to Fieffes*'.

Friday, March 23rd was designated a 'rest day' for the brigade:

'*Sat March 24th/17: Fieffes to Ecquedecques (nr Lillers)*'. [Less two companies at Lespesses]

'*Sun March 25th/17: Ecquedecques to Calonne and Merville*'.

On March 26th, the 94th Brigade resumed their training. The emphasis appeared to have been placed on close-quarter fighting – probably in preparation for the forthcoming attack at Oppy Wood. The 11th East Lancashires' war diary recorded that the training consisted of 'Battalion training in Wood fighting, Musketry, Bombing, Bayonet fighting. Specialist training'.[10] The battalion war diary also listed the casualties for the month of March as '4 killed, 18 wounded, 3 missing'.[11]

From March 30th, the 31st Division was placed in reserve to XI Corps in case of attack on their front line. The brigade continued with their training and the 11th East Lancashires reconnoitred routes to the support lines between Neuve Chapelle and Festubert as part of their own training programme. On April 8th, the bulk of the battalion marched to Fouquereuil, but four officers and 50 other ranks were sent to XIII Corps' reinforcement camp at Robecq: 'These were selected from personnel to be left behind when the battalion took part in any offensive action'.[12] It is likely that these were 'Category B' soldiers, who were considered not fit enough for the rigours of front line service.

10 TNA WO 95/2366/1: 11th East Lancashire Regiment war diary.
11 TNA WO 95/2366/1: 11th East Lancashire Regiment war diary.
12 TNA WO 95/2366/1: 11th East Lancashire Regiment war diary.

Jack recorded the subsequent moves in his own diary:

> '*Sun April 8th/17: Left Merville for Fouquereuil* [near Bethune]'.

> '*Wed April 11th/17: Fouquereuil to Houchin*'.

> '*Sat April 14th/17: Houchin to Magnicourt* [Magnicourt en Comte]'.

The 11th East Lancashires remained at Magnicourt until April 29th – and during that period, they practised formation attacks at platoon, company and battalion strength:

> '*Sun April 29th/17: Magnicourt to Ecoivres*'.

> '*Mon April 30th/17: To Maroeuil*'.

Oppy Wood

On Monday, April 30th, warning orders were issued to the 94th Infantry Brigade concerning a proposed attack on Oppy Wood, which was to be carried out by the First and Third Armies during the early hours of May 3rd. The portion of the enemy line to be assaulted by the 31st Division ran from just north of the wood on the left of the line, to the southern outskirts of Gavrelle on the right of the line. For the purposes of the attack, the 94th Infantry Brigade – less the 11th East Lancashires, the 12th York & Lancasters and the 94th Machine Gun Company – would be held in divisional reserve. The dividing line between the 92nd Infantry Brigade and the 93rd Infantry Brigade was along Link Trench, which was situated roughly 500 yards to the south of Oppy Wood – and running from west to east. The assault to the north of Link Trench would be carried out by the 92nd Infantry Brigade, with the 11th East Lancashires and the 94th Machine Gun Company attached. The 11th East Lancashires' role in the forthcoming battle was to provide support for the attacking battalions of the 92nd Infantry Brigade. The assault to the south of Link Trench would be carried out by the 93rd Infantry Brigade, with the 12th York & Lancasters attached.

On May 1st, the 11th East Lancashire Regiment left their billets at Maroeuil and moved to the lines situated to the east of Roclincourt, where they stayed overnight:

> '*Tue May 1st/17: Maroeuil to Roclincourt (in trenches)*'.

> '*Wed May 2nd/17: Went into the line at Oppy (4 Yorks Div)*'.

Although Jack mentions moving to Oppy on May 2nd, the 11th East Lancashires actually assembled to the west of Bailleul, where they waited to take over the front line trench close to Oppy Wood. During the early hours of May 3rd, the 10th, 11th and 12th Battalions of the East Yorkshire Regiment moved towards their assault positions – and as they went forward, the 11th East Lancashires moved in and took over the line. The stretch of trench which the 11th East Lancashires was now holding ran from a point roughly 500 yards north of Oppy Wood and down to the Bailleul-Gavrelle railway (situated on the north-western side of Gavrelle). Two companies occupied the front line, with one company positioned further back in support and with the remaining company held in reserve at Bailleul. At approximately 1:40 a.m., the enemy artillery opened up on the men of the East Yorkshires after they were observed moving towards their assembly points for the assault. At 2:55 a.m., distress flares began to climb into the sky from the German trenches in Oppy Wood, as they became increasingly alarmed by the extra activity along their front: 'The effects of these barrages when battalions were reaching point of assembly, were disastrous, especially to rear waves of 11th E. Y. R. and the whole of 12th E. Y. R. who were then taking up their positions. It was impossible to get the waves thoroughly organised under this fire'.[13]

By now, the whole front was in a high state of alert – and to the south of the line in the 93rd Infantry Brigade area, the German artillery and machine guns put down a heavy barrage on the British front line after observing the West Yorkshires moving to their forward positions in readiness for the attack. The moon was particularly bright that night and the ground below was illuminated to such an extent that the Germans were able to observe the troops assembling for the attack. Casualties soon started to mount, as the enemy shells found their target amongst the tightly-packed ranks of the West Yorkshires, with scenes of unimaginable horror before the attack had even got under way. The 93rd Infantry Brigade report said of the situation: 'The result was that some men about to get into position were killed and wounded, but the remainder continued to get into position by crawling, some having to crawl over the dead bodies of their comrades'.[14]

At 3:45 a.m., the British guns opened up on the German lines and the first and second waves of the attack went in – closely following the creeping barrage as it moved forward. In the front line trench, the Accrington Pals watched the East Yorkshires going over the top. For Jack and the other few survivors of the attack on Serre, it surely must have brought back terrible memories of their doomed assault on the fortified village where so many of their friends were killed, but this time they were mere spectators to the death and destruction taking place some 500 yards to their front.

13 TNA WO 95/2342/3: 'Report of the Action of May 3rd, 1917'.
14 TNA WO 95/2342/3: 'Report of Events in Connection with Operations on the 3rd Inst.'.

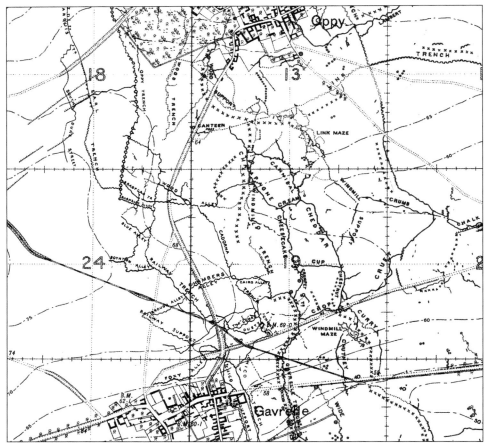

Map 2 – A trench map showing the area around Oppy Wood and Gavrelle. (Map used with kind permission of the Lancashire Infantry Museum, Preston)

At the northern end of the line attacked by the 92nd Infantry Brigade, the 'Right' assaulting battalion – the 10th East Yorkshire Regiment – were immediately met with a ferocious fusillade of rifle and machine gun fire from the heavily-defended trenches as they advanced towards the enemy wire. Despite this, they succeeded in breaching the enemy lines and advancing some distance towards their first objective, but in the end they were beaten back by the heavy fire from the enemy machine guns and had to withdraw to their assembly trenches.

The battalion account said of the attack:

Our barrage opened and was almost instantaneously answered by a heavy enemy Artillery barrage and machine Gun fire. The waves moved forward to attack behind the barrage. As soon as the barrage left the front trench more

M.G. fire as well as rifle fire opened from this trench, which was strongly held. It is impossible to give an accurate account of what happened after this as the four Company Commanders are casualties, and the darkness, thick dust and smoke made it impossible to see any distance. It was found impossible to get forward or to consolidate inside the German Line, so the Battalion took up a position in the assembly trench and shell holes in its vicinity.[15]

The 'Centre' assaulting battalion – the 11th East Yorkshire Regiment – fared no better. 'B' Company – on the right – were driven back on their first attempt to reach the German line, but showing great courage and determination, they attacked again; that too resulted in failure. One of their platoons even tried a third time, but this was also beaten back. The two front waves from 'C' Company, the 'Centre' company, managed to advance a considerable distance into Oppy Wood, but were then cut off from the following waves.

The battalion report said of 'D' and 'A' Companies:

"D" Coy. On the left not having been able to organise itself into waves, advanced at ZERO hour. This Company it is thought lost direction and went off too much to its right into the wood; where it got to is unknown. All the Officers of this Company are missing and 84 O.R. of which a considerable number have been evacuated wounded.

"A" Coy. My support Company had less casualties than the others, only losing about 30 men. This Company never formed up in its proper position on account of hostile barrage, it tried to capture the German front line but failed.[16]

The 'Left' assaulting battalion – the 12th East Yorkshire Regiment – advanced forward; the first wave of the 'Right' company entered the German trenches close to the northern edge of the wood. The enemy held the line in considerable strength along this stretch and put down a heavy concentration of fire on the advancing troops. Hardly anyone from the second wave managed to make it across – and they were forced to withdraw due to their heavy losses and the sheer weight of the enemy fire. The 'Centre' company captured a stretch of trench situated a short distance in front of the sunken road which ran along the northern edge of the wood, but they were subjected to repeated counter-attacks from enemy

---

15 TNA WO 95/2342/3: 'Report of Operations on the 10th (Service) Bn. East. Y. R. on the Night of 2nd/3rd May, 1917'.
16 TNA WO 95/2342/3: 'Report of Attack on Oppy Wood and Village on 3rd May, 1917', which was written by Lieutenant Colonel S.H. Ferrand, CO 11th Battalion, East Yorkshire Regiment.

bombing parties who were using the sunken road as cover. Eventually, their position became untenable and they were also forced to withdraw.

The 'Left' company of the 12th East Yorkshire Regiment was already in a state of disarray before they even went in. Their company commander had been killed in the enemy shelling as they tried to assemble into their attacking waves before zero hour. They advanced over open ground and pushed forward over an empty trench just yards away from where the 'Centre' company was pinned down by the enemy bombing parties. After occupying a trench about 250 yards to the left of the crossroads situated north of Oppy, they came under a sustained counter-attack from the enemy and were eventually forced to retire to the empty trench they had previously passed over. They immediately started to dig in and strengthen their defences, but were subjected to increasingly heavy fire – and their losses started to mount; every officer from the company was either killed or injured. Their right flank had no supporting troops and was wide open to attack, and so the decision was taken to withdraw back to their assembly points. Of the 46 officers and 1,416 other ranks from the three assaulting battalions of the 92nd Infantry Brigade, 34 officers and 758 other ranks were listed as casualties.

To the south of Link Trench, the 93rd Infantry Brigade prepared to go in. Under cover of the bombardment from their artillery, the 16th West Yorkshire Regiment advanced towards their first objective: Windmill Trench. Within minutes, however, they came under heavy fire from nests of enemy machine guns positioned on their right (near the windmill on the northern outskirts of Gavrelle), the top end of Wood Trench on their left and from the direction of Link Maze to their front. These machine gun positions succeeded in inflicting heavy casualties on the battalion and broke up the momentum of the attack. By now, the German artillery had opened up in reply to the distress flares from their own troops. Owing to the darkness, smoke and the general confusion caused by the barrage, the 16th West Yorkshires found it almost impossible to maintain visual contact with the assaulting battalions on their left and right flanks. Amidst all the chaos, elements of the 16th and 18th West Yorkshires lost their bearings and several of their companies became mixed together.

The failure of the assault by 10th East Yorkshires on the northern side of Link Trench left the 16th West Yorkshires wide open to a counter-attack on their left flank, and so the battalion commander – Lieutenant Colonel Croydon – took the decision to consolidate and defend the stretch of trench which they had entered: 'I immediately ordered my Adjutant to organise two bombing parties, composed of Headquarters Signallers Runners and Servants and an Artillery Liaison Officer, to block the trench'.[17] Several minutes later, a large group of the enemy were observed advancing along Wood Trench (situated to the rear of their position).

---

17 TNA WO 95/2342/3: 16th (S) Battalion, West Yorkshire Regiment document ('Report on Operations of 3rd May, 1917').

The two parties of bombers, under the command of Lieutenant Stanley, climbed out of their trench and proceeded to attack the approaching enemy from behind – and succeeded in driving them off. The Germans launched a second assault – and this too was driven off by Stanley's men. About 50 Germans were captured in the failed attacks – and as they were taken to the rear, many of them fell victim to their own artillery and machine gunners. Shortly after the assault, Croydon's men were joined by a party of stragglers, who came running down the trench to their left after being forced out of their line by the advancing Germans. They were immediately put to use in defending the left and right flanks of the battalion line. By 5:15 a.m., Croydon had managed to establish a better line of defence and was able to start evacuating the wounded to the rear. He had previously detailed a bombing party to deal with the troublesome Link Maze in the initial stages of the assault, but the strongpoint continued to inflict heavy casualties on his men. After making line contact with Brigade HQ, he sent an SOS request for reinforcements and for a barrage to be put down on the Link Maze.

As Croydon continued to consolidate his position, the enemy artillery opened up with their large-calibre weapons – and such was the ferocity of the bombardment that the trench they were defending was almost completely blown in and levelled. Their situation was so grave that it was becoming impossible for them to hold out much longer. The German machine gunners were finding easy targets amongst his men, who by now, had virtually no cover at all – and so the decision was taken to withdraw to the south side of the Bailleul-Gavrelle railway. About 100 yards behind the railway track ran a short stretch of trench, which had been chosen by the battalion commander of the 18th West Yorkshires – Lieutenant Colonel Carter – as their new line of defence. Croydon immediately started withdrawing his men in small groups towards the new position, but the enemy machine gunners firing from the top end of Wood Trench and from Windmill Trench on their right inflicted heavy casualties as the men fell back to the new line. Here they were eventually joined by 'B' Company, 18th Durham Light Infantry (DLI), who were sent up after the SOS request for reinforcements. One platoon was sent forward to establish a strongpoint on the north side of the railway track, while 'D' Company from the 18th DLI covered the north-eastern sector of the defensive line. Later in the day, Lieutenant Colonel Croydon attempted to return to his original position (which he had occupied earlier), but owing to the continuous bombardment from the enemy machine guns and artillery, he was unable to get any further than the railway. Eventually, he set up two defensive outposts which were garrisoned by machine gunners and bombing parties. The enemy launched several counter-attacks against his positions, but despite suffering heavy casualties, Croydon's men stood their ground and succeeded in beating off all the enemy assaults.

On the right of the line, the 15th West Yorkshires pushed forward towards the enemy positions. Their first objective was a line of unconnected posts garrisoned by enemy snipers and bombers which ran along the eastern side of Gavrelle. Despite suffering heavy casualties during the advance, the battalion made good progress and soon reached their first objective. As they closed in, several of the German garrisons surrendered and others fled to the rear in some disarray. The following waves were not so fortunate and suffered heavy casualties at the hands of nests of German machine gun emplacements in South Gavrelle Trench, Willie Trench (to the right of the cemetery) and from a strongpoint situated close to the Gavrelle-Fresnes Road on the eastern outskirts of the village. These machine guns had remained silent as the barrage and the first waves passed over them, and had waited for the succeeding waves to cross before opening up in a deadly fusillade of heavy fire from both flanks and the rear.

On the north side of Gavrelle (in the area around the windmill), elements of 'B' Company from the 18th West Yorkshires advanced as far as their second objective at Windmill Support Trench and started working along its length. Here they met a group of men from 'A' Company, who were beating a hasty retreat from a large party of advancing enemy soldiers, who were firing on them as they withdrew. 'C' Company reached the wire in front of their first objective to the right of the windmill, but were unable to advance any further. They were forced to withdraw after enemy troops started working around their flanks. 'D' Company advanced towards their first objective, but they too were caught by the machine guns situated in the ditch and on the main Gavrelle-Fresnes Road. The first two waves were practically wiped out by the concentrated fire from their right; only one man succeeded in reaching the first objective.

By 5:30 a.m., the 15th West Yorkshires' HQ still had no information on the progress of the attack and sent out runners to try and make contact with the forward companies. The news was not good: although the first waves had managed to reach their objective (while suffering considerable casualties), the following waves were virtually wiped out from the concentrated fire of the enemy machine guns. The Germans had also succeeded in capturing the windmill, along with four Vickers machine guns and two Stokes mortars, and Brigade HQ ordered its immediate retaking. By now, there was the very real possibility that Gavrelle and the high ground to the north and south of the village could fall into German hands if they launched a counter-attack. The battalion commander of the 15th West Yorkshires, Lieutenant Colonel Taylor, immediately set up a defensive line along their assembly trenches close to the cemetery and blocked off both flanks with whatever men he could spare. All he had at his disposal to hold the line were around 80 men he had managed to gather together from 'runners, signallers and stragglers'.[18] By this time, the enemy had started withdrawing in the direction of Fresnes along the Gavrelle-Fresnes Road, but it wasn't long before they realised that the British assault had ground to a halt.

---

18 TNA WO 95/2342/3: 15th West Yorkshire Regiment report.

At 6:45 a.m., 2nd Lieutenant Hitchin of 'C' Company, the 18th DLI attacked the windmill in two waves across open ground – completely devoid of any cover. To the right of the windmill, the enemy started launching distress flares, which immediately brought down a heavy barrage of shrapnel on Hitchin's men. Upon crossing the railway track to their front, they were subjected to a hail of machine gun fire from guns positioned along the Gavrelle-Fresnes Road on their right, and were forced to pull back to their start point. On their third attempt, they managed to get within 50 yards of the windmill, where they paused before making their final assault.

All along the line, there were signs that the enemy were preparing to counter-attack. Large numbers of their infantry were observed gathering just north of Hollow Copse and Railway Copse in readiness for an assault on the position held by Lieutenant Colonel Taylor's men of the 15th West Yorkshires, but Taylor had managed to establish contact with the British gun batteries, who proceeded to subject the advancing Germans to a heavy barrage of shrapnel – as well as succeeding in breaking up the attack. At 7:00 a.m., Taylor was joined by one officer and about 100 men from the 18th West Yorkshires, who had been forced to withdraw after their own failed attack on the left flank. With these extra men at his disposal, he was able to extend his defensive line to cover the main portion of the village. At 8:00 a.m., the defenders were further strengthened when they were joined by a platoon from the 12th King's Own Yorkshire Light Infantry (KOYLI); these men were immediately sent to seal the left flank.

To the west of Gavrelle – and on the southern side of the Gavrelle-Arras Road – one half of 'A' Company, DLI and one company from the 12th York & Lancasters took up position in a stretch of trench to give extra support to the left flank. A further two companies of the 12th York & Lancasters occupied Hill 80. Shortly afterwards, the Germans launched another assault on Taylor's men, but were again driven back by the British gun batteries and two machine guns positioned on an embankment approximately 400 yards south of the village cemetery. Several hours later, two companies of the 18th DLI arrived to help in the defence of the village. One company was positioned to cover the Gavrelle-Fresnes Road on the left of the line, with a defensive flank extending to the north-east corner of the village; the second company took position in a ditch on the eastern side of the village.

Back at the windmill, the enemy had started to pull out at around 9:00 a.m., but their movement attracted the attention of the British artillery spotters, who immediately proceeded to direct a heavy barrage of 4.5-inch howitzer shells upon the retreating Germans. Hitchin was forced to pull back to the railway track after the barrage started to fall amongst his own men – causing appalling losses in the process. By now, he had lost about half of his attacking force – and for his final assault, he organised the remainder of his company into small fighting sections. After regrouping, they gradually moved forward to attack once more: 'Creeping from shell hole to shell hole, and finally stopped at a point previously pointed out from the road. On reaching destination every other man of the party fired whilst the second man consolidated'.[19]

The enemy were still putting up a stubborn resistance from a house to the south of the windmill, but by 11:30 a.m., they had been driven out by volleys of rifle grenades. At 1:10 p.m., Hitchin was finally able to report to his battalion commander that the windmill had been retaken. By that afternoon, the whole line along the brigade front had become more or less stable. The last entry in the 18th West Yorkshire Regiment war diary for May 3rd reported: 'Night comparatively quiet'.[20]

In a brigade report written shortly after the battle, the conclusions reached for the failure of the attack were:

a)   The extent of the front was very much too great for a Brigade, as it permitted of no depth in the attack.

b)   Owing to ZERO hour being so early the darkness and the ground mist, together with dust and smoke prevented the attackers seeing where they were, or what they were doing while the defence knew the ground, and only had to handle their many machine Guns with firmness to cause very many casualties.

c)   Owing to the bright moonlight in the early part of the night, the enemy must have seen our troops lining up on the tapes. Enemy put up S.O.S. signal near OPPY WOOD and barraged our lines about 1.30a.m, causing many casualties, which, however, did not prevent arrangements being carried out.

d)   I think previous barrages a mistake as the enemy got practice in putting down his barrage, which came down quicker each time. He is stated to have put down his barrage in 30 seconds after ZERO hour.[21]

On May 4th, the 94th Infantry Brigade took over the line from the battered remnants of the 93rd Infantry Brigade. In all, they suffered a total of 1,900 casualties on that single day of fighting.

'Anthem for Doomed Youth'

What passing-bells for those who die as cattle?
- Only the monstrous anger of the guns.
Only the stuttering rifles' rapid rattle
Can patter out their hasty orisons.

---

19 TNA WO 95/2342/3: 'Report by 2nd Lieut Hitchin? [*sic*] D.S.O. (18th D.L.I.) on Capture of Windmill Gavrelie [*sic*], 3rd May, 1917'.
20 TNA WO 95/2362/2: 18th West Yorkshire Regiment war diary.
21 TNA WO 95/2342/3: 'Report of Events in Connection with Operations on the 3rd Inst.'.

No mockeries now for them; no prayers nor bells;
Nor any voice of mourning save the choirs, -
The shrill, demented choirs of wailing shells;
And bugles calling for them from sad shires.

What candles may be held to speed them all?
Not in the hands of boys, but in their eyes
Shall shine the glimmers of goodbyes.
The pallor of girls' brows shall be their pall;
Their flowers the tenderness of patient minds,
And each slow dusk a drawing-down of blinds.[22]

The 11th East Lancashires were relieved in the support trenches by the 13th East Yorkshires and withdrew to the railway cutting on the western side of Bailleul, where Jack caught his first sighting of a British Mk1 tank: *Fri May 4th/17: Moved back a little out of the trenches. Came across the tanks'*. The 11th East Lancashires' war diary entry for Saturday, May 5th recorded the battalion's return to the front: 'Moved to trenches in H. 1. c,[23] becoming supporting battalion to 94th Infantry Brigade, which was holding Gavrelle'.[24]

On the night of May 5th, the German artillery started to bombard Gavrelle and the trench lines around the village. Shortly afterwards, the British guns retaliated and shelled Oppy Wood. The following day started with heavy artillery fire around the southern sector of Gavrelle – and that evening, the 14th York & Lancasters took over the windmill from the 13th York & Lancasters. The German guns resumed firing on Gavrelle and the Gavrelle-Arras Road to the west of the village – and in the early hours of the 7th, the British 18 pdr guns opened up with a continuous barrage on the German defences. On the night of May 7th/8th, the 11th East Lancashires rejoined the 94th Infantry Brigade after relieving the 10th East Yorkshires in the trenches. The battalion was instructed to set up a post 'at or close to the Northern boundary of the brigade area'.[25]

'Mon May 7th/17: Moved into front line'. During the night of May 7th/8th, the German artillery shelled the reserve lines with lachrymatory shells (tear gas) for more than two hours – and at around 7:00 p.m. on the evening of the 8th, large formations of enemy infantry were observed advancing from the north-east towards Windmill Hill. The right supporting battalion immediately launched SOS flares to summon assistance from their artillery. Within minutes, the British gunners had responded with pinpoint accuracy: 'Our artillery barrage came down in the right place, and the enemy who had reached the ridge in C. 19. b.

22 Poem by Wilfred Owen (1893-1918).
23 West of Bois de la Maison Blanche.
24 TNA WO 95/2366/1: 11th East Lancashire Regiment war diary.
25 TNA WO 95/2363/5: 94th Infantry Brigade Operation Order No.140.

and C. 19. c.[26] disappeared into the folds of the ground'.[27] Later in the evening, the support and reserve areas were subjected to a barrage of 200 gas shells from the German artillery. The British guns quickly opened up in reply and targeted Oppy, the support lines and the enemy artillery positions. On May 9th, the 11th East Lancashires were relieved by the 13th York & Lancasters and moved back into the support line situated in the railway cutting on the west side of Gavrelle: *'May 9th/17: Relieved'*.

At approximately 3:45 p.m. on May 10th, the enemy were reported to be gathering between Oppy and Neuvireuil. Fearing that an attack may be imminent, the 11th East Lancashires and the 14th York & Lancasters were put on a five-minute warning until further orders. At 7:45 p.m., a heavy bombardment opened up to the north of Oppy at Arleux. The British guns shelled Neuvireuil and extended the bombardment to the eastern side of the village and back towards Gavrelle. At 8:40 p.m., the 13th York & Lancasters sent up SOS flares after suspecting the enemy were about to launch an attack. The British guns opened up to protect the forward line, but were gradually stood down after the attack failed to materialise. A short while later, the British guns were in action again when they fired gas shells into the enemy lines on the southern outskirts of Oppy village.

At around 2:40 a.m. on May 11th, a patrol from the 13th York & Lancasters launched an attack on a stretch of the German front line on the southern side of Oppy Wood. After a short barrage from Stokes mortars, the bombing party entered Oppy Trench and worked their way forward towards the edge of the woods; they eventually succeeded in driving out the enemy and capturing almost 100 yards of trench. Throughout much of the day, Gavrelle and the trench systems to the west of the village were subjected to intermittent artillery fire from the German large-calibre guns. The 31st Division's war diary made an observation on the continual shelling of Gavrelle: 'NOTE whenever there is any activity North of the Scarpe, the Enemy promptly retaliates on Gavrelle. This makes it very difficult for working parties to reach their work and causes heavy casualties amongst parties at work'.[28] During the evening of May 12th, the 11th East Lancashires relieved the 13th York & Lancasters in the line. Jack recorded the changeover in his diary: *'Sat May 12th/17: Into the Line again'*.

For much of the day, the German artillery had been very active – their guns targeting Gavrelle and the trench systems on the western edges of the village. During the evening, the windmill and the village were heavily shelled – and then during the early hours of May 13th (at around 2:10 a.m.), a party of about 40 Germans launched a raid on a stretch of line being held by the 11th East Lancashires to the south of Oppy Wood. The defenders stood their ground and fought back with their Lewis Guns and rifle grenades, and succeeded in driving

26 The approximate position of Windmill Support Trench.
27 TNA WO 95/2363/5: 94th Infantry Brigade war diary.
28 TNA WO 95/2342/3: 31st Division war diary.

the enemy back towards their own trenches. Moments later, the German artillery and machine guns put down a heavy barrage on their own wire and to the rear of the British trenches to deter any counter-attack.

During the early hours of May 14th, a bombing party led by Second Lieutenant Lott of the 11th East Lancashires entered Oppy Trench and started working towards an enemy strongpoint situated 50 yards beyond the junction of Oppy Trench and Bird Alley. Upon reaching their target, they found it to be heavily wired and it was impossible to gain entry. The 94th Brigade war diary entry said of the raid: 'The garrison was bombed and groans and cries were heard, but an entrance was not affected. Our bombing stop was advanced up to the enemy's wire, which fills the trench for some distance. Two of the enemy were killed by our sniper and Lewis Gun fire in addition to the casualties resulting from our bombs'.[29] At around noon that day, the German artillery opened up with a blind barrage along the length of Wood Trench. Some of the shells succeeded in hitting (or landing very close to) the post raided just hours earlier by 2/Lt Lott's men – much to the consternation of the enemy garrison manning it – and they immediately started launching red distress flares to bring the barrage to a halt. Throughout that afternoon and late into the evening, the British guns targeted the village of Oppy, while the heavy batteries concentrated on the Fresnes-Rouvroy defences and Neuvireuil areas.

On the night of May 14th/15th, the 11th East Lancashires launched a further raid against the German strongpoint near Bird Alley. Two bombing parties led by 2/Lt Lott and 2/Lt McKenzie worked their way up Oppy Trench and Wood Trench – under cover of a heavy barrage of Stokes mortars and rifle grenades. They closed in and attacked from both flanks, but were once again thwarted by the heavy wire covering the trench. They eventually resorted to bombing the position with grenades after failing to break through – and after a furious engagement lasting about 20 minutes, the raiding party withdrew back to their own lines.

At 5:30 a.m., the enemy launched a counter-attack on the bombing post situated at the southern end of the line held by the 11th East Lancashires. A brief engagement took place, which was later described as 'very hot',[30] and the enemy suffered several casualties. According to the 94th Brigade war diary, they were 'seen carrying their dead and wounded away under a red cross flag'.[31]

Shortly after midnight on the 16th, the German guns opened up on Hill 80 and the railway cuttings at Bailleul with a barrage of shrapnel shells. The heavy artillery laid down a barrage on Neuvireuil, Oppy and the German strongpoint situated near Bird Alley.

On the night of May 16th/17th, a third attempt was made by the 11th East Lancashires to capture the strongpoint near Bird Alley:

---

29 TNA WO 95/2363/5: 94th Infantry Brigade war diary.
30 TNA WO 95/2363/5: 94th Infantry Brigade war diary.
31 TNA WO 95/2363/5: 94th Infantry Brigade war diary.

SITUATION. Last night we made a further attempt to seize the line from B. 18. d. 3. 3. to B. 18. d. 7. 2 but were unsuccessful. After advancing over the forward block, bombing party was challenged. Bombs were thrown by enemy in large numbers, both from right flank and front, also a machine gun opened fire from a position in rear of enemy's post. After quarter of an hour's heavy bombing it became quite evident, [sic] that the enemy were in some force and fully prepared, and that a further frontal advance along OPPY trench would serve no useful purpose. In view of the fact that the mud was so heavy as to prevent any rapid movement by the men, and the darkness being such that a man two yards away could not be seen, it was decided that an attack over the top would have little or no hope of success, especially as any element of surprise was out of the question; party was therefore withdrawn.[32]

Shortly after the attempt to take the strongpoint, the 11th East Lancashires were relieved in the line by the 13th York & Lancasters and returned to the support lines situated in the railway cutting at Bailleul. Between May 12th and May 17th, the battalion casualties were two officers and eight men killed, and a further 36 other ranks wounded, with one reported missing. Jack did not have much to say about this period in the trenches, although he and his battalion undoubtedly saw a great deal of action throughout the month. Three simple words give a glimpse to the horrors which he must have witnessed: *'Thurs, May 17th/17: Relieved from Front Line after about 3 weeks in… A rough time'.*

How these brave young men coped with such horrific scenes of slaughter is difficult to comprehend. The reality of life in the trenches, where death was never far away – and where men saw their friends turned into bloodied bits of flesh – drove some soldiers over the edge and into the horrors of madness.

> I dropp'd here three weeks ago, yes – I know,
> And it's bitter cold at night, since the fight –
> I should tell you if I chose, - no one knows
> Excep' me and four or five, what ain't alive
> I can see them all asleep, three men deep,
> And they're nowhere near a fire – but our wire
> Has 'em fast as fast can be. Can't you see
> When the flares go up? Ssh boys; what's that noise?
> Do you know what these rats eat? Body-meat!
> After you've been down a week, an' your cheek
> Gets as pale as life, and night seems as white
> As the day, only the rats and their brats

---

32 TNA WO 95/2363/5: 94th Infantry Brigade war diary.

Seem more hungry when the day's gone away –
An' they look as big as bulls, an' they pulls
Till you almost sort o' shout – but the drought
What you hadn't felt before makes you sore.
And at times you even think of a drink ...[33]

The attack on Gavrelle Trench

The British front line which ran through the eastern edge of Gavrelle was, by now, being shelled on an almost daily basis by the German gun batteries. The position of the front line amongst the ruins on the edge of the village made it an easy target for enemy artillery spotters and reconnaissance aircraft to pinpoint with a high degree of accuracy – and the resulting barrages were having a devastating effect on the defenders. Therefore, the 93rd Infantry Brigade was ordered to capture a 350-yard stretch of Gavrelle Trench, which had originally been one of the first objectives of the failed attack on May 3rd. If this section of trench could be secured, it would enable the brigade to advance their front line outside the boundaries of the village and to establish a support line – something which they had previously been unable to construct within the confines of the village. A second aim was to further strengthen their hold on the ground immediately to the north-east of the village by linking Gavrelle Trench to the line held around the windmill.

The 2nd Field Artillery Brigade was due to leave the area on May 18th – and as they would be needed for the bombardment of the enemy positions, the decision was taken to launch an attack that night. The 18th DLI was to carry out the actual assault – and as soon as they went over the top, approximately two companies of the 18th West Yorkshires would occupy the front line trench. If required to do so, they would advance to Gavrelle Trench upon its capture and help consolidate the line. Prior to the assault, the British guns put down a heavy barrage on the German trench systems situated in Oppy Wood and to the south of Gavrelle. The ground in front of Gavrelle Trench had previously suffered three days of shelling from the British heavy guns and was already badly churned up and cratered. The initial intention had been to use gas shells against the known enemy machine gun emplacements, but in the hours leading up to the attack, the wind changed direction and this ruled out their use. Shortly after midnight on May 18th, the British guns opened up on the German lines – and at 12:30 a.m., two companies of the 18th DLI climbed out of their trenches and advanced in three successive waves under cover of a heavy machine gun barrage from two MG companies which were under the direct command of 93rd Infantry Brigade. The 17th Division supplied a further eight machine guns to cover the right flank – and towards the

---

33 Passage taken from the poem 'The Mad Soldier' by E. Wyndham Tennant (1897-1916).

north around Oppy Wood, the machine guns of the 5th Division joined in the feint attack on the wood, which it was hoped would confuse the Germans as to where the attack was actually going to take place.

All along the front (from Gavrelle in the south, to Oppy in the north), the enemy SOS flares climbed into the night sky. The response from the German artillery was swift and accurate, but much of the shelling passed over the front-assaulting platoons and landed to the rear. The 'Right' attacking company was already at a disadvantage after their commanding officer was killed shortly before the assault went in. As they approached the enemy wire, they came under a furious bombardment of stick grenades and small arms fire – forcing them to lie down and take cover in front of the trench. The bombing party which was responsible for attacking the right flank lost direction and went too far over to the right; a second party was hurriedly organised and they managed to force their way into one of the fire bays and killed the garrison of 12 men, but after coming under increasingly heavy grenade attacks and machine gun fire from the right flank, the officer in charge took the decision to pull back from the trench and withdraw his men away from the glare of the flares, which were presenting the enemy machine gunners with easy targets. He reasoned that after losing the element of surprise, there would be little to gain in making any further frontal assaults on the trench.

The attack on the left was a little more successful, although the assaulting companies found it hard-going over the badly-cratered ground. The left half of the company failed to break into the trenches and withdrew to their own lines; they reorganised before going forward again on the right half, where the attack had succeeded in breaking through. The acting company sergeant major took command after all the officers became casualties and managed to secure a 60-yard stretch of trench, which they initially succeeded in holding. Fierce grenade battles now broke out between defenders and raiders, as the enemy attacked from both flanks. At great personal risk, the company sergeant major made his way through the hostile barrage and back to Battalion HQ to brief the commanding officer on the situation. After hearing how the trench was almost levelled by the bombard-ment, which was meant to neutralise the machine guns, and how (in the opinion of the company sergeant major) it would be impossible to hold the position in daylight, the commanding officer took the decision to withdraw his men.

As it was, the men of the 18th Battalion were already starting to withdraw to their own lines even before their commanding officer had taken the decision to pull back. They were facing increasingly heavy counter-attacks, and the machine guns on their flanks were causing appalling losses. If the reinforcements from the 18th DLI and the 18th West Yorkshires had been sent forward earlier in the assault, there was a chance that the line might have been held, but the reports filtering back to HQ suggested that the line was already secured. As a conse-quence, the officer commanding the support company took the decision to hold his men back.

There appears to have been some criticism at first from Brigade HQ of the decision taken by the commanding officer of the 18th DLI to withdraw his men from Gavrelle Trench. The brigade commander commented in his report:

> By the time the report of the situation had reached the O.C. battalion, our men were coming back from the trench on which the enemy's bombers made constant bombing attacks, more especially from the right flank. It was just getting light at this time and he considered that he would not be justified in making a fresh attack with the men in our old front line who though somewhat disorganised were most eager to be allowed to advance again. I think he was right in not doing so then, but I have told him to report why he did not do so before. Communication with him today is only by telephone and he has replied that he does not feel justified in sending it.[34]

Throughout much of the day, the German artillery shelled the reserve lines at the railway embankment on the western edges of the sugar factory and Bailleul. German spotter planes were very active in the area and flew several low-altitude sorties over the front line. That evening, the British guns opened up on the German trenches to the east of Gavrelle and between the Neuvireuil and the Izel-Vitry Road after reports of large groups of enemy troops on the move. On the evening of May 19th – and fearing that the enemy might launch a counterattack in the Gavrelle sector – the 11th East Lancashires were brought forward and 'stood to' until daybreak in a stretch of the support line (the 'Red Line') situated on the eastern side of the sugar factory and Bailleul. On the following day, the 190th Infantry Brigade took over the Gavrelle/Oppy sector from the 94th Infantry Brigade. The 11th East Lancashires finally came out of the line after being relieved by the 4th Bedfordshire Regiment and moved with the rest of the brigade to their new camp at Mont St Eloi. Here they remained for the next week, where much of their time was devoted to further training: *'Sun May 20th/17: Went to Saint Eloi'*.

On May 27th, the 94th Infantry Brigade relieved the 93rd Infantry Brigade at Roclincourt – and each night from 10:00 p.m. onwards, the brigade was put to work on the 'Green Line' and the communications trenches to the east of le Point du Jour along the Arras-Gavrelle Road. According to the 11th East Lancashires' war diary: 'Working parties of 300 strong provided each night for work in H. 3. d.'.[35] That figure represented almost half of the battalion strength. Even when not on duty in the front line, there was little time for rest; there were always trenches to be repaired and new defensive works dug.

34 TNA WO 95/2342/3: 31st Division S.G. 104/169.
35 TNA WO 95/2366/1: 11th East Lancashire Regiment war diary.

'*Sun May 27th/17: St Eloi to Roclincourt*'.

'*Tue May 29th/17: Lt Lonsdale went home on leave*'.

On June 10th, the 94th Infantry Brigade moved back into the line and the 11th East Lancashires took over the Oppy sub-sector from the Hawke Battalion of the 63rd Royal Naval Division: '*Sun June 10th/17: Into the Line again*'.

Since the battalion was last in the line, the area had considerably quietened down – and by now, there was growing speculation that the Germans might be about to pull out of the area. On June 11th, Brigade Operation Order No.152 – concerning the anticipated withdrawal of the Germans – was issued:

1. Information indicates that the enemy is intending shortly to move back opposite the CANADIAN Corps front, and his eventual withdrawal from our front to the DROCOURT – QUEANT line may also be expected.
2. Any signs of the enemy's intention to withdraw will be carefully noted and reported immediately.
3. Any opportunity given of occupying his trenches will be immediately seized, and the neighbouring units as well as Brigade H.Q. informed. As soon as there is any indication of retirement, strong patrols will be pushed forward to reconnoitre. Battalion Commanders in the line will be responsible that the necessary support is given to these patrols in the first instance, so as to ensure that any ground won is made good, and that the enemy's initial retirement is not unmolested.[36]

The sector remained unusually quiet, with the enemy firing just a few light mortar shells at the British lines during the early morning – and the following day, was much the same. Later that evening, patrols ventured out again and '… two night posts established and occupied in 'no man's land' near Gavrelle-Oppy Road'.[37] On June 13th, three more posts were established on the Gavrelle-Oppy Road and the night patrols were increased to keep the enemy lines under observation for any signs of the anticipated withdrawal. For Jack Smallshaw though, the constant days spent in the trenches had taken their toll, and he went down with another attack of trench fever. This time, his condition was quite serious: '*Wed June 13th/17: This afternoon had a bad attack of Trench Fever. Stayed all night at M.O.'s dugout (105)*'.

On June 14th, the battalion was relieved by the 13th York & Lancasters and moved back to the railway cuttings and trenches to the east of Bailleul. Meanwhile, 'W' Company took over the defences situated on Hill 80. For Jack though, there would be no return to the trenches: '*Thu June 14th/17: Carried*

36 TNA WO 95/2363/5: 94th Infantry Brigade Operation Order No.152.
37 TNA WO 95/2363/5: 94th Infantry Brigade war diary.

to 94th Ambulance and then to 93rd and again to 95th'. The 93rd, 94th and the 95th Field Ambulance Units of the Royal Army Medical Corps were attached to the 31st Infantry Division; they were responsible for the care and evacuation of the casualties within the division. 'Field Ambulance' (FA) was a descriptive term applied to the mobile army medical units who established advanced dressing stations – usually situated 400 yards or more behind the regimental aid posts. These units were housed within any suitable building or tented accommodation – and their role was to provide care to the less seriously wounded and sick, who could then be returned to their units. The more badly injured were evacuated from the advanced dressing stations to the main dressing stations, which were situated further back from the front and out of range of the artillery. When out of the line, these units would set up divisional rest centres for the treatment of minor ailments such as skin diseases and the more serious complaints of trench fever and similar conditions. Bath units would be set up to allow the men to delouse and have their clothing properly laundered and repaired: '*Sun June 17th/17: My 21st Birthday. Still in ambulance*'.

For the past week, the British heavy artillery had been pounding away at the German front line as the build-up to the anticipated assault on their lines continued. On the night of June 18th/19th, the 12th York & Lancasters succeeded in driving forward a sap from the windmill defensive line and establishing a post a mere 60 yards from the enemy trenches. On June 19th, the battalion was relieved by the 11th East Yorkshires and moved to their camp near Ecurie, where they prepared for their part in the forthcoming assault on the German positions planned for June 28th. It is likely that Jack would have been taken to Ecurie by the 95th Field Ambulance Unit when they came out of the line with the brigade: '*Tue June 19th/17: Battalion relieved tonight*'.

By June 20th, Jack's condition had worsened – and the decision was taken to evacuate him to No.5 General Hospital at Rouen.

> '*Wed June 20th/17: I went by motor from "F.A." to 42nd C.C.S.*[38] *at Orbigney* [*sic*]'.

> '*Mon June 25th/17: Entrained at Aubigney and arrived at Rouen*'.

On June 28th at 7:10 p.m., the 94th Infantry Brigade launched their attack on the German lines. The brigade war diary recorded that:

> Brigade instructions were carried out to the letter. Our men met with little resistance and very few casualties. They report the barrage as excellent.

---

38 Casualty Clearing Station.

Prisoners, wounded and unwounded, 61. Estimated dead (not including those killed by M.G. fire at long range) 133. Our guns kept up desultory shelling all night, whilst the brigade dug itself in, in the old enemy front line and established posts at the front. At dawn the following day, it was possible to get into, and go round the whole of the front line by daylight.[39]

Compared to the losses suffered in the attacks on May 3rd and again on May 18th, the casualty figures for the actual assault were remarkably light. Between June 27th and June 30th, the 94th Infantry Brigade casualty figures were four officers and 48 other ranks killed, 12 officers and 319 other ranks wounded, and four other ranks missing. Out of these totals, the losses suffered by the 11th East Lancashires were 11 other ranks killed and four officers and 92 other ranks wounded during the same period. One of the officers wounded during the attack was Lieutenant Lonsdale of 'W' Company; he was later awarded the Military Cross for his actions on that day. Jack apparently heard of his injury whilst still at Rouen: '*Thu June 28th/17: The Battalion went over. Lt. Lonsdale is wounded*'.

By mid-July, Jack was showing no signs of improvement – and the decision was taken to send him back to England for further treatment: '*Mon July 16th/17: Embarked at Rouen and arrived at Southampton the next morning*'. The following day, Jack arrived in London and was taken to Middlesex Hospital in Mortimer Street. During the Great War, the hospital was used as a section of the Third London General Hospital and provided about 60 beds for sick and injured servicemen: '*Tue July 17th/17: By train from Southampton to London. Middlesex Hospital 4.pm*'.

Jack's health started to gradually improve and he became sufficiently recovered to be allowed out of hospital and to go for the occasional stroll around the city. He eventually got in touch with his brother Archie, and they both made arrangements to meet up in London. Over the next few days, they enjoyed several outings together:

'*Thu Aug 9th/17: Went out with Archie for a stroll round London. Had tea on the Strand*'.

'*Sat Aug 11th/17: Down Hounslow at the Playing Fields, had an enjoyable afternoon*'.

'*Sun Aug 12th/17: Went to Richmond with Archie on the canal*'.

'*Wed Aug 15th/17: Went to Raffers*'.

'*Tue Aug 21st/17: Went to the Empire*'.

---

39 TNA WO 95/2363/5: 94th Infantry Brigade war diary.

A photograph of Jack's friend, Leo.
Written on the back is: '*With my
very best wishes. Good Luck. Leo*'.

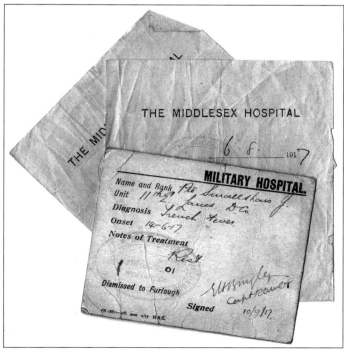

Jack's diagnosis from
Middlesex Hospital.

On August 23rd, Jack was discharged from the Middlesex Hospital and trans-ferred to the Third London General Hospital at Trinity Road, Wandsworth. By May 1917, this hospital was able to accommodate almost 2,000 military patients and even had its own temporary railway station at the front of the building to enable the wounded to be ferried straight to the hospital from the south coast. The Third London General achieved quite astonishing results with their care of the injured servicemen:

> By November 1917 some 897 officers and 987 enlisted men were being treated. At this time, of the 40,000 patients who had been admitted since the beginning of the war, only 270 had died.[40]

> *Thu Aug 23rd/17: Discharged from Middlesex Hos and went to Wandsworth Hospital*.

> *Fri Aug 24th/17: Went to see the 'Better Ole' at Oxford*.

A few days later, Jack was sent to convalesce at Bleakdown Auxiliary Military Hospital at Byfleet, Surrey. The 46-bed hospital was housed in the dining room at the former Bleakdown Golf Club and run by the nurses of the Voluntary Aid Detachment (VAD): *Mon Aug 27th/17: From Wandsworth to V A D at Byfleet in Surrey*.

Back at home in Accrington, there was a bereavement in the family when Jack's mother passed away at the age of 51. She had been suffering from breast cancer for some time, and although back in England, Jack still hadn't been considered well enough to make the journey to visit his dying mother. Although the death was expected, it still came as a great shock to Jack and the rest of the family.

Two days after receiving word of her death, he discharged himself from the convalescence hospital and set off for Accrington:

> *Thurs Sept 6th/1917: I had sad news this morning of my poor mother's death; she died at 7.15am*.

> *Sat Sept 8th/17: I discharged myself from Convalescent and went on my 10 days' Hospital leave and landed home same night*.

> *Tue Sept 11th/17: We buried poor Ma today at 2.15pm*.

The next two diary entries are rather obscure – and the place names mentioned are illegible. Jack's younger brother, Joe, was a driver in the Army Service Corps

---

40 'Lost Hospitals of London'; accessed at: <www.ezitis.myzen.co.uk>

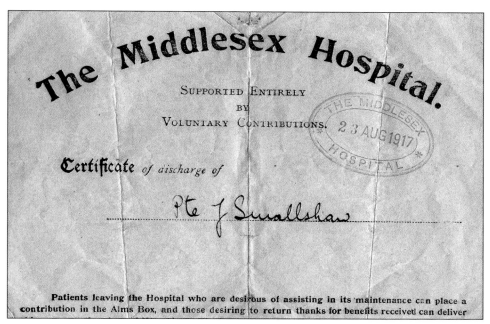

Jack's certificate of discharge from Middlesex Hospital.

(ASC) at the time – and his army records show that in December 1916, he was based at Grove Park; he also spent some time in Lincoln at the ASC garage depot. It is likely that at this period, he was home on compassionate leave for the funeral of his mother and returned back to his base a few days later:

'*Wed Sept 12th/17: Archie went back to G…..* [illegible] *today*'.

'*Thu Sept 13th/17: Joe went back to G…..* [illegible]'.

Shortly after the death of his mother, Jack wrote a letter to Lieutenant Lonsdale's wife to enquire about his recovery since receiving his injury in the fighting at Oppy Wood the previous June. A few days later, Jack received an invite to visit him at the Queen's Hydro Hotel in Blackpool, where he was convalescing:

Dear Smallshaw,
My Wife who is staying down here tells me that she had received a letter from you and told me all about it. I am exceedingly sorry to hear of your Mother's death & feel glad for your sake that you were not in France at the time. At least her last days were free from anxiety on your behalf.
    I had wondered often how you were getting along & whether you had got to Blighty or not, but as I left the Batt. soon after you did I lost touch with

Bleakdown Auxiliary Military Hospital.

A photograph of Jack's
mother, Janet.

A photograph of Jack's brother, Joe. Written on the back is: *'The fed-up one'*.

the means of getting to know. I am jolly glad to hear that you got over here alright. You will probably have heard that my wound is only slight, a bullet thro' the right wrist & really nothing to worry about. The hand is practically useless & it may be some time before it is quite right again. I am told that it will be all right in time. At present my left hand does all that it is called upon to do, even to writing letters.

I am a convalescent patient down here having 'beaucoup' massage & electricity & I am here for another month or two, so I am told. Prior to being here I was two months in Manchester. I saw a good deal of Mr Jackson who is also here.

If you are thinking of visiting this district during your leave don't fail to let me know for I should like to have a chat with you.

Kindest regards, best of luck & may you be some little time before you cross the water again.

Believe me to be,

Yours sincerely,

W F Lonsdale

Queen's Hydro. Hotel,

South Promenade,

Blackpool.

18. 9. 17.

TELEPHONE: No. 730.
TELEGRAMS: "PROGRESS."

RESIDENT MANAGER: B. C. SLACK.

Dear Smallshaw,

My Wife who is staying down here tells me that she has received a letter from you & told me all about it. I am exceedingly sorry to hear of your Mother's death & feel glad for your sake that you were not in France at the time. At least her last days were free from anxiety on your behalf.

I had wondered often how you were getting along & whether you had got to Blighty or not, but as I left the Batt. soon after you did I lost touch with the means of getting to know. I am jolly glad to hear that you got over here alright. You will probably have heard that my wound is only slight, a bullet thro' the right wrist & really nothing to worry about. The hand is practically useless & it may be some time before it is quite right again. I am told that it will be all right in time. At present my left hand does all that it is called upon to do, even to writing letters.

The letter to Jack from Lieutenant Lonsdale.

Although Lieutenant Lonsdale referred to his wrist wound as only being 'slight', it was still serious enough to keep him out of the fighting for the rest of the war: *'Sun Sept 18th/17: I went to Lt Lonsdale's at Blackpool and stayed till next day'.*

The following day, Jack set off for Knowsley Command Depot at Prescot, Liverpool. These command depots were another stage in the rehabilitation of injured soldiers, who although no longer requiring convalescence, were still considered too unfit for deployment back to the front.

Whilst at the depots, the servicemen underwent a gradual fitness regime of sports and gymnasium workouts, which were designed to gradually build up their strength and bring them back to full health, before finally returning them back to their own units for further training:

'*Mon Sept 19th/17: Went to the Command Depot at Knowsley'.*

'*Tue Dec 25th/17: Xmas Day. Still at Knowsley. Had a good Xmas dinner at Camp'.*

*'Always your affectionate brother,
Jack. Sept/17'.*

A few days later, Jack underwent a medical examination and was deemed fit enough to be returned to his unit for further training. On December 29th, he was posted to Saltburn Camp to undergo a one-week course of musketry with the 3rd (Reserve) Battalion, East Lancashire Regiment: '*Sat Dec 29th/17: Left Knowsley for Saltburn in Yorks; landed at 5 pm*'.

Part 5: 1918

RETURN TO FRANCE

By New Year's Day, Jack had completed his musketry course – and he appears to have done remarkably well. For his proficiency on the ranges, he was awarded the coveted marksman's badge of crossed rifles: '*Wed Jan 1st 1918: New Year's Day. At Saltburn (3rd E.L.R.). We fired our course in three days here (MARKSMAN)*'.

Within a week, he was on his way back home again on 10 days' embarkation leave:

'*Mon Jan 7th/18: I went on draft leave home from Saltburn*'.

'*Tue Jan 16th/18: Went to St Helens*'.

A photograph of Jack (front row, far right, kneeling) proudly displaying his marksmanship badge and wound bar.

'Wed Jan 17th/18: Came home from Wigan'.

'Thu Jan 18th/18: Set off for Saltburn, turned back at Halifax'.

'Fri Jan 19th/18: Went back to Saltburn'.

The diary entries for January 20th to January 28th are missing – the pages having been deliberately ripped out. The next entry mentions Jack's departure from Saltburn Camp to rejoin his unit in France:

'Tue Jan 29th/18: We left Saltburn for France at 5 p.m. this afternoon and landed at Folkestone at 5 a.m'.

'Wed Jan 30th/18: Embarked at 8 a.m. at Folkestone and arrived at Boulogne at 1 p.m. and went by bus to Etaples (22nd I.B.D.)'.

The infantry base depot at Etaples (also known as the 'Bull Ring') earned a formidable reputation over the years that it was in operation. The Red Caps (military police) and the instructors (known as 'canaries' because of the yellow armband they wore) were known for their sadistic brutality towards the servicemen. Many (like Jack) were still recovering from illness or injury when they passed through the camp before rejoining their unit. In September 1917, it had been the scene of a mutiny amongst the troops, which started after one of the military policemen opened fire with his pistol following an altercation with the New Zealanders and killed a soldier from the Gordon Highlanders. Fortunately for Jack, he appears to have spent just a few days there before returning to his unit:

'Sat Feb 2nd/18: Left Etaples at 8 am and entrained for Pernes; landed at Floringhem'.

'Mon Feb 4th/18: Sent letters to home'.

Jack recorded the names of the recipients of his next batch of letters (sent on February 7th) within his diary, but then he seems to have changed his mind – scrubbing all five names out. There is also reference to providing a firing party at a military funeral at Lapugnoy Military Cemetery. The very fact that the individual was accorded a gun salute suggests that he was probably a person of some standing: *'Thu Feb 7th/18: Sent letters to home. A dozen of us went on a firing party to Lapugnoy to the Military Funeral of one of the D.L.I.s.'.*

Jack's diary entries covering February 10th to the 12th have been scrubbed out – and the next entry is for February 13th: *'Feb 13th/18: Floringhem Canteen. About 9 of us gave a 2 hour sketch entitled: 'Umpteen Miles behind the Lines.' A kind of 'Better 'Ole' show. I was as a Staff Officer. The show was a success. Lt Lowe – the writer, Ashworth, Cooper, Crooks, Dillon, Haddock, Hindle, Jordan'.*[1]

The next page of the diary has been torn out, which presumably covered the dates from February 14th to March 7th. Jack makes no reference to when he actually rejoined his battalion – and the first time he mentions the 11th East Lancashires was in his diary entry for March 8th. During Jack's absence, the 94th Infantry Brigade had been broken up and the 11th East Lancashires now came under the command of the 92nd Infantry Brigade. Jack appears to have rejoined the battalion while they were still at rest camp, where they had been since March 4th. The Headquarters Company, with two companies (probably 'Y' and 'Z'), were at Marquay; the two remaining companies were billeted at Bailleul aux Cornailles. The war diary for March 4th recorded that the battalion was 'employed training – Route Marching – Battalion and Brigade Attack Schemes – Musketry – Bombing'.[2]

'Fri March 8th/18: We moved from here at Floringhem and went to Marquay where I was attached to Z Coy 11th E.L.R. The Batt being out on rest'. The pages containing the diary entries covering March 9th to March 15th have been ripped out. Jack's actual whereabouts between these dates is not known, but from here on, his diary entries seem to indicate that he was probably attached to the transport section for the remainder of the war. There is a likelihood that Jack never fully recovered from his last bout of trench fever and, as a result, was reclassified as a 'Category B' soldier and kept out of the front line: *'Sat March 16th/18: I took over Batman for Capt the Revd Meskel at Bailleul'.*

The German spring offensive

The pages covering March 17th to March 20th have been ripped out of Jack's diary. The removal of these pages – and parts of other pages – from the diary appear to have been done by Jack himself. The reason for their removal, along with the deliberate scrubbing-out of names in previous diary entries, is not known. The next entry in Jack's diary is dated 'March 21st', in which he mentions the opening of the 'Bosch Offensive', although it is likely that this entry – and the ones he made later – were actually written a few days *after* the battle started: *'Thu March 21st/18: The Opening of Bosch Offensive (20 mile front) between Arras and la Fère. Received two letters from home. Sent letter to Archie'.*

By this stage of the war, the British and French Armies were suffering from severe manpower shortages after the heavy losses suffered in the battles of 1917. The British philosophy had always been one of constantly being on the attack, but by 1918, they found themselves having to adopt a totally different strategy of defence: Field Marshal Haig correctly reasoned that the area of greatest strategic

1   This was probably the list of the cast for the play.
2   TNA WO 95/2358/1: 11th East Lancashire Regiment war diary.

A photograph of the missing diary entries.

importance to the Allies lay in the north, which contained the main routes to the Channel ports – and it was there he decided to concentrate the largest part of his forces. The line to the south was defended by the severely depleted Fifth Army, which was under the command of General Gough. He had at his disposal just 12 infantry divisions to protect a front of 42 miles – extending from Flesquières to La Fère in the south. By the middle of March, it was becoming increasingly apparent to the British that the Germans were preparing for an attack on the lines to the south of Arras after aerial reconnaissance photographs revealed newly-constructed supply roads and the installation of heavy '*Minenwerfer*' mortar batteries along the enemy front lines. Over the next few nights, the British guns started targeting the German front and reserve areas in an attempt to disrupt the build-up of troops, as concerns grew over the increased activity along the front.

At 4:40 a.m. on March 21st, the heavens were suddenly filled with a thunderous roar, as the German artillery opened up with a furious bombardment on the Allied lines between Arras and la Fère. Over a period of five hours, approximately 10,000 artillery pieces and heavy trench mortars pulverised the

British front and rear lines: Operation 'Michael' had begun. The British defences crumbled under the sheer weight of the artillery barrage, as a mixture of gas, smoke and high-explosive shells crashed down on the forward trenches. At 5:40 a.m. (and under cover of thick fog), the *Stosstruppen* of the German Second and Eighteenth Armies broke through and made rapid advances into the British rear areas of Gough's Fifth Army – sweeping all before them as they pushed forward. By the end of the first day of the battle, the Germans had captured some 500 field guns and taken 21,000 prisoners. In the northern sector – and just to the south of Arras – General Haldane's VI Corps of the Third Army grimly hung on against the might of the German Seventeenth Army.

At the time of the opening of the German offensive, the 92nd Infantry Brigade was still training in the divisional area prior to their planned return to the front line in the Roclincourt sector on the northern outskirts of Arras. Just before midnight on March 21st, 31st Division Headquarters received a phone call warning them of a probable move; at 1:50 a.m. on March 22nd, they received a further phone call ordering them to move by transport to join Haldane's VI Corps in the Boisleux area to the south of Arras; at 9:00 a.m., the 11th East Lancashires boarded a fleet of buses which rushed them towards Bailleulval, where they remained until that evening before moving on to the front line. The men of the transport section, to which Jack appears to have been attached, were not so fortunate… ahead of them lay a long, gruelling march to catch up with the rest of the battalion: '*Fri Mar 22nd/18: We made a quick march from Bailleul,*[3] *through Avesnes,*[4] *on to Bailleulval. A lovely day for the march of about 26 kilos* [kilometres]. *Arrived at 10pm at Bailleulval. The Battalion went straight into support for The Guards*'.

By now, the situation in the corps area was critical. The 4th Guards Brigade and the 93rd Infantry Brigade were ordered to move by bus to the north-west of Boiry St Martin. The 92nd Infantry Brigade was ordered to 'dig and consolidate in depth subsequently the Green (Army) line'[5] running from the eastern side of Boisleux St Marc in the north, to a position approximately 700 yards due east of Hamelincourt. The 11th East Lancashires were ordered to hold the left of the line, with the 11th East Yorkshires on their right, and the 10th East Yorkshires holding the switch line some 500 yards to the rear.

At 11:00 p.m. that night, the 11th East Lancashires left Bailleulval and marched towards the 'Green Line', but upon their arrival during the early hours of March 23rd, they found the trenches were already occupied by the Guards Division. They were immediately ordered to pull back and establish a position straddling the railway line on the western side of Boisleux St Marc. Tired – and somewhat dispirited by the undeniable chaos caused by the German assault – the battalion

---

3   Bailleul aux Cornailles.
4   Avesnes-le-Comte.
5   TNA WO 95/2356/3: 92nd Infantry Brigade Operation Order No.207.

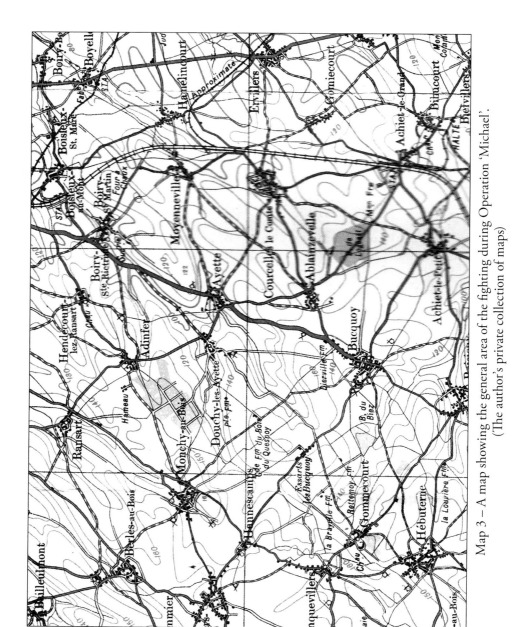

Map 3 – A map showing the general area of the fighting during Operation 'Michael'. (The author's private collection of maps)

reached their new position by 6:00 a.m., but at least for a short while they were able to grab some badly-needed rest.

Much of that day saw heavy fighting on the 31st Division front, with the divisional account of the fighting reporting that: 'During the 23rd [of] March there was heavy fighting on our front and also on the Division on our right round Mory. The 111th Division (Hanoverians and Hamburgers) were first of all opposed to us, but after suffering very heavy losses, the 2nd Guards Res. Div. took over from them'.[6] By mid-morning, the enemy were observed advancing in considerable numbers north and south of St Leger, but this attack was broken up by the artillery of the 92nd and 93rd Infantry Brigade. A short while later, another attack was launched from the south of St Leger, but again this was repulsed by the divisional artillery. Shortly after 2:00 p.m., a further attack developed to the north of St Leger, with large formations of enemy cavalry gathering on the right of the line. To the south-east of the line, the 40th Division was driven out of Mory by the advancing German hordes. The loss of this village left the right flank wide open to attack, and so the 92nd Infantry Brigade was ordered into the 'Green Line', which ran northwards from Ervillers, to cover the right of the 4th Guards Brigade. The 11th East Lancashires took up position to the right of the 18th DLI of the 93rd Infantry Brigade, while the 11th East Yorkshires occupied the remainder of the line running down to the eastern edge of Ervillers and to the southern boundary of the 31st Division area. The 10th East Yorkshires were placed in reserve some 500 yards to the rear; while holding the 'Green Line', the 92nd Infantry Brigade was placed in divisional reserve.

Shortly after midnight on March 24th, the German artillery opened up on the positions held by the Guards Division. By the morning of March 24th, the enemy had taken full control of Mory and, as a result, the right flank of the 4th Guards Brigade became completely exposed. Between 9:00 a.m. and 12:00 p.m., the enemy launched repeated attacks in the 93rd Brigade area and succeeded in capturing some of the high ground on the western side of St Leger. Further attacks were launched throughout the afternoon and evening – and the corps line to the east of Ervillers was captured after suffering from constant shelling and assaults on that front. As the enemy gained ground, the retreating formations withdrew to Ervillers, where they were organised by the 11th East Yorkshires for the defence of the village. The brigade's narrative recorded that: 'These troops were very tired and did not prove a very effective help'.[7] Meanwhile, the 4th Guards Brigade fell back and dug in along the St Leger-Ervillers Road and linked up with the 92nd Brigade line at the village.

---

6   TNA WO 95/2343/2: 'Narrative of Operations of 31st Division between March 22nd and April 1st, 1918'.
7   TNA WO 95/2356/3: 'Narrative of Operations around Ervillers & the Aerodrome, from March 23rd to 27th Inclusive'.

Reinforcements had been requested for the retaking of the corps line on the eastern side of Ervillers, but due to the precarious situation around the southern side, this request was refused. Every available man was needed to plug the gap left by the withdrawal 'without orders' of the remnants of other battalions positioned there by the 11th East Yorkshires. Enemy formations were, by now, advancing up the Mory-Ervillers Road – and to counter this latest threat, two companies of the 10th East Yorkshires were brought out of reserve to strengthen the defence of the village and to extend the right flank to the south and south-east.

At about 10:00 p.m. on the night of March 24th, three enemy battalions of the *91st Reserve Infanterie Regiment* launched a heavy attack and succeeded in pushing forward into the village. This attack exposed the 4th Guards Brigade positioned along the St Leger-Ervillers Road to harassing fire from their rear, but the 10th East Yorkshires succeeded in driving the Germans back out. By now, there were growing signs of panic amongst some of the troops defending Ervillers, as sporadic fighting broke out in the streets: 'About this time an enemy patrol of 1 officer 13 O. R. and a Light Machine Gun were captured at Battalion Headquarters in Ervillers, and desultory fighting was occurring all over the village'.[8] Such was the state of the confusion amongst the troops gathered there that German patrols were making forays into the village virtually unchallenged: 'During the evening, an enemy patrol had penetrated to the Ervillers position, so that distinction between enemy patrols and retiring bodies of troops from other Divisions in the Corps Line was difficult'.[9]

At dawn on March 25th, the remnants of a battalion of the Welsh Regiment – believed by the brigade to be the 18th Battalion – were withdrawn from the corps line and organised into a defensive line on the southern flank of the village. A short while later, the village was subjected to a heavy bombardment from the German artillery, and enemy formations were observed gathering for an attack to the east and south-east of Ervillers and near Mory. Ten machine guns were hurriedly brought up to defend the right after touch was lost with the 42nd Division. Four guns were immediately taken forward and placed in defensive outposts along the line – and for the next three hours, they were in almost continuous action as they engaged targets over open sights from ranges of 300 to 1,500 yards. At 10:00 a.m., the 10th Manchesters of the 42nd Infantry Division filled the gap on the right flank of the 11th East Yorkshires 'and took over that part of our right flank which was evacuated without orders or notice about that time by the remainder of the Welsh regiment above mentioned'.[10]

8   TNA WO 95/2356/3: 'Narrative of Operations around Ervillers & the Aerodrome, from March 23rd to 27th Inclusive'.

9   TNA WO 95/2356/3: 'Narrative of Operations around Ervillers & the Aerodrome, from March 23rd to 27th Inclusive'.

10   TNA WO 95/2356/3: 'Narrative of Operations around Ervillers & the Aerodrome, from March 23rd to 27th Inclusive'.

Jack commented in his diary on returning to Douchy at this time: '*Mon Mar 25th/18: Went to transport lines at Douchy* [Douchy-les-Ayette]'. The afternoon was relatively free of further attacks on Ervillers, but at about 6:00 p.m., the enemy opened up with a heavy barrage on the village and the higher ground to the north. At 7:30 p.m., a renewed attack was launched, which succeeded in breaking through to the western end of the village, but again, they failed to capture it after meeting with fierce resistance from the men of the East Yorkshires. Orders were issued for the 92nd Brigade to withdraw from the army line at 9:30 p.m. that night and fall back to the 'Yellow Line' and the railway line on the eastern side of Courcelles to cover the withdrawal of the Guards Brigade and the 93rd Brigade, but due to the sheer speed of the enemy advance – and the breakthrough on the right flank – the withdrawal commenced almost immediately and Ervillers was successfully evacuated with hardly any losses.

Although it was recorded that during the withdrawal, shelling from the British heavy guns was falling on the ground on which the British troops had to cross, the division's narrative of the situation recorded that:

> Orders were received from the VI Corps that owing to the situation farther south we were to withdraw to a line from Moyenneville inclusive to Ablainzeville, where we were to gain touch with the 42nd Division. Orders were issued for this withdrawal to be carried out by Brigades in succession, making use of the line constructed E. of Courcelles, which was held by part of 92nd Bde. as a covering position. The 92nd Bde. reinforced by the 12th K. O. Y. L. I (Pioneers) and the 3 Field Coys. R.E., were ordered to cover the right flank, whilst the Guards Bde., and subsequently the 93rd Bde., fell back to their new line, which was to be held by the 93rd Bde. on the left and the 92nd Bde. on the right. The 4th Guards Bde. in reserve were to hold a position N. E. and S. E. of Ayette.[11]

Gradually, the 4th Guards Brigade and the 93rd Infantry Brigade started to fall back to their new positions, while the remaining two companies of the 10th East Yorkshires; two companies of the 11th East Lancashires, the 12th Battalion, KOYLI; and three field companies of the Royal Engineers formed the defensive line facing south to cover the withdrawal. The two remaining companies of the 11th East Lancashires had pulled back from the north-east of Ervillers in artillery formation, where they rejoined the battalion on the ridge. It was because of the stubborn resistance of the 11th East Lancashires – in the face of overwhelming enemy attacks, while defending this line – that the withdrawal of the

---

11 TNA WO 95/2343/2: 'Narrative of Operations of 31st Division between March 22nd and April 1st, 1918'.

93rd Brigade and the 4th Guards Brigade was successfully carried out: 'During this retirement the enemy put strong pressure on the 92nd Brigade who, however, successfully held their own and thus secured the safe withdrawal of the other two Brigades, which would have been jeopardised had the 92nd Bde. given way'.[12]

By 10:00 p.m. that night, the withdrawal had been completed and the new line established. The brigade's narrative of the withdrawal reported the situation as:

> Parts of the Welsh Regiment, Middlesex Regt, Suffolks, and East Surreys, were found in our area without orders during this withdrawal, and were ordered to report to the 11th. E. Lan. R. in the Yellow Line.
>
> The order of battle from South to North at 10.pm on the 25th. was as follows:-
> 3 Field Companies R. E. South-East of Courcelles, facing Gomiecourt-
> 12th. Bn. K. O. Y. L. I. facing South-East with their left about 500 yards from the railway, thence,
> 10th. E. York. R. and 11th. E. Lan. R. garrisoning Railway Line and Yellow Line.
> 11th. E. York. R. in reserve, West of the embankment.
> Trench Mortar Battery at the Level Crossing East of Courcelles.
> 93rd. Inf. Bde. On our left.
> 126th. Inf. Bde. (42nd. Divn.) on our right.[13]

At 1:00 a.m. on March 26th, further orders were issued for the 92nd Infantry Brigade to move into a new defensive line running from Ablainzeville in the south, to Moyenneville in the north. To their left was the 93rd Infantry Brigade and to their right, the 126th Infantry Brigade of the 42nd Division (with the 4th Guards Division held in reserve at Ayette). The 11th East Lancashires took up a position on the right of the line along the Ablainzeville-Moyenneville Road to the point where it reached the Courcelles-le-Comte-Ayette Road. The left of the line was held by the 11th East Yorkshires, with the 10th East Yorkshires held in reserve on the aerodrome spur north-east of Ayette. Outposts were established about 300 yards forward of the line, with the machine guns of 'A' Company, the 31st Machine Gun Battalion positioned along the defences. By 9:00 a.m., the rearguard of the 10th East Yorkshires' Trench Mortar Battery and 'A' Company, the 31st Machine Gun Battalion had passed through the line and taken up their new positions. Courcelles-le-Comte was, by now, empty – the remaining defenders having withdrawn to their new line while subjected to desultory small arms fire from the enemy as they moved through the village. Jack mentions his leaving

---

12 TNA WO 95/2343/2: 'Narrative of Operations of 31st Division between March 22nd and April 1st, 1918'.
13 TNA WO 95/2356/3: 'Narrative of Operations around Ervillers & the Aerodrome, from March 23rd to 27th Inclusive'.

Douchy for Bienvillers aux Bois, just over four miles away. This would presumably have been with the transport section of the battalion: '*Tues Mar 26th/18: From Douchy to Bienvillers. Out in the open all the time*'.

Throughout the afternoon of March 26th – and into the early hours of the 27th – the brigade lines came under sporadic shelling from the German guns. The brigade continued to dig in and strengthen their defences, but had no barbed wire at their disposal to protect their front from infantry attack. To make matters worse, they continued to fall victim to their own heavy gun batteries from another division, who were still dropping shells well short of the enemy lines. Twice in the night, the defenders had to send up SOS flares to bring down their artillery on large formations of enemy troops gathering to their front. To the right of the line, the 11th East Lancashires and one company of the 10th East Yorkshires extended their frontage by 1,200 yards on their right flank to link up with the left of the 126th Infantry Brigade in order to plug the gap created by the 10th Manchesters after they failed to reach their allotted position. On the left of the brigade line, the 93rd Infantry Brigade had also failed to reach their new positions – and the enemy had, by now, captured Moyenneville.

At 11:20 a.m., the enemy started shelling the brigade lines with heavy concentrations of fire. The defenders were still falling victim to their own heavy artillery, with the British guns still falling short of their targets. At noon, the defenders started launching SOS flares as the enemy infantry surged towards their lines, which were completely bare of any barbed wire defences. For almost five hours, there was vicious close-quarter fighting, where positions were lost and retaken several times during the course of the battle. The remainder of the 10th East Yorkshires – less one company – were brought forward from reserve to help restore the line. On the left of the line, the 15th West Yorkshires fell back and exposed the 92nd Infantry Brigade line to heavy enfilade fire on their left flank. To their right, Ablainzeville had, by now, been occupied by enemy troops, which exposed the right flank to attack from their machine guns.

Throughout the remainder of the afternoon, the 92nd Infantry Brigade came under further attacks at extremely close quarters, where many assaults were driven back at the point of the bayonet and heavy rifle fire. By 4:30 p.m., the situation was grave: the line was holding, but only just. Both flanks were exposed and the enemy prepared to launch another attack in the centre of the line. The commanding officer of the 11th East Lancashires, Lieutenant Colonel Rickman (the senior battalion commander), was instructed by the GOC, 92nd Infantry Brigade 'to use his own initiative if communications were out, and circumstances arose which could not be dealt with by the Brigadier himself'.[14]

---

14 TNA WO 95/2356/3: 'Narrative of Operations around Ervillers & the Aerodrome, from March 23rd to 27th Inclusive'.

By this time, the enemy had penetrated along both the left and right flanks as far back as the aerodrome – and after consultation with the other battalion commanders, Lieutenant Colonel Rickman took the decision to pull back to the Ayette Line. Such had been the scale of the fire put down by the British artillery on the German troops, the batteries of the 165th and 170th Brigades, Royal Field Artillery were down to just 12 rounds for each gun. The 11th East Lancashires started to fall back in artillery formation towards the new line, with the 11th East Yorkshires on their left flank, while a detachment of the 10th East Yorkshires – under the command of Major Cattley (11th East Yorkshire Regiment) – remained at Ayette with the 4th Guards Brigade to cover the withdrawal of the 92nd Infantry Brigade.

Some confusion arose within the battalions as to whether they were meant to hold the Ayette Line or the 'Purple Line', which ran between Adinfer Wood and Douchy, but eventually the decision was taken to fall back towards Adinfer Wood, while the 4th Guards Brigade held the Ayette Line. The division narrative of the withdrawal commented on the stubborn resistance shown by the 92nd Brigade as they withdrew: 'The 92nd Inf. Bde. fell back fighting every inch of the ground till evening when they were ordered to reform behind the Guards Bde. which was astride of Ayette, and to man the Purple Line running from Adinfer to Essarts'.[15]

At approximately 5:00 p.m., the 92nd Trench Mortar Battery withdrew to the 'Purple Line' to establish a skeleton force within the defences until the arrival of the remainder of the brigade. The brigade narrative recorded the dispositions of the battalions at 6:00 p.m. on March 27th as:

> 4th. Guards Brigade on the Ayette Line, with both flanks in the air, as far as they were aware.
> 92nd. Infantry Brigade established in the Purple Line, as follows from South to North:-
> 92nd. Trench Mortar Battery.
> 10th. East Yorks Regt.
> 11th. East Yorks Regt.
> With 11th. East Lancs Regt. in support in Adinfer Wood, and 'A' Company, 31st. M. G. Battn, covering the position with eight guns, the remaining eight being utilised for the defence of Ayette.[16]

By 7:00 p.m., the 11th East Lancashires had moved out of reserve after being replaced by three field companies, Royal Engineers and took up a position in

---

15 TNA WO 95/2343/2: 'Narrative of Operations of 31st Division between March 22nd and April 1st, 1918'.
16 TNA WO 95/2356/3: 'Narrative of Operations around Ervillers & the Aerodrome, from March 23rd to 27th Inclusive'.

the 'Purple Line' running north from Quesnoy Farm to the Douchy-Monchy Road. Meanwhile, the situation at Ayette remained critical: the village was being subjected to continuous heavy shelling from both sides, with many shells from the British guns also falling between Ayette and Douchy. The commanding officer of the 2nd Battalion, Irish Guards made an urgent request for reinforcements to help him defend the gap to the right at the village – and at around 9:00 p.m., the composite battalion (made up of 'Category B' soldiers from the brigade) had reached Adinfer. They were immediately guided down to Ayette to help in the defence of the village, but by the time of their arrival, the situation had slightly improved and only 120 men were required to fill the gap on the right. The decision was taken to retain a composite company of the 11th East Lancashires and to send the rest back to the 'Purple Line'.

At around midnight on March 29th/30th, the remainder of the composite battalion and Major Cattley's men, who had earlier covered the withdrawal of the 92nd Brigade, were relieved of their duties and pulled back through the lines of the 4th Guards Brigade to rejoin their own units, which they reached at around 1:00 a.m. on the 30th. With them they brought back 350 rounds of badly-needed artillery shells, which had been abandoned earlier in the withdrawal.

Jack Smallshaw commented in his diary on the fighting of the past few days – and although the diary entry was dated for 'March 22nd' (because of the reference to the fighting at Ayette), it is likely that it was actually written several days later:

From Friday March 22nd/18: The Battalion were fighting hard at Croiselles, Bullecourt and Ayette. A very trying time for all the Division or rather several Divisions who were rushed up on this front. We were specially mentioned in the G.O.C. Despatches as having fought well in spite of overwhelming strength of the enemy who drove us back a fair distance; but what a hard time of it the lads are having up to today.

More pages removed from the diary:

'Sat March 30th/18: Eight days and nights of it so far. Just fancy how the 3rd and 65th armies stuck it up against 7 Divisions of the enemy'.

It was because of the courage and bravery of all the officers and men of the 11th East Lancashires – and indeed, all of the 31st Division – that the might of the German Army failed to break through in the Arras sector. The 11th East Lancashires paid a heavy price for their stubborn defence of the line: four officers and 28 other ranks lost their lives, while seven officers and 177 men were wounded. A further 134 other ranks were recorded as missing. One of those officers who lost their lives during the withdrawal of March 26th and March 27th was 2/Lt Basil

Arthur Horsfall of the 11th East Lancashires. He was posthumously awarded the Victoria Cross for his gallant actions over those two days.

Lieutenant Colonel Rickman wrote the following letter to Horsfall's father:

> In the action fought between Ablainzeville and Mayannaville [*sic*] on 26th and 27th March 1918, my Battalion (11th East Lancs.) was holding the ridge which runs between Ablainzeville and Mayannaville [*sic*]. My left was on the road which runs from Courcelles le Comte Le Ayette [*sic*]. The enemy attacked very heavily on the dates mentioned. Your son was commanding the left platoon of my left company. The 11th East Lancs. prolonged the line towards Moyenneville. The 11th East Lancs. were driven off the ridge but your son continued to hold his position. I received a message from him saying that he had been driven back but that he was counterattacking which he most successfully did, driving the enemy back and gaining his objective. He being severely wounded at the time. Hearing that two other platoon commanders on the ridge were both killed and the other platoon commander wounded he refused to leave his men. Throughout the day a very heavy fight continued. Twice your son lost his position but each time he counterattacked, driving the enemy back. He held his ground though his company had lost 135 out of 180 engaged. In the evening when both my flanks were driven in on to my headquarters. I sent written instructions to your son to retire on to the line at Ayette. He received the instructions and carried them out, himself remaining behind to supervise the retirement. During the retirement he was unfortunately killed close to the ridge which he had so gallantly held for two days. His body had to be left where he fell, and the ridge has been in possession of the Germans ever since. By his splendid example and devotion to duty undoubtedly a very critical situation was saved. The division on my right had been driven in. The bridge on my left had evacuated its position and the troops under my command held two German divisions for two and a half days and nights – and then with both flanks in the air they only retired 1,000 yards which the line is today held.
>
> There is little that I can say that befits the glorious record of your son's death, and the battalion and all the regiment are so righteously proud of the glorious deeds in which won for your son the highest award of fame that can be granted to a soldier. On the award being received I paraded the battalion and called them to attention to hear the record of the deed which won for the Regiment this undying reward.
>
> Alas your son has gone in earning for his battalion the undying fame of a Victoria Cross.
>
> Beloved by all, respected by all. A magnificent example of cool bravery, splendid endurance and a record of the greatest gallantry under the most

adverse conditions. His name will be forever remembered by his regiment and by all who had the honour to know him.

I can only add my deepest sympathy to you in your loss, and I can assure you if there is anything I can do for you, I should only be too pleased.

I have lost a personal friend and an officer whose deeds will forever go down to posterity.

With my deepest sympathy

Believe me, yours sincerely,

(Sgd,) Arthur Rickman, Leut. Col.[17]

'The Anxious Dead'

O guns, fall silent till the dead men hear
Above their heads the legions pressing on:
(These fought their fight in time of bitter fear,
And died not knowing how the day had gone.)

O flashing muzzles, pause, and let them see
The coming dawn that streaks the sky afar;
Then let your mighty chorus witness be
To them, and Caesar, that we still make war.

Tell them, O guns, that we have heard their call,
That we have sworn, and will not turn aside,
That we will onward till we win or fall,
That we will keep the faith for which they died.

Bid them be patient, and some day, anon,
They shall feel earth enwrapt in silence deep;
Shall greet, in wonderment, the quiet dawn,
And in content may turn them to their sleep.[18]

On the night of March 31st/April 1st, the 11th East Lancashires were relieved in the 'Purple Line' by the 1st Dorset Regiment of the 32nd Infantry Division and went by march-route to St Amand. By 4:10 a.m. on the morning of April 1st, they had reached their billets, where they rested for a short while before setting off once more. It is likely that Jack Smallshaw remained at Bienvillers after going there on March 26th and rejoined the battalion at St Amand.

---

17 This letter was posted on the BBC's First World War 90th Anniversary Remembrance Wall by Hannah Mehiri on 11 November 2008; accessed at: <www.bbc.co.uk/remembrance/wall/record/12158>
18 Poem by John McCrae (1872-1918).

*'Sun March 31st/18: Served Mass in Church. Moved from Bienvillers to St
Amand. A long journey and raining'.*

'Mon April 1st/18: Left St Amand at 1p.m. and marched to Sus-St-Leger'.

*'Tue Apr 2nd/18: Left Sus-St-Leger and marched about 5 kilos then got on Buses
and arrived at Bailleul again where we were before we got marched up the line'.*

That same day, the battalion was on the move again; they 'embussed on the
Frevent-Avesnes le Comte Road and proceeded to Bailleul aux Cornailles'.[19] They
remained in the XIII Corps area for several days while they reorganised, were
brought back up to strength and underwent training: *'Wed April 3rd/18: Still at
Bailleul. 1st Army, 13th Company'.*

Operation 'Georgette'

After the failure of Operation 'Michael' and the attempt to capture Amiens, General
Ludendorff next turned his attention towards the major communications centre
of Hazebrouck in the north. On the evening of Sunday, April 7th, the Germans
opened up with a terrific artillery bombardment on the British front line running
from Festubert in the south towards Armentieres in the north. At 4:15 a.m. on
Tuesday, April 9th, the German *Sixth Army* launched their attack. The Portuguese
2nd Division (near Neuve Chapelle) bore the brunt of the assault – and their lines
crumbled under the onslaught of Operation 'Georgette', as the German armies
swept forward five miles. The British divisions to the left and the right grimly hung
on as the enemy advanced. On April 10th, the German Fourth Army launched
their attack in the northern sector. Armentieres was captured, along with much of
the Messines Ridge, which had already been the scene of three costly battles during
the course of the war. The enemy were, by now, closing in on Hazebrouck.

Between April 10th and April 13th, the 31st Division was heavily involved in
the fighting to the east of Hazebrouck. The following account is the author's brief
summary of the actions carried out by the 11th East Lancashires throughout that
three-day period… With the situation deteriorating by the hour, a warning order
was issued by XIII Corps for the 31st Division to prepare to move to the XV
Corps area – and at 7:00 p.m. on April 10th, the 92nd Infantry Brigade boarded a
fleet of buses and headed towards Vieux Berquin. Jack Smallshaw went to Borre,
presumably with the transport section, where he remained while his battalion
went in the line: *'Wed Apr 10th/18: Off again at a minute's notice, we leave Bailleul
at 6 p.m. by buses thro' Lillers on to Borre. The lads went forward into the line. A
long journey'.*

---

19 TNA WO 95/2358/1: 11th East Lancashire Regiment war diary.

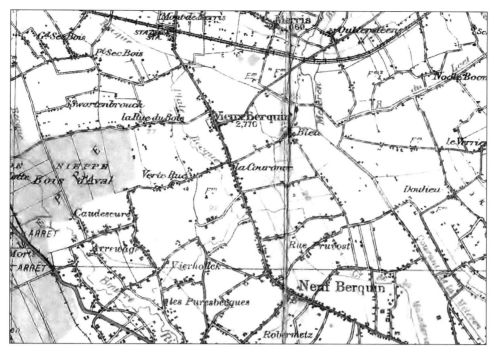

Map 4 – A map showing the area of operations during Operation 'Georgette'.
(The author's private collection of maps)

During the early hours of April 11th, the brigade reached the Strazeele-Vieux Berquin Roadway, where they hurriedly dismounted from the buses. The 11th East Lancashires made their way through La Couronne and on to the hamlet of Bleu, and started to dig in. Two companies set up a line on the eastern edge of the village, with the remaining two companies forming a defensive flank facing south. The 11th East Yorkshires dug a line of outposts to the south of 'les 3 Fermes' ('the 3 Farms'), with the 10th East Yorkshires taking up a position in support near Haute Maison.

On the left of the 92nd Infantry Brigade line to the north of the Rau du Leet, the 93rd Infantry Brigade established a string of defensive outposts to the east of Outtersteene. Shortly after 11:00 a.m., the 92nd Infantry Brigade received orders to hold a new line running in a southerly direction from the Rau du Leet in the north, to the road junction[20] lying approximately 750 yards to the east of Prince Farm. The 93rd Infantry Brigade advanced and dug in along the Rau du Leet, with the right of their line joining up with the 11th East Yorkshires of the 92nd Infantry Brigade, and with the left of their line resting opposite Blanche Maison.

---

20 Marked on some trench maps as 'Acton Cross'.

The 11th East Lancashires took up a position further back, in support of the East Yorkshires, with the right of their line facing due south towards Prince Farm.

That same day, Field Marshal Sir Douglas Haig issued his 'Special Order of the Day' to all troops serving in France and Flanders. In it he made it quite clear that he expected every man to stand his ground in the face of the German onslaught – and to fight it out to the very 'last man':

TO ALL RANKS OF THE BRITISH ARMY IN FRANCE AND FLANDERS

Three weeks ago to-day the enemy began his terrific attacks against us on a fifty-mile front. His objectives are to separate us from the French to take the Channel ports and destroy the British Army.

In spite of throwing already 106 divisions into the battle and enduring the most reckless sacrifice of human life, he has yet made little progress to his goals.

We owe this to the determined fighting and self-sacrifice of our troops. Words fail me to express the admiration which I feel for the splendid resistance offered by all ranks of our Army under the most trying circumstances.

Many amongst us now feel tired. To these I would say that Victory will belong to the side which holds out the longest. The French Army is moving rapidly and in great force to our support.

There is no other course open to us but to fight it out. Every position must be held to the last man: there must be no retirement. With our backs to the wall and believing in the justice of our cause each one of us must fight on to the end. The safety of our homes and the Freedom of mankind alike depend upon the conduct of each one of us at this critical moment.[21]

At 6:00 p.m., the 10th East Yorkshires reported that they were 'in touch with the 50th M. G. C. on their right'.[22] Lieutenant Colonel Rickman reported that 'troops of 50th DIV. continually retiring on his right & asks for information about his right flank'.[23] At 6:50 p.m., a warning order was issued for the 92nd Infantry Brigade to prepare to relieve the 40th Division 'about Le Verrier';[24] and then at 7:00 p.m., the 29th Division reported that their right flank had been turned and the enemy were advancing towards Neuf Berquin. To protect that flank, two companies of the 11th East Lancashires moved forward to link up with the right company of the 10th East Yorkshires and extend the line to the west

---

21 Passage taken from the 'Special Order of the Day' held at the National Army Museum, London.
22 TNA WO 95/2356/3: 'Operations. 10th – 15th April'.
23 TNA WO 95/2356/3: 'Operations. 10th – 15th April'.
24 TNA WO 95/2343/3: 'Summary of Operations of 31st Division from 10th April to 14th April, 1918'.

through Prince Farm. Further to the left of the line in the 93rd Infantry Brigade area, a counter-attack was launched 'with the object of driving the enemy out of LA BECQUE and gain touch with the 40th Division in LE VERRIER'.[25] This operation was a complete success, which resulted in the re-taking of la Becque, la Rose Farm and Farm du Bois. Just before daybreak on April 12th, the 29th Division took over the line being held by the 11th East Lancashires – whereupon the battalion immediately withdrew to the line which they had previously held during the evening of April 11th.

The 10th East Yorkshires had, by now, taken over from the 40th Division and were holding the line running from the roadway near Acton Cross to the crossroads at Pont Werneau. From here, the 11th East Yorkshires extended the line further to the left at le Verrier, where they linked up with the 93rd Infantry Brigade. At 8:00 a.m., the enemy attacked in great strength along the 4th Guards Brigade front in the south; this attack also extended along the line held just hours earlier by the 11th East Lancashires. At 9:10 a.m., the 93rd Infantry Brigade reported that large formations of enemy troops were making preparations for an assault from the area of la Becque – and by 9:30 a.m., the whole of the 93rd Infantry Brigade front was under attack. The 11th East Lancashires' war diary said of the situation: '9.15Am: [*sic*] The enemy attacked and troops on each flank gave way. The two right companies were moved over in artillery formation to extend the support line to the North through F22 c and a'.[26, 27]

At 10:30 a.m., the 10th & 11th East Yorkshires started to withdraw towards the Rau du Leet, with the 11th East Lancashires covering them as they fell back. Such was the ferocity of the rifle and machine gun fire put down by the battalion, the enemy attack was brought to a halt and they were forced to dig in.

After completion of the withdrawl, the 11th East Lancashires took up a new line running from Labis Farm on their right, to Haute Maison on their left, where they linked up with the 10th East Yorkshires – but further to the left, a gap had been left in the line:

> The 11th E York Regt were to extend still further to the left but did not take up this position thus leaving the left of the 10th E York R. exposed. Information was then received that the enemy were advancing along the railway and consequently the 10th E York R. threw their left back and took up a line HAUTE MAISON – Railway F 8 d.[28, 29]

25 TNA WO 95/2343/3: 'Summary of Operations of 31st Division from 10th April to 14th April, 1918'.
26 Grid reference F 22 c and a: the line held just west of Farm du Bois.
27 TNA WO 95/2358/1: 11th East Lancashire Regiment war diary.
28 Grid reference F 8 d: the railway line immediately south of Outtersteene.
29 TNA WO 95/2358/1: 11th East Lancashire Regiment war diary.

Stretching from La Couronne to le Pont de Pierre in the east, the enemy onslaught continued throughout much of the day. The 93rd Infantry Brigade was gradually falling back towards Meteren whilst under intense pressure from enemy assault troops and heavy machine gun fire. Near Clapbanck, they reached an outpost line of the 33rd Division – and from here, they eventually moved to a position lying to the east of Meteren, where they 'came under the orders of the 19th Inf. Bde., covering METEREN'.[30] At 12:30 p.m., the 11th East Lancashires were ordered to bring the right of their line towards Bleu and gain touch with the 29th Division.

Meanwhile, the 10th East Yorkshires had swung the left of their line towards 'les 3 Tilleuls' ('the 3 Trees') in the north, but by then, the enemy were already occupying Outtersteene – and the capture of this village forced them to pull back even further. To the west of Merris, the 92nd Composite Battalion was digging in. By 6:55 p.m., the 11th East Lancashires were holding a new line running from Labis Farm to the railway line just north-west of Celery Copse, where they linked up with the 10th & 11th East Yorkshires. By 10:55 p.m. that night, the 11th East Lancashires had established outposts on the eastern edge of Celery Copse.

At 1:00 a.m. on April 13th, the line was further strengthened when an outpost with 20 men and one machine gun was established on the eastern edge of Merris. By 8:30 a.m. that morning, the enemy were once again renewing their assaults on the British lines, with the whole of the divisional front coming under attack. At Celery Copse, the outposts set up by the 11th East Lancashires on the eastern edge of the wood were driven back, but due to the intense artillery barrage being put down by the British guns, the enemy were unable to make any further progress. At around 3:00 p.m., Lieutenant Colonel Rickman reported that his line was still holding out, 'but whole road VIEUX BERQUIN to PARADIS full of 29th Div. & K.O.Y.L.I. who report Guards have fallen back'.[31] Rickman was then ordered to gather together any stragglers and form a defensive position in front of Paradis facing towards Vieux Berquin, with the instructions: 'This line will not withdraw'.[32]

At approximately 3:20 p.m., Rickman reported that his Battalion HQ was coming under heavy machine gun fire along the Vieux Berquin Road – and he had observed 'about 1,000 men with some officers'[33] retreating towards Paradis from the direction of Vieux Berquin, which had, by then, been captured by the enemy. To the north of the line, the Germans had also taken Merris. At 3:40 p.m., Rickman was informed that the Australian Division had dug a new line to the west of their position – and if he was forced to retire, he was to swing his

30 TNA WO 95/2343/3: 'Summary of Operations of 31st Division from 10th April to 14th April, 1918'.
31 TNA WO 95/2356/3: 'Operations. 10th – 15th April'.
32 TNA WO 95/2356/3: 'Operations. 10th – 15th April'.
33 TNA WO 95/2356/3: 'Operations. 10th – 15th April'.

right flank towards the southern end of this line. At 5:30 p.m., it was reported that the Guards Brigade was in danger of being surrounded, and that they had been ordered to withdraw and pass through the Australian lines. Rickman was then ordered to bring back his right flank, but at 6:45 p.m., a 'Staff Captain 86th Bde. reported to Col. RICKMAN that situation in VIEUX BERQUIN in hand and asks him to hold on to his present line'.[34]

At 8:10 p.m., Rickman was again ordered by the brigadier general to bring back his right flank – and after driving off further assaults on his front, he finally swung the right of the line to rest at a position about 200 yards south-west of Tern Farm. By the early hours of April 14th, the 1st Australian Division had established a new line of defence and took over the front. The 92nd Infantry Brigade withdrew through this line – the 11th East Lancashires pulling out at approximately 4:00 a.m. and moving to billets at Pradelles. Later that day, at around 4:00 p.m., the battalion marched to camp south-east of Hondeghem. Jack mentioned moving out of the line to the camp on 'April 13th', but this was probably another of his errors with dates in his diary. The brigade casualties for this period were put at around 950, 'but very heavy casualties were inflicted on the enemy':[35] *Sat April 13th/18: Moved from Borre and landed at Nr Hondeghem at 2.30 a.m.*'.

From April 14th to April 17th, the battalion was at rest in billets to the east of Hondeghem, where they re-equipped and reorganised. During this period, a composite brigade was formed from units of the 92nd and 93rd Infantry Brigade. The 11th East Lancashires amalgamated with the 13th York & Lancaster Regiment to form the 94th Composite Battalion, which was under the command of Major Lewis MC. On April 17th, the 94th Composite Battalion moved into the line on the eastern side of Hazebrouck, where they spent the next few days working on strengthening the defences, but the amalgamation of the 11th East Lancashires and the 13th York & Lancasters was only brief. On April 19th, the composite battalion was disbanded 'and 11 E. Lan. R. reorganised into 4 companies forming 10 platoons. 11 E. Lan. R. took over portion of front line held by 8th Australian Infantry Batt.'.[36] The line they were holding stretched from Seclin on the eastern edge of Aval Wood and ran north-east for approximately 1,000 yards. The battalion remained here until the night of April 25th/26th, when they moved into support after being relieved by the 10th East Yorkshires. Two days later, they moved into corps reserve. Jack recorded the battalion going into the line, but he did not go with them. Instead, he went to Wallon Cappel on the western side of Hazebrouck. During this period, he was still batman to Captain The Reverend Meskel – and it is likely that he would have had to accompany him on his visits to the sick and injured. Again, there are several pages removed from his diary – and nothing is known of Jack's movements between April 20th and May 11th: *'Fri*

---

34 TNA WO 95/2356/3: 'Operations. 10th – 15th April'.
35 TNA WO 95/2356/3: 'Operations. 10th – 15th April'.
36 TNA WO 95/2358/1: 11th East Lancashire Regiment war diary.

Apr 19th/18: Moved from Hondeghem and went to Wallon Cappel. The Battalion go into front line again tonight'.

The battalion losses for April were two officers and 33 other ranks killed, nine officers and 149 other ranks wounded, and 47 other ranks missing. The 92nd Infantry Brigade remained in corps reserve until May 8th – and throughout that period, the 11th East Lancashires continued to supply working parties for the strengthening of the Hazebrouck defences. On the night of May 9th, the 92nd Infantry Brigade relieved the 2nd Australian Brigade and moved into divisional support in the Meteren sector. The 11th East Lancashires took over from the 5th Australian Battalion and moved into billets to the south of Caestre. For the next five nights, Jack's battalion provided working parties for the repair and strengthening of the reserve line and the Roukleshille Switch Line. Jack mentions writing home during this period, but again, there is evidence of Jack censoring some of the contents of the diary. He mentions who he sent the letters to, but then he appears to have changed his mind and crossed out the names: *'May 12th to 15th/18: 5 letters sent to* [names crossed out]'.

'Bombed last night' (song)

Bombed last night, and bombed the night before.
Going to get bombed tonight if we never get bombed anymore.
When we're bombed, we're scared as we can be.
Can't stop the bombing from old Higher Germany.

They're warning us, they're warning us.
Thank your lucky stars there are no more of us.
So one of us can fill it all alone.

Gassed last night, and gassed the night before.
Going to get gassed tonight if we never get gassed anymore.
When we're gassed, we're sick as we can be.
For phosgene and mustard gas is much too much for me.
They're killing us, they're killing us.
One respirator for the four of us.
Thank your lucky stars that we can all run fast.
So one of us can take it all alone.[37]

On the night of May 15th, the 92nd Infantry Brigade took over from the 93rd Infantry Brigade in the line. Throughout the period of the relief, the relieving battalions were subjected to sporadic shelling from both gas and shrapnel along

---

37 Lyrics by Anon.

the tracks and roadways as they made their way to the trenches. Shortly after 2:00 a.m. on the morning of May 16th, the 11th East Lancashires had taken over from the 15th West Yorkshires in a stretch of line which ran from the northern outskirts of Meteren and headed in a south-westerly direction towards the Meteren Becque. For Jack though, there would be none of the discomforts of trench life. Being batman to The Reverend Meskel had its advantages! '*Wed May 15th/18: We moved from Hondeghem and arrived at Caestre where we billeted and had the Mess in the farm house. The French came this afternoon to billet here but we didn't budge. The Battalion went into the Line last night*'.

During the early hours of May 21st, the 11th East Lancashires launched a trench raid on the German lines 'in order to try to obtain an identification & inflict casualties on the enemy'.[38] After moving into position opposite their target, a few enemy shells fell amongst them – causing several casualties. In the confusion that followed the shelling, the enemy launched several flares and opened up with their machine guns on no man's land. Under such heavy fire, the raiding party was left with no option but to withdraw back to their own lines. On the night of May 21st/22nd, the battalion finally came out of the line and moved into reserve near Rouge Croix. Throughout the period the battalion was in the line, Jack remained at Caestre: '*Eight days at the Billet near Caestre.*[39] *Glorious weather. Enjoyed the place. Excellent. Cecile, the young girl was very good to us. We are sorry to leave this place*'.

On May 23rd, the brigade came out of reserve and moved to the Lumbres area. The 11th East Lancashires moved by bus to Val de Lumbre Camp, where they underwent training.

The losses for the battalion for the whole of May were six other ranks killed, one officer and 15 other ranks wounded, and one other rank missing:

Thu May 23rd/18: We left Caestre at 11pm by Motor Buses relieved by the 9th Div; and arrived at the Brigade Camp at Lumbres (nr St Omer) through Hazebrouck, which was being shelled. A lovely moonlight night but very chilly. We passed through some very nice scenery. Landed at Lumbres about 1.30 a.m. and everyone under canvas. Arthur and I won a couple of tents and stuck them up in a wood near the Battalion camp for the Padre and Lt Armstrong. The other we put over us both only to waken up and find it raining hard about 5 a.m. Then we set to and erected the tent after we were wet through and slept in our wet clothes until 10 a.m. A Mess on our own of two Arthur and I. SOME cooks. In the middle of a wood, under canvas cooking for the Padre and Lt Armstrong.

---

38 TNA WO 95/2356/4: 92nd Infantry Brigade war diary.
39 Caestre is situated approximately four miles north-west of Meteren.

'Fri May 31st/18: The Padre said Mass for my Mother (it being her birthday if she had lived) in Lumbres Church this morning at 8 a.m.'.

The 11th East Lancashires remained at Val de Lumbre until June 8th. The time spent there was 'devoted to musketry, company and battalion training'.[40]

On June 8th, there was a further move when the battalion went by march-route to Racquinghem, where they spent another week of intensive training at company and battalion level:

'Sun June 2nd/18: Mass in the Church at Lumbres this morning a beautiful day too'.

'Sat June 8th/18: Reveille at 4 a.m. We moved this morning very early and went through Avre and on to Racquinghem where we got a Billet at a little house near the camp (Padre, Lt Armstrong and the Interpreter). It was a march of about 16 miles in the hot sun. We had a few halts and landed about dinner time'.

'Sun June 9th/18: Mass this morning at 9.30 in the Church and also Benediction'.

On June 15th, the 11th East Lancashires moved with the brigade to Wallon Cappel, where they remained on standby until June 17th. Their orders were to man the West Hazebrouck defences or the Le Peuplier Switch Line in the event of an enemy attack. According to Jack Smallshaw, the Spanish Flu pandemic which was sweeping throughout Europe at that time had severely affected the battalion – and as a consequence, around half the men had to stay behind at Racquinghem when the battalion moved to Wallon Cappel.

Jack himself fell victim to the virus:

'Sat June 15th/18: The Battalion moved to Wallon Cappel. Padre goes as well with them. As I am down with Influenza, which at this time is going through the troops, half of the battalion are left behind on account of this, I stayed behind with M Armstrong and Arthur and the Interpreter and Joe Sharrocks at the Billet'.

'Mon June 17th/18: Down with the Influenza still. Sent a letter to Wigan. My 22nd birthday and I am feeling rotten. Still at the Billet at Racquinghem'.

On June 17th, the battalion moved to billets at Blaringhem, where they stayed until June 21st. Jack rejoined his unit on the 18th after finally recovering from the flu virus:

---

40 TNA WO 95/2358/1: 11th East Lancashire Regiment war diary.

'*Tue June 18th/18: We left Racquinghem and arrived at Blaringhem about 10 p.m. Joe Arthur and myself*'.

'*Thu June 20th/18: I took over as Batman for the Interpreter Lefrerve (as well as for the Padre). Left Blaringhem and arrived under canvas at Le Crinchon near Wallon Cappel. Left this place and landed at Morbecque, 2 kilos distant and out in the open*'.

'When this lousy war is over'
(sung to the tune of 'What a friend we have in Jesus')

When this lousy war is over no more soldiering for me,
When I get my civvy clothes on, oh how happy I shall be.
No more church parades on Sunday, no more begging for a pass.
You can tell the sergeant-major to stick his passes up his arse.

When this lousy war is over no more soldiering for me,
When I get my civvy clothes on, oh how happy I shall be.
No more NCOs to curse me, no more rotten army stew.
You can tell the old cook-sergeant to stick his stew right up his flue.

When this lousy war is over no more soldiering for me,
When I get my civvy clothes on, oh how happy I shall be.
No more sergeants bawling, 'Pick it up' and 'Put it down'
If I meet the ugly bastard, I'll kick his arse all over town.[41]

Nieppe Forest

On June 21st, the battalion returned to the front line and relieved the South Wales Borderers in the trenches on the eastern edge of Aval Wood. They remained in the line until June 25th and then moved to a camp close to the small hamlet of Le Grand Hazard: '*Sun June 23rd/18: Received letter and photo from Cash's. Received letter and parcel of cakes, milk and cocoa from Wigan*'. On the same day that the battalion came out of the trenches, a warning order was issued by the GOC of XI Corps for an assault to be carried out by the 31st and 5th Divisions on the enemy lines to the east of Nieppe Forest on June 28th. At around 6:00 p.m. on the night prior to the attack, the 92nd Infantry Brigade moved into their assembly trenches on a frontage of approximately 1,500 yards – stretching from Volley Farm in the north to the outskirts of Caudescure in the south. On their left flank was the 15th West Yorkshire Regiment of the 93rd Infantry Brigade, and on their right was

---

41 Lyrics by Anon.

the 12th Gloucester Regiment of the 95th Infantry Brigade. Jack recorded the battalion going into the line: '*Thu Jun 27th/18: Went into the line again tonight*'.

The 92nd Brigade was using three battalions for their part in the assault, with the 11th East Yorkshires on the left of the line, the 11th East Lancashires taking the centre and the 10th East Yorkshires on the right of the line. At 6:00 a.m., the British guns opened up on the German trenches and fortifications – and Operation 'Borderland' got under way. To the left of the brigade area, the 15th West Yorkshires of the 93rd Infantry Brigade advanced towards the enemy lines and were met with very little resistance from the defenders – soon reaching their final objective.

In the 92nd Brigade area, there were considerable casualties caused through the attacking battalions sticking too close to the creeping barrage – and on the left flank, a gap opened in the line between the left and right attacking companies of the 11th East Yorkshires after the left attacking company strayed towards the 93rd Brigade area: 'An N. C. O. of the support company acting on his own initiative immediately rushed his platoon forward to fill the gap and capture the final objective simultaneously with the right company'.[42]

On the right of the line, the 10th East Yorkshires were subjected to heavy machine gun fire from the direction of Gars Brugghe Farm – and for a short while, the assault stalled until the right attacking company managed to turn the flank. A Stokes mortar was brought to bear on the enemy machine gun and put it out of action – and shortly afterwards, the position was taken. However, it was the centre attacking battalion which was given the hardest task of all: at the formidable strongpoint of Beaulieu Farm, 'Z' Company of the 11th East Lancashires moved forward – under cover of the creeping barrage – and took the German garrison completely by surprise because of their own close proximity to the barrage. As soon as the guns lifted and moved on to their next target, the enemy garrison emerged from their deep shelters – with their machine guns – only to find the men of the Accrington Pals already upon them; the strongpoint was captured.

The second objective of the 11th East Lancashires was Gombert Farm – and this proved to be a much tougher obstacle to take… While 'Z' Company consolidated Beaulieu Farm, the men of 'W' Company advanced towards Gombert Farm. The German defenders opened up with a murderous fusillade of machine gun fire as they crossed the open ground, but eventually the strongpoint was finally captured – although at a terrible price. The two remaining companies of 'X' and 'Y' pressed on to the final objective – and again, the cost was high: 'One of the assaulting companies of the centre Battalion losing all its Officers and was reduced to a strength of one N. C. O. and 34 O. R. on reaching its objective.

---

42 TNA WO 95/2356/4: 'Narrative of Operations Carried by the 31st Division on the 28th June, East of Foret de Nieppe'.

Another company of the same Battalion which took the final objective came out
with only one Officer and 42 O. R.'.[43] By the end of the day, all the objectives
had been taken by the brigade. The list of captured enemy weapons was also
quite impressive, which the 11th East Lancashires' war diary duly recorded: 'The
following material [sic] was captured – 10 light machine guns, 2 heavy machine
guns, 1 heavy Trench mortar, 2 medium Trench mortars, and 2 light field guns'.[44]

During the course of the battle, the 92nd Infantry Brigade suffered a total
of 680 casualties, but the greatest loss was borne by the 11th East Lancashires,
with two officers and 38 other ranks killed, seven officers and 195 other ranks
wounded, and 11 other ranks reported as missing.

Earlier in the month, there had been other casualties, when two officers lost
their lives and 17 other ranks were wounded. Jack recorded the success of the
battle – and also the deaths of some of his friends:

> Fri June 28th/18: The Battalion went over the lid this morning at 6 a.m. a
> pretty successful stint. The lads were "digging in" by 6.30 p.m. (Nieppe Forest)
> and a good many prisoners were taken. Bill Mortimer was killed in this advance
> also Mick Morgan and Dan Brady. 400 prisoners were taken. 12 machine guns
> and 2 field guns 3.1/2 miles of an advance in length and above a mile in depth.
>   (Saxons and Prussians).

After holding the newly-captured ground for two days, the battalion was relieved
by the Royal Welsh Fusiliers on June 30th and moved to camp at Grand Hasard,
where they remained until July 4th:

> 'Sun June 30th/18: Our Battalion was relieved late tonight and "came to" near
> Hazebrouck'.

> 'Mon July 1st/18: Two years ago today (by date) we went over the top at Serre
> (on the Somme)'.

Vieux Berquin

On July 4th, the 92nd Infantry Brigade moved back into the line and occupied the
trenches to the west of Vieux Berquin. The 11th East Lancashires took over from
the 13th York & Lancasters in brigade reserve just north of Petite Marquette. On
the night of July 8th/9th, the battalion relieved the 10th East Yorkshires in the
front line. Jack recorded the move and noted the recent sinking of the *Llandovery
Castle* – the ship which had brought the battalion to France early in 1916: '*Mon*

---

43 TNA WO 95/2356/4: 'Narrative of Operations Carried by the 31st Division on the 28th June,
    East of Foret de Nieppe'.
44 TNA WO 95/2358/1: 11th East Lancashire Regiment war diary.

July 8th/18: Our Battalion goes into supports tonight. The Llandovery Castle sank (by Bosch) on its voyage from Canada as a Hospital Ship'.

The RMS *Llandovery Castle* was built by Barclay, Curle & Co. of Glasgow for the Union Castle Line and was launched in September 1913. After being completed in January 1914, the ship worked the London-East Africa routes before switching to the London-West Africa routes in August 1914. Shortly after she had taken the 11th East Lancashires to France in March 1916, she was requisitioned by the Canadian Navy and converted for use as a hospital ship. In July 1916, she was recommissioned as HMHS *Llandovery Castle*. On 27th June 1918, the ship was torpedoed by the submarine SM *U-86* while off the coast of Southern Ireland and heading towards Liverpool. At the time of the attack, the ship clearly displayed her status as a hospital ship and was sailing with all lighting switched on. Under the rules of The Hague Convention of 1907, military hospital ships had to be painted in a distinct livery of all white, with large red crosses and a broad green band. They could be stopped and searched, but it was considered a war crime to carry out a deliberate attack. After the sinking of the ship, the commander of *U-86* – *Kapitänleutnant* Helmut Brümmer-Patzig – brought his submarine to the surface and proceeded to ram and sink the lifeboats in a deliberate and cold-blooded attempt to cover up his crime. He was determined that there would be no-one left alive to tell what happened – and Patzig ordered his crew to open up on the survivors with their machine gun as they clung to wreckage in the water. However, one lifeboat survived the onslaught... Out of a total of 258 passengers and crew, just 24 people lived to tell the tale of Patzig's war crime. This barbaric attack on an unarmed hospital ship was one of the worst atrocities of the Great War.

'*Mon July 14th/18: France's Day'.* On July 16th, the battalion came out of the line after being relieved by the 12th Royal Scots Fusiliers and moved to divisional reserve at Le Grand Hazard, but it would not be long before they were back at the front – and on July 22nd, they returned to the trenches opposite Vieux Berquin and relieved the 18th DLI: '*Mon July 22nd/18: The Battalion goes into the line again tonight'.* After a relatively quiet spell in the line, the battalion was relieved by the 11th East Yorkshires and moved back into brigade reserve. The casualty list for the whole of July was fairly light, with eight other ranks killed, and one officer and 36 other ranks wounded.

On the night of August 2nd/3rd, two fighting patrols from the 10th East Yorkshires and the 11th East Lancashires ventured out into no man's land under cover of small arms fire and a short artillery barrage. In front of Gars Brugghe Farm, the patrol from the 10th East Yorkshires entered two short stretches of trench, which were found to be unoccupied. A little further on, they captured two German soldiers from *Infanterie Regiment 187* in a machine gun post, which was apparently missing its gun. The 11th East Lancashires reached their point of entry by midnight. At zero hour, they continued to crawl forward towards the enemy post under cover of the barrage – and as soon as the guns lifted to their next target, they rushed the short stretch of trench, but by then, the garrison had already fled and were seen running towards another post set further back. A quick search of the captured trench was carried out, but nothing of value was found. By now, the enemy had been alerted to the raids along their front – and the distress flares started arcing into the night sky as they called for artillery support. The decision was taken to return to their own lines, and both patrols made it back without losing a single man – their only casualty being one soldier with a slight wound. On August 3rd, the brigade moved into divisional reserve and into billets at Morbecque. Between August 3rd and August 9th, the brigade carried out various training schemes – one of which involved aircraft from 4th Squadron, RAF for the purpose of practising communications between aircraft and ground troops. After almost two weeks of silence, Jack finally writes a brief note in his diary: '*Sun Aug 4th/18: The fourth year of the war by date*'.

On the night of August 9th/10th, the brigade went back in the line and took over the right brigade sector from the 93rd Infantry Brigade. The 11th East Lancashires relieved the 15th West Yorkshires in the 'R 1' sub-sector, with two companies in the outpost line and two companies in the main line of resistance: the 'Z' Line. On the night of August 13th/14th, the divisional boundaries were reorganised and the 92nd Infantry Brigade took over the centre sector.

The 11th East Lancashires were relieved by the 15th Battalion, KOYLI and moved into brigade reserve:

'*Mon Aug 12th/18: Padre went to 2nd Irish Guards this morning (Doullens) for a fortnight, their Padre being on leave*'.

'*Tue Aug 13th/18: Received letter from Archie. Sent letter to Dad*'.

'*Wed 14th to Sat 17th/18: Sending and receiving letters to Archie. Aunt Judith. From H Cash*'.

On the night of August 15th/16th, the 11th East Lancashires relieved the 10th East Yorkshires in the front line in the 'R 3' sub-sector. Throughout this tour in the trenches, a new policy of advancing the line was adopted.

In the brigade notes for 'Operations around Vieux Berquin', it outlined the tactics which were used:

The policy to be employed was, that enemy territory was to be occupied without serious fighting. To do this the battalions were ordered to send out strong patrols to take up definite lines. These patrols would send back word when they had accomplished their task, and parties would then be sent out to consolidate a line about 50 yards in the rear.[45]

---

45 TNA WO 95/2356/5: 'Operations around Vieux Berquin'.

During the early hours of August 16th, patrols went out to probe the enemy lines, but were unable to make much progress due to heavy machine gun fire coming from a group of fortified houses on the Vieux Berquin-La Couronne Road. During this two-day period, the 11th East Lancashires were subjected to heavy gas shelling from the enemy guns and suffered several casualties as a result of these gas attacks. The following day, a fresh attempt was made on the German lines. A few of the British outposts closest to the enemy strongpoints withdrew, while their artillery put down a barrage along the Vieux Berquin-La Couronne Road. Shortly after the barrage lifted, the patrols ventured back out in an attempt to advance their posts further into no man's land. On the left flank, the 11th East Lancashires again encountered heavy hostile fire from the direction of the buildings on the roadway, while on the right, the 11th East Yorkshires managed to push further forward and establish a new line of posts.

At 11:00 a.m. on August 18th, the 29th and 9th Divisions attacked and captured the high ground at Hoegenacker and Outtersteene approximately two miles north-east of the 92nd Infantry Brigade positions. Throughout that evening, several patrols from the 10th East Yorkshires and 11th East Lancashires probed the German lines for signs of movement. To the south, the enemy had already started to pull back – and it was anticipated that this withdrawal would eventually spread all along the front. At 5:00 p.m. on August 19th, the 94th Infantry Brigade and the 86th Infantry Brigade launched an attack on the salient between Outtersteene and Vieux Berquin. The 11th East Lancashires provided one platoon to protect the right flank of the 94th Infantry Brigade during the attack – and it is this attack which Jack is most likely to have observed (probably from Battalion HQ): 'Mon Aug 19th: Our lads went over a short distance at 5 p.m. this evening, what a good barrage it was'.[46]

On the night of August 19th/20th, the 11th East Lancashires came out of the line – after being relieved by the 11th East Yorkshires – and moved into brigade reserve at Le Souverain. During this spell in the trenches, they had succeeded in pushing forward their front line by approximately 200 yards.

On August 21st, the battalion moved to camp near Wallon Cappel – and according to Jack's diary, this was at La Brearde. Three days later, they took over from the 12th Battalion, the Norfolk Regiment in brigade and divisional reserve:

'Wed Aug 21st: Lt Armstrong goes on leave this morning'.

'Thu Aug 22nd: Reserve Capt. J. A. Guideless came to replace Capt Meskel while he is in with the S Guards. My old chum Harold Crookes wins the Distinguished Conduct Medal. Captures a Bosch out-post along with another chap'.

---

46 Information compiled by the author from the following sources: TNA WO 95/2356/5: 'Operations around Vieux Berquin'; TNA WO 95/2358/1: 11th East Lancashire Regiment war diary.

'*Sat Aug 24th/18: The Battalion were continually in and out of the line up to this date. After dinner today we moved from Morbecque (to the Meteren Front where we went into the line again) to La Brearde nr Hondeghem 8 kilos away. Under canvas. M' Maurier (Interpreter) joined us today and also Fr. Gribluin, a few days ago*'.

'*Sun Aug 25th/18: Said Mass with Fr. Gribluin in his billet this morning*'.

The 11th East Lancashires remained in camp at La Brearde until August 31st, when at 10:30 a.m., they set off by march-route to camp just west of Meteren in preparation for their impending move back to the front line. Casualty figures for the month were given as: 'Killed, 11 O.R. Wounded, 10 Offrs, 79 O.R. Wounded & missing, 3 O.R. Missing, 1 O.R.'.[47]

Sun Sept 1st/18: Left La Brearde and were dumped in a field (as usual!) between Fletre and Meteren Road. At this time we were on the look out for Bosch who was rapidly retiring towards his old Hindenburg Line, probably Armentieres, way from the front we were on. Behind his lines scores of villages and ammunition dumps we have seen on fire lately, evidence of his rapid retreat.

The following verse was found written in the back of Jack's first notebook; it is the chorus from a marching song:

> *There's a friend in every milestone*
> *All along the old road home*
> *Can't you read their friendly greetings?*
> *You've one less mile to roam*
> *There's a cosy place, a smiling face,*
> *To crown your journey's end.*
> *So we'll pass each milestone gaily saying*
> *Welcome home Friend.*[48]

Operations along the Warnave River

During the evening of September 4th/5th, Jack's battalion relieved the 10th East Yorkshires in the line – and at around 4:30 a.m. on September 5th, strong fighting patrols went out and pushed forward to probe the German lines in front of the Warnave River. By noon, the battalion was occupying the hamlet of Pontceau on the right and had succeeded in driving out the German garrison at Riga Farm on

---

47 TNA WO 95/2358/1: 11th East Lancashire Regiment war diary.
48 Lyrics by Anon.

the left of the line. To the centre, Oostove Farm was found to be deserted, but further progress became impossible due to heavy fire coming from the fortified enclosures and farms close to Soyer Farm. Because of the intensity of the machine gun fire, the decision was taken to make a further attempt under cover of an artillery barrage. Prior to the bombardment starting, the platoon occupying Riga Farm were withdrawn to a safe distance and 'Y' Company was brought forward out of support in preparation for the assault.

At 5:00 p.m., the first waves went over the top – sticking close to the barrage – with 'Z' Company attacking on the left of the line, 'Y' Company in the centre and 'X' Company (less two platoons) on the right of the line. Immediately the barrage started to fall, the enemy machine guns were brought in to action – their fire being heaviest on the right flank. However, as the first waves got closer to their objectives, the enemy started to withdraw towards Soyer Farm, where they attempted to make a stand before finally surrendering. On the right of the line, 'X' Company encountered two thick belts of barbed wire as they advanced towards their objective. They suffered heavy casualties when machine guns opened up on them as they tried to find a way through the second belt of wire – and they failed in their attempt to reach their objective. The left and centre attacking companies had made good progress – and by 5:40 p.m., they were consolidating their positions to their front and along the Warnave River, although no contact was established with 'X' Company on their right.

The battalion report covering the action said:

> Before touch could be made, the enemy counter attacked the centre company. Enemy approached in 'blobs' from the hospital up the road through C. 7. c.[49] central and gradually worked round the right flank of the centre company.
>
> The left flank held and the company gradually swung back to the road immediately in the rear. The whole of the right platoon were either killed or captured. Further progress of the enemy was stopped by Lewis Gun and Rifle fire. The line was then handed over to the 11th E. York. R.[50]

Jack briefly mentioned the two attacks in his diary: '*Thurs Sept 5th/18: Over the lid this morning and also over at 5 o'clock this evening. Two houses in between Fritz and our lads were very harassing. The Battalion was relieved this evening*'.

After being relieved by the East Yorkshires, the battalion moved to camp southeast of Bailleul near Mit Cottage. Jack and his comrades caught up with them the following day. In his diary, he gives a vivid description of the destruction caused by the recent fighting:

49 Grid reference C. 7. c: Mortelette Chapelle.
50 Information compiled by the author from TNA WO 95/2356/5: 'REPORT ON OPERATION CARRIED OUT BY THE 11TH E. LAN. RGT. 5-9-18'.

Fri Sept 6th/18: From this field (S-W) of Bailleul we moved our quarters nearer the Line by about three or four Kilos. What a horrid place this vicinity is, only a few days ago the Germans had left this part and no wonder, he must have been like living in Hell. Our shell holes round here are literally touching each other. As I was coming along the road this afternoon, the smell was awful of dead men and horses. As I'm writing this, there's a house in the corner of the field which is still burning from when the enemy set fire to it, and also a Bosch Convoy of transport 'put out' by the roadside.

We are having some rainy weather just now, just had the tent over with a storm. What a place Bailleul is now, there is hardly a stone upon a stone to be seen. 'Jerry' must have had a hot time of it whilst he was the 'holder' of this town. On this front a couple of our chaps are recommended for the V.C. for their pluck in bringing into our Batt H.Q, a couple of Bosch Machine Gun teams by themselves!

On the night of September 12th/13th, the battalion finally came out of the line after spending a further two 24-hour spells in the trenches. They marched to Bailleul, where a fleet of buses were waiting to transport them to camp southwest of La Brearde: '*Thu Sept 12th/18: From near Meteren we moved down to an old billet of ours near Hondeghem, how glad we were to get back there after the awful places we have been 'dumped' in (Old Jerry's ground up to lately). Padre is in a Nissan Hut and Interpreter is billeted in Hondeghem*'.

Between September 13th and September 23rd, the battalion was in divisional reserve and then moved to billets at Hazebrouck. Jack commented in his diary that it was '*for one night only*' before they moved on to Bailleul prior to going back in the line:

'*Sat Sep 14th/18: Col Rickman pins the D.C.M. on Crookes*'.

'*Sun Sept 15th/18: Mass in the Church and also at the windmill this morning and Benediction at 6 this evening in Hondeghem Church*'.

'*Mon Sept 23rd/18: After about 10 days' stay at Hondeghem we moved this morning to Hazebrouck, a fairly large place not far away. We had some fine billets here, the only discomfort we suffered was the absence of the windows which Bosch had kindly removed by his shelling and bombing of the place. The 'Brasserie-Moderne' is a fine place, not much harm has come to this building, or the Church either considering the stuff which has been sent into Hazebrouck!*'

'*Tue Sept 24th/18: At Hazebrouck for 'one night only' we moved up in front of Bailleul (by train). The ground over which we travelled gently reminded us of the hard scrapping which had taken place round here not long ago, but now the old R.O.D.[51] shrilly whistles on its way up the line with their cargos of troops and guns, stores etc. When we landed here what lovely 'billets' we had, the ever open-fields under 'bivvies.[52] The Batt is in the line tonight.*

Crookes modestly tells me of his D.C.M. and how he locates a German Outpost. Bombing them (himself and ....) they bring in the German Officer and two of his men'.

A move to the Ploegsteert sector

Since the beginning of September, the German Army had suffered a series of defeats at the hands of the Allies – from which they were never able to recover. The first blow was the Saint-Mihiel offensive of September 12th, when a joint force of American and French colonial troops launched an attack on the German positions around Saint-Mihiel. By the following day, all the objectives had been taken. On September 26th, the French Second and Fourth Armies – fighting alongside the American I, III and V Corps – launched an attack in the Meuse-Argonne sector; then on September 27th, the British First and Third Armies launched their attack towards Cambrai. The next major battles would be around the Ypres salient.

On the night of September 24th/25th, the 92nd Infantry Brigade relieved the 94th Infantry Brigade in the line around the Ploegsteert sector. The 11th East Lancashires moved to Aldershot Camp and relieved the 12th Norfolk Regiment in brigade support. Two companies from the battalion then moved to the GHQ line in the Nieppe System and came under the command of the 10th and 11th Battalions, the East Yorkshires. On September 26th/27th, there were more changes in the front line after the brigade boundaries were extended further north in preparation for the assault planned for the following day. The 11th East Lancashires moved out of brigade support and relieved part of the 2/16th London Regiment in the left of the line at Hill 63, while the 10th East Yorkshires took over the right of the line from the southern side of Hill 63 to Hyde Park Corner (a notorious crossroads prone to heavy enemy shelling). The 11th East Yorkshires were held in reserve in the Nieppe System, with instructions to move forward and take over Hill 63 once the assaulting companies had moved out: *'Thu Sept 26th/18: Harold goes on 'Boulogne rest' today'.*

At 5:30 a.m. on Saturday, September 28th, the Belgian Army and the British Second Army – under the command of General Plumer – attacked the German defences across the old battlefields of Passchendaele and made spectacular gains as they broke out of the salient. Just over eight miles to the south, the 92nd Infantry Brigade faced an anxious wait as they prepared to attack later that day. At 11:00 a.m., the battalions finally received warning orders that zero hour would

---

51 A reference to the trains operated by the Railway Operating Division of the Royal Engineers.
52 'Bivvies' is army slang for bivouac, or tent.

be at 3:00 p.m. The Germans – already alerted by the fighting further north – started shelling the surrounding roads, back areas and Hill 63 with a mixture of gas and high-explosive shells in an attempt to disrupt the assault that they knew would eventually come. Finally, at 3:00 p.m., the attack went in. Within minutes, the German artillery had opened up in response and proceeded to put down a heavy barrage on Hill 63 and the Ploegsteert Wood trench systems. On the left of the line, the 11th East Lancashires advanced under cover of their barrage and two sections of machine guns, with their left flank covered by the 2/16th London Regiment of the 30th Division. On the right of the line in Ploegsteert Wood, the 10th East Yorkshires advanced towards their first objective. By 3:35 p.m., 'X' and 'Y' Companies of the 11th East Lancashires were making good progress towards their first objectives – and it was reported that six prisoners from *Infanterie Regiment 156* were taken: 'Attack going well on the higher ground N. of the wood. (This high ground provides a width of some 600 yards defiladed from the wood and screened from Messines Hill by smoke barrage. But the going is appallingly bad – a tangle of old shell holes, wire, trench systems and concrete emplacements.)'[53]

To the left of the 92nd Brigade area, the 2/16th London Regiment of the 30th Brigade was still trying to drive the enemy out of Petite Douve Farm and Donnington Hall. Enemy machine gun fire continued to pour in towards the left flank of the 11th East Lancashires from the direction of the farm and the wood on their right. By 4:00 p.m., 'W' Company was closing in on its final objective at La Douve Farm, although the progress of 'Z' Company – on the right – was much slower. By 4:46 p.m., contact had finally been made with the 10th East Yorkshires on the right of the brigade area, but the news was not good: the right attacking company of the East Yorkshires had come under very heavy machine gun fire from the north and were unable to advance towards their objectives to the south of the wood. This failure to reach their objectives exposed the right flank of the 11th East Lancashires to an enemy counter-attack – and although all the objectives on the left were successfully taken by the battalion, it came across stiff opposition on its right flank.

At around 5:00 p.m. – and despite heavy machine gun fire continuing to pour in from the northern part of Ploegsteert Wood – 'W' Company of the 11th East Lancashires consolidated its position at La Douve Farm after successfully holding out against strong enemy counter-attacks. To the right of the line, 'Z' Company was still slowly pushing forward. The brigade report of operations recorded the situation: '5.46 p.m. 11th E. Lancs Regt right front counter-attacked, supported by M. G. s of 31st Bn. M. G. Corps, but gap W. of them – back to the held up coys. of 10th E. Yorks Regt makes their situation difficult. Our artillery shell

53 TNA WO 95/2356/5: 'Report of Operations Carried Out by the 92nd Infantry Brigade'.

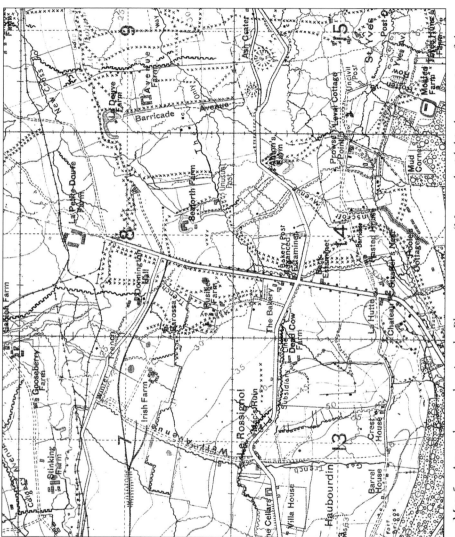

Map 5 – A trench map showing the Ploegsteert sector. (Map used with kind permission of the Lancashire Infantry Museum, Preston)

enemy near ULTIMO CRATER'.[54] With 'Z' Company facing increasingly heavy resistance from the woods, the decision was taken to turn the line on the right and form a defensive flank facing south. At 6:20 p.m. – and under cover of a 15-minute artillery barrage – 'Z' Company swung the line back 400 yards north of the woods between Prowse Point and La Hutte to plug the gap left by the failure of the 10th East Yorkshires to push forward. Enemy machine gunners situated in the northern edges of the woods continued with harassing fire as the new defensive line was established. At 6:45 p.m., the British guns switched their attention back to Ultimo Crater and Broken House – and a heavy barrage was put down on the two positions in an attempt to drive the enemy out. Although the line was successfully turned, a gap still existed between the right company of the 10th East Yorkshires and 'Z' Company of the 11th East Lancashires.

Further north, reports were coming in that the enemy were withdrawing from the eastern side of the Messines-Wytschaete Ridge:

> *Sat Sept 28th/18: Our Brigade went over this afternoon at 3 o'clock under cover of a smoke-barrage. They made pretty good. Our Battalion advanced somewhere about 3 to 5 kilos but a couple of Companies, 'Y & Z', were held up a little and went over the lid later on, when they were successful this time. Many machine guns, some prisoners and one or two field guns were taken. This stunt is at Messines, and was carried on for miles along the line.*

Throughout the night of September 28th/29th, the German guns continued to pound away at Hill 63 and the surrounding roads and tracks. At about 3:00 a.m. on September 29th, 'the 10th E. Yorks Regt.'s position was ascertained. Little progress'.[55] Faced with heavy machine gun fire from the right, they had been unable to move forward, but by 8:00 a.m., the situation had somewhat changed when it was suspected that the enemy had withdrawn from the woods. With the 18th DLI advancing on their right, the 10th East Yorkshires started to push forward and finally gained entry to the woods. By that afternoon, Ploegsteert Wood was captured by the brigade and outposts were set up to the south and east of the woods: *'Sun Sept 29th/18: The 93rd and 94th went over the top today. Very rainy just now – especially today! It was on this show that Messines Ridge was taken by us. This operation may mean also the falling of Cambrai and St Quentin. (Also this advance was under the command of King Albert and Gen. Plumer (2nd Army)'.*

On the night of September 29th/30th, the line held by the 11th East Lancashires was taken over by the 10th East Yorkshires and the 18th DLI. The battalion pulled back to the old front line at Hill 63 and counted the human cost of its stubborn

---

54 TNA WO 95/2356/5: 'Report of Operations Carried Out by the 92nd Infantry Brigade'.
55 TNA WO 95/2356/5: 'Report of Operations Carried Out by the 92nd Infantry Brigade'.

determination to evict the enemy from their positions north of Ploegsteert Wood. During the course of the battle, three officers and 41 other ranks lost their lives; a further six officers and 258 other ranks were injured, and four officers and 46 other ranks were reported as missing.

The following day – September 30th – the situation in the brigade sector was given as:

> 10th E. Yorks Regt. advance S to line of the WARNAVE RIVER. 18th D. L. I. advance towards the LYS, E of the wood in the centre of the Brigade Sector. 12th Royal Scots Fus. Advance to the LYS on the left of the Sector, keeping touch with the 94th Infantry Brigade who have been brought in between 93rd Infantry Brigade (now advancing S. E. on WARNETON) and ourselves. Not much opposition. Enemy withdrawing his annoying ARMENTIERES groups of artillery. Shell fire on our roads much less. Captures to date:- 1 Officer, 65 O. R.; 1 Field Gun (77mm), 2 T. M. s and about 20 M. G. s. Estimate 50 enemy killed.[56]

The 11th East Lancashires remained in brigade support until October 3rd, with 'W' Company occupying La Petite Munque Farm and the remaining three companies in the deep dugouts at Hyde Park Corner. Whilst in support, they supplied salvage and working parties to recover the detritus of war from the battlefield. By the beginning of October, it was becoming apparent to the German High Command that the war was lost – and that the only way left open to them was to negotiate a peace settlement with the Allied Powers.

For Jack Smallshaw and his battalion, the end was finally in sight:

> *Tues Oct 1st/18: News of Ostend being captured – also St Quentin and other places. In the latter mentioned places over 9,000 prisoners and many guns were also taken. Also of course the village of Warneton which we took. (Right of Messines and Ploegsteert).*
>
> *About this time (the latter part of September) Bulgaria asks for a 48 hrs [sic] armistice, which I don't wonder at not being granted them. The Allies are doing splendidly on the Eastern (Palestine) Front in fact, too well for the Bulgars!*

On October 3rd, the battalion returned to the front line in the Ploegsteert sector. Throughout the day and night, patrols were sent out to probe along the west bank of the Lys River – and at one point, even succeeded in crossing over a damaged bridge during daylight and advancing for some distance on the east bank of the river without making contact with the enemy. By night, the German machine gunners put down heavy concentrated fire and prevented any further excursions

---

56   TNA WO 95/2356/5: 'Report of Operations Carried Out by the 92nd Infantry Brigade'.

by the battalion onto the east bank. The following day, the battalion was relieved by the 15th West Yorkshires and moved to camp near Neuve Eglise: '*Sat Oct 5th/18: Colonel Rickman went to England today on a 'Brig Gens' Course. Germany is asking for terms with the object of Peace from President Wilson; also for an armistice from us on Land, Air and Sea. This was posted outside our Orderly Room too. Good News*'.

On October 6th, the 92nd Infantry Brigade went into divisional reserve. The 11th East Lancashires moved to camp at Bailleul, where they remained until October 12th. Whilst at the camp, the battalion underwent small arms training with Lewis Gun and rifle on a 30-yard rifle range, which they had constructed on the outskirts of the camp:

'*Sun Oct 6th/18: We moved to the top of a hill outside Bailleul, under canvas and "bivvies." Splendid view of the surrounding country round about here from the hill*'.

'*Thurs Oct 10th/18: Joe's* [Jack's brother] *birthday (in hospital)*'.

'*Fri Oct 11th/18: Fr. Gribluin came to see us today (on the hill here)*'.

On October 12th, the battalion returned to the front in the Ploegsteert sector and relieved the 12th Norfolk Regiment in the trenches. Jack stayed with the transport section at La Romarin, which lay just under two miles to the west of the line being held by his battalion. Two companies ('W' and 'Z') occupied the front line, with 'X' and 'Y' Companies held in support. The battalion war diary recorded that: 'An enemy withdrawal was expected and the Lys was extensively patrolled and efforts made to cross and form bridgeheads'.[57]

'*Sat Oct 12th/18: We moved to Le Romarin near Neuve-Eglise. The Batt. Went into the line at Ploegsteert sector tonight.*
    All day scrounging timber and stuff, making a "HOME"!'

'*Sun Oct 13th/18: Mass this morning in a little hut at the R.A.F. Camp. Great excitement is prevailing just now on account of Germany having accepted Pres. Wilson's 14 points of his Terms of Peace. Some people in fact were under the impression the war was Napoo*'.[58]

Patrols continued all along the west bank of the Lys – constantly probing all the crossing points – but the Germans continued to hold the east bank in considerable

---

57 TNA WO 95/2358/1: 11th East Lancashire Regiment war diary.
58 'Napoo' is a slang word for 'finished'.

strength, with bridges defended by nests of machine guns. The enemy shelling which had been targeting the company lines and Battalion HQ throughout the night began to die out by the morning of October 14th – and on the following day (October 15th), the battalion received orders that in the event of a withdrawal by German troops, they were to prepare to advance and establish a new line along the Quesnoy-Comines railway. The advance was to be carried out in two 'bounds': the first bound would be carried out by 'W' and 'Z' Companies – and their orders were to establish a line running from Deûlémont to Frelinghien. Once this line was secured, 'X' and 'Y' Companies would pass through and take the final objective along the Quesnoy-Comines railway.

On the night of October15th/16th, patrols from the 11th East Lancashires established bridgeheads on the west bank of the Lys River at Pont Rouge, and at another crossing point 500 yards further south. The battalion war diary recorded how the enemy were 'very quiet'[59] that night as the companies started to cross the river on rafts. Once they were established on the east bank, both 'W' and 'Z' Companies pushed forward to their first objective, which they took without meeting any opposition. Following up close behind, 'X' Company passed through the new positions and advanced to the second objective, with 'W' Company advancing on their right. Both companies reached the Quesnoy-Comines railway and secured the line, with 'W' Company ordered to hold the position and the remaining three companies held in reserve. After the Battalion HQ had been established at Quesnoy, the transport section started to bring up the rations to the west bank of the Lys by limbers; then after transferring the supplies onto pack mules, they were taken over an old footbridge and on to the companies manning the line on the east bank. The 92nd Infantry Brigade continued to push forward through the small hamlets and farms recently vacated by the retreating German Army. On October 17th, the 11th East Lancashires, now in brigade support, reached and crossed the Deûle River 'in single file'[60] by means of duckboard bridges.

After a short rest in some of the nearby farms, the battalion received orders to move on to Bondues, which lay to the east of their positions. By 10:00 p.m. that night, the move was completed and Battalion HQ was set up at Chateau Du Lasserre. Jack recorded the recent events in his diary:

Thu Oct 17th/18: Moved from Le Romarin – still on scent of Fritz! We marched about 14 kilos, and crossed the River Lys (a very immortalised place at the moment) by means of a temporary pontoon bridge over which the transport passed. The lads of the Battalion crossed this river by rafts, four at a time, and advanced oh! Umpteen miles without finding the enemy. It's rumoured that the

---

59 TNA WO 95/2358/1: 11th East Lancashire Regiment war diary.
60 TNA WO 95/2358/1: 11th East Lancashire Regiment war diary.

Bosch has retired back by rail, he has gone so quickly. As I am writing this I'm thinking how strange it is to think that only late yesterday (Wednesday), the Germans were occupying the same spot as we are in. 'Dumped' in an open field, but Lewis and I soon 'scrounged' some timber and etc.

At approximately 5:00 a.m. on October 18th, the battalion left Bondues and passed through the line held by the 10th East Yorkshires – continuing with the advance. Accompanied by 'C' Battery of 170 Brigade, RFA and 'C' Company of the 31st Machine Gun Battalion, they formed the vanguard of the brigade advance on Tourcoing, with 'W' Company given the honour of leading the column. The town was reached without meeting any opposition from the enemy – the streets lined with waiting citizens eager to catch their first glimpse of the liberating Allied armies. They exploded into a thunderous roar of applause as 'W' Company straightened their backs, shouldered their rifles and marched through. Everywhere the soldiers were mobbed by crowds overcome with emotion at finally being freed from the tyranny of the German forces of occupation – hugging and kissing the Tommies, who were in complete awe of the rapturous reception they received. Wine, beer and food was pushed into their hands as they filed through; they had never witnessed anything like it. Now they dared to believe that the war would soon be over:

Fri Oct 18th/18: Left this place (near Warneton) and tramped to Mouvaux [approximately three miles from Tourcoing] *where the civilians gave us 'Bon' beds and every hospitality, even bouquets of flowers, gallons of wines, beer, coffee, oh! all sorts. The people of this town were so happy at being released from the Germans who commandeered about everything ever since they occupied Mouvaux.*

The battalion continued on through to Wattrelos, with 'Z' Company in support. As they passed through, the German artillery opened up with gas shells and heavy machine gun fire, but 'enemy resistance was gradually overcome and all companies attained their objectives'.[61] A new line was established running from Herseaux towards the canal, which lay approximately 4,000 yards to the south.

On October 19th, the 11th East Yorkshires took over the role of advance guard for the brigade and passed through the line held by the 11th East Lancashires. The battalion war diary recorded that they came out of the line and 'withdrew to billets between Tourcoing and Wattrelos'.[62]

Jack mentions a move to Roubaix in his diary – and it is probable that this was the same location where the rest of the battalion moved into billets:

---

61 TNA WO 95/2358/1: 11th East Lancashire Regiment war diary.
62 TNA WO 95/2358/1: 11th East Lancashire Regiment war diary.

Sat Oct 19th/18: Left Mouvaux at 1 p.m. and marched thro' the town on to Roubaix, a very big place. We stopped the other side of the Canal where Padre Mr Smith, Lewis and I had splendid beds, at a big house there. On this march the people lined the streets and were giving us everything; on the road, they made an awful fuss of us, and civvies were among us in the ranks, walking with us all the way. When we landed at Roubaix we got another lovely billet, only the 'Madame' in the whole place, who gave myself and Fran Lewis a nice bed, also the Q.M. and Padre were billeted here as well.

On October 20th, the 92nd Brigade moved into divisional support, with the 11th East Lancashires remaining at their billets near Tourcoing. The battalion war diary recorded that 'the inhabitants continued to show their appreciation of their relief from enemy control'.[63] For the men though, there would be little rest – and training at company and platoon level continued until October 25th, when the battalion moved by road to Cuerne.

In this part of the diary – covering the events towards the end of October – there are some discrepancies in the dates used by Jack. The author has left the entries exactly as they were written at the time:

Fri Oct 24th/18: We had a fine time during our stay here and were very sorry indeed to leave this town which was like "home from home". We left Roubaix and went across the frontier to Belgium a good distance away by road and arrived at Cuerne where we got a little billet, but unfortunately I got a dose of Gas here, so I was glad to get away from the place as it was reeking in Gas.

In later years, this exposure to gas would ultimately lead to Jack's death through respiratory problems and heart failure: '*Sat Oct 25th/18: Left this place this afternoon at a moment's notice and went to a big farm by Harlebeke*'.

'Dulce et Decorum Est'

Bent double, like old beggars under sacks,
Knock-kneed, coughing like hags, we cursed through sludge,
Till on the haunting flares we turned our backs
And towards our distant rest began to trudge.
Men marched asleep. Many had lost their boots
But limped on, blood-shod. All went lame; all blind;
Drunk with fatigue; deaf even to the hoots
Of tired, outstripped Five-Nines that dropped behind.

---

63 TNA WO 95/2358/1: 11th East Lancashire Regiment war diary.

Gas! GAS! Quick, boys! – An ecstasy of fumbling,
Fitting the clumsy helmets just in time;
But someone still was yelling out and stumbling,
And flound'ring like a man in fire or lime…
Dim through the misty panes and thick green light,
As under a green sea, I saw him drowning.
In all my dreams, before my helpless sight,
He plunges at me, guttering, choking, drowning.

If in some smothering dreams you too could pace
Behind the wagon that we flung him in,
And watch the white eyes writhing in his face,
His hanging face, like a devil's sick of sin;
If you could hear, at every jolt, the blood
Come gargling from the froth-corrupted lungs,
Obscene as cancer, bitter as the cud
Of vile, incurable sores on innocent tongues. –
My friend, you would not tell with such high zest
To children ardent for some desperate glory,
The old Lie; *Dulce et Decorum Est*
Pro Patria Mori.[64] [65]

On October 26th, the 11th East Lancashires moved back in the line. The battalion war diary said of the situation:

> The battalion relieved the Scottish Rifles and R Scotch Fusiliers in the line in the INGOYGHEM sector W and Z Coys in the front line and X and Y Coys in support – The enemy was in great strength in machine guns and was very active in artillery fire – especially every morning from 4 a.m. to 7 a.m. a large proportion of gas shells was used. Belgian civilians remained in their farms in many cases in the shelled area. The line of posts was advanced about 700 yards but the enemy maintained strong machine gun fire.[66]

On Sunday, October 27th, the battalion was relieved by the 12th Royal Scots Fusiliers and moved to billets at Harlebeke, where they remained until October 31st. The casualty figures for the whole of the month were remarkably light when compared to previous months, with just five other ranks killed, and two officers and 57 other ranks wounded:

---

64 *Dulce et Decorum Est*': 'It is Sweet and Honourable to Die for One's Country'.
65 Poem by Wilfred Owen (1893-1918).
66 TNA WO 95/2358/1: 11th East Lancashire Regiment war diary.

Sun Oct 26th/18: Off to Church here with the Padre this morning, still feeling the awful effects of the Gas. Another move again today to the Fabrise (Harlebeke) where we got our Mess in a large house attached to the Fabric factory recently occupied by Bosch and where he has left an awful big 'dump' of timber, cement, sheeting, stones, picks and other material behind him. He bombed us here tonight by 'plane' and also the following night of Mon, and Tues; the latter day he dropped three bombs right in front of the house much to our discomfort. The Battalion at this time has been in the line since Friday and are being relieved tonight, Tuesday 28th Oct.

Have just heard that Austria has 'thrown the sponge up,' hope it's true. We're having a rough time with bombs at the Factory here, near Courtrai. This place is getting it very hot tonight by bombing. The Batt is at Harlebeke.

On November 1st, the battalion left Harlebeke and moved to fresh billets at Ingoyghem – closely following the advance of the 94th Infantry Brigade. For the next few days, they cleared the battlefield of weapons and munitions – 'bringing in a considerable amount of material [*sic*] including 10 machine guns',[67] which had been abandoned by the fleeing Germans. Once the battlefield had been cleared, the battalion moved back to billets at Harlebeke. On November 3rd, the battalion moved to fresh billets at Halluin, where they remained until November 7th:

'Sun Nov 3rd/18: Left this factory this morning (which was a very big 'dump' of "Jerrys" before the advance) and went back to Halluin. A decent place but it's been heavily bombed by both the British and Germans too. It is only 10 kilos from Roubaix and 7 kilos from Tourcoing. Good Billets here!'

'Mon Nov 4th/18: Austria has apparently finished her lot in this war, chucked the sponge up'.

On November 7th, the battalion moved to billets near Kloosterhoek in close support of the 12th Yeomanry Battalion, the Norfolk Regiment. That same night, 'W' Company advanced with the 12th Norfolks and crossed over the Den Ryjtgracht Canal at Rugge to establish posts on the west bank of the Escaut River. The battalion war diary reported that 'the condition of the ground was very bad and there was considerable hostile fire,[68] but eventually the Germans withdrew and posts were established along the east bank of the canal: *'Thu Nov 7th/18: Left Halluin and landed at St Louis. The Batt are 7 kilos further on from Transport lines'*.

---

67 TNA WO 95/2358/1: 11th East Lancashire Regiment war diary.
68 TNA WO 95/2358/1: 11th East Lancashire Regiment war diary.

On the night of November 8th/9th, the battalion took over from the 12th Norfolks at Avelghem, with 'Y' Company covering the left of the line, 'X' Company on the right and 'Z' Company held in support at the rather aptly-named village of 'Bosch'. Meanwhile, 'W' Company carried out a minor operation against the enemy lines. Under cover of artillery, trench mortar and machine gun fire, they pushed forward and established a line of posts along the west bank of the Escaut River: *Fri Nov 8th/18: Rumour has it that there is a 'Peace Conference' to be held today on the battlefield'*. The 31st Division continued with their advance – and on November 9th, the 11th East Lancashires reached the Escaut River. About 500 yards south of Rugge, a successful crossing was made by 'Y' Company, who used the girders of a bridge destroyed in the German retreat. Further downstream at Escanaffles, 'X' Company crossed by raft. The two companies then advanced towards Mont de l'Enclus, 'which was re-occupied by noon. The battalion received orders to halt and allow the 11th Bn E. Yorkshire Regt. to take up the advance'.[69]

After the East Yorkshire Regiment passed through the line, the 11th East Lancashires moved to billets at Amougies, where they were held in support:

> *Sat Nov 9th/18: Left St Louis and went to a little village called 'Bosch' where we shifted again under an hour then on again as soon as the bridge was ready for us to go over; we passed over this bridge (River Scheldt) at 4 a.m. the following morning (the 'Bosch' had retired a few hours before, blowing the bridges up as he went). We were on the march all day until 8 p.m., the first British to go through the villages which we passed thro' and the Belgians gave us a fine welcome. We eventually went through Renaix and on to Ronse. Still on the heels of the Hun. He's only a few hours in front of us.*
>
> *Our Batt entered Mont de l'Enclus at the point of the bayonet. This place is a fairly large town and when the lads went through it the civilians were jumping for joy (the Germans had only just evacuated this town). What an ovation we got, the folks dragged us about in their joy and excitement. Terribly short of fags on these moves lately.*

By the evening of November 10th, the 92nd Brigade had established a new line running across the high ground on the eastern side of Mont de Rhodes. The 11th East Lancashires, still being held in support, moved to billets at Quesnau: 'Sun Nov 10th/18: Been on the go all week almost and now this morning off again (over the ridges) early, landing late at night at Quesnau'. During the early hours of November 11th, the 11th East Lancashires were informed of the impending cessation of hostilities: 'Orders were received with the information that the enemy had accepted the terms on which the Allied governments were prepared to grant an armistice and that hostilities would cease at 11.00 hours'.[70]

The battalion was ordered to set up a line of posts to the east of Goeferdinge, with instructions that no-one was to be allowed to approach them from the enemy lines, and no-one was to be allowed to proceed further east.

This was it: the day everyone had been hoping for after four long and bitter years of bloodshed. In the minutes leading up to 11:00 a.m., there were still the occasional skirmishes – and lives still needlessly lost along the front – but at the stroke of 11:00 a.m., the guns suddenly fell silent and peace reigned once more:

Mon Nov 11th: A Great Day. At 1 a.m. this morning we were officially informed that an Armistice would commence at 11 a.m. which it did! Fancy! Not a sound of a gun, all peaceful. At 12 noon we got orders to again pursue the Germans so we were on the advance all day again. 7 p.m. this evening found us at Goeferdinge where we received a hearty welcome once more. The Nuns at the Convent here made scores of us soup and etc., also providing sleeping rooms for the lads. A strange incident occurred at this village this morning when the French patrol entered; one of the soldiers was sniped by a couple of Boschs at five minutes to eleven, only five minutes before the Armistice started; it was a great pity as probably this unfortunate chap will be the last to lose his life in the War.

However, we are in a 'Bon' billet tho.' Heaven knows how long we shall be here. We are only seven kilometres from Ghent, at this place, what a rapid advance it is, but still it is one of the points of the Armistice that the Allies shall keep in close contact with the enemy, and we are doing it too, but its [sic] jolly stiff work. Very little time for anything at all on this novel 'stunt'. Can see us at our 30 kilos destination over the German territory soon if Peace does not come quickly!

'And There Was A Great Calm'

(On the Signing of the Armistice, 11 Nov. 1918)

There had been years of Passion – scorching, cold,
And much Despair, and Anger heaving high,
Care whitely watching, Sorrows manifold,
Among the young, among the weak and old,
And the pensive Spirit of Pity whispered, "Why?"

Men had not paused to answer. Foes distraught
Pierced the thinned peoples in a brute-like blindness,

---

70 TNA WO 95/2358/1: 11th East Lancashire Regiment war diary.

Philosophies that sages long had taught,
And Selflessness, were as an unknown thought,
And "Hell!" and "Shell!" were yapped at
Lovingkindness.

The feeble folk at home had grown full-used
To "dug-outs", "snipers", "Huns", from the war-adept
In the mornings heard, and at evetides perused;
To day–dreamt men in millions when they mused-
To nightmare-men in millions when they slept.

Waking to wish existence timeless, null,
Sirius they watched above where armies fell;
He seemed to check his flapping when, in the lull
Of night a boom came thencewise, like the dull
Plunge of a stone dropped into some deep well.

So, when old hopes that earth was bettering slowly
Were dead and damned, there sounded "War is done!"
One morrow. Said the bereft, and meek, and lowly,
"Will men some day be given to grace? yea, wholly,
And in good sooth, as our dreams used to run?"

Breathless they paused. Out there men raised their glance
To where had stood those poplars lank and lopped,
As they had raised it through those four years' dance
Of Death in the now familiar flats of France;
And murmured, "Strange, this! How? All firing stopped?"

Aye; all was hushed. The about-to-fire fired not,
The aimed-at moved away in trance-lipped song.
Once checkless regiment slung a clinched shot
And turned. The Spirit of Irony smirked out, "What?
Spoil peradventures woven of Rage and Wrong?"

Thenceforth no flying fires inflamed the gray,
No hurtlings shook the dewdrop from the thorn,
No moan perplexed the mute bird on the spray;
Worn horses mused: "We are not whipped today,"
No weft-winged engines blurred the moon's thin horn.

Calm fell. From Heaven distilled a clemency;
There was peace on earth and silence in the sky;
Some could, some could not, shake off misery:
The Sinister Spirit sneered: "It had to be!"
And again the Spirit of Pity whispered, "Why?"[71]

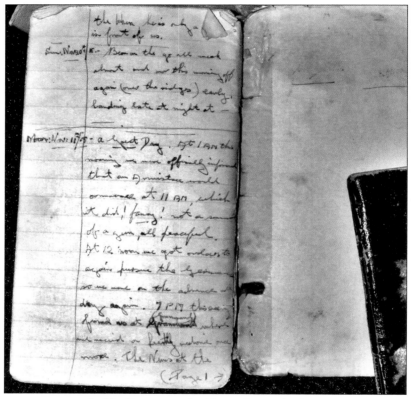

Jack's diary entry for November 11th 1918.

On November 13th, the 92nd Infantry Brigade rejoined the Fifth Army. The 11th East Lancashires moved into billets at Quesnau after being relieved by a battalion from the 41st Division:

'*Wed Nov 13th/18: Left Grammont (where we had outposts on the outskirts of the village as Jerry was going back according to his terms of Armistice) and went back to ------- [illegible] where I saw three British prisoners who had escaped just before the Armistice came into action. Tho' we met hundreds of them later on this week on their way to England. On this march a German Staff Car passed*

---

71 Poem by Thomas Hardy (1840-1928).

*us containing three High German Officers, flying the white flag, probably they
were Delegates. A British Staff Car was in front'.*

*'Thu Nov14th/18: Again we were on the move, went through Renaix and landed
for the night at Amougies. At this place I made more good friends, an old man
and his missus, they would give me any mortal thing they possessed so great was
their joy at the 'Hallemans'[72] evacuating the place, and our lads (as usual) were
the first to enter the village as has often been the case in this present advance. We
moved scores and scores of miles in Belgium about this period'.*

*'Fri Nov 15th/18: Off again this morning back to Bosch.[73] Stayed the night here
and off once again the following morning'.*

On November 16th, the battalion moved to billets at Marke, where baths were set
up for the men and uniforms were cleaned; they remained here until November
25th. During their stay – on November 23rd – 'a ceremonial parade of the Brigade
was held when the Divisional Commander presented medal ribands to officers
and men who had received awards since June 27th last'.[74]

*'Sat Nov 16th/18: Landed at Marke this morning and got a good billet again
Why we are going backwards I don't know, but rumour has it that we are being
transferred from the good old 2nd Army (in which the East Lancashires have
distinguished themselves) to the 5th Army. However we are at Marke for a day
or two for a rest after numerous moves and shifts'.*

*'Sun Nov 17th/18: Church Service this morning at 10-30 a.m. in the Church
here at Marke'.*

On November 25th, the 31st Division started to pull back – the senseless slaughter
now at an end, and the once-warring nations at peace. The 92nd Brigade set off
on their long journey back towards the coast – passing through the battle-scarred
landscape surrounding Ypres, where so many had lost their lives defending the
ancient city.

Jack recorded the route taken by his battalion in his diary, as they made their
way towards the cavalry barracks at St Omer:

---

72 'Hallemans' is probably a misspelling by Jack of the British soldiers' slang word 'Alleyman', which
     was used to describe the German soldier; it is derived from the French word 'Allemande', which
     means 'German'.
73 A reference to Banhout Bosch.
74 TNA WO 95/2358/1: 11th East Lancashire Regiment war diary.

'*Mon Nov 25th/18: Quite a usual day for us moving (raining). We shifted at 9 o'clock this morning and went as far as Menen only about six kilos but we're off again tomorrow morning*'.

'*Tues Nov 26th/18: Left Menen at 8 this morning and troudged [sic] along thro' the ruins of old Ypres, past the Cathedral and Cloth Hall and over the old lines (and once the hottest part of the line) Oh! What a terrible sight, the late battle-field of Ypres, nothing but shell-holes and tanks on either side of the road. We did a march of 22 kilos today arriving at Vlamertinge about 3 or 4 p.m*'.

'*Wed Nov 27th/18: On the road again bound for St Eloi (or Abele) this small village was just on the Frontier of Belgium and France*'.

'*Thurs Nov 28th/18: Left St Eloi this morning again, had a good tramp to near Ebblinghem*'.

'*Fri Nov 29th/18: Left Ebblinghem and landed at St Omer, where we were in the Barracks there. The Padre is billeted at the Hotel-de-France on the Grand Place*'.

'*Sun Dec 1st/18: I served Mass with Padre this morning at 9 a.m. in the Cathedral at St Omer, it's a lovely church. Benediction at four this evening too*'.

'*Thurs Dec 5th/18: The Padre left us today at St Omer, he is for [sic] home for good, having finished his three years' active-service with our Regiment. I shook hands with him, wished him "Good-Bye". Am very sorry to lose him. He asked me to go over to Cahir (Tipperary) when I get home again. I'd very much like to visit him, maybe I might do so, some old day when "Peace reigns Supreme" once again!*
   Still at St Omer!'

'*Sun Dec 15th/18: Took over Batman for Capt. Wilton, O.C. Z. Coy. This makes the fourth job offered me since I joined my Company*'.

'*Wed Dec 25th/18: Xmas Day. Having a Bon-time this Christmas time, but am feeling too ------ [sic] to record it! Ring Off. Still on for Wilton!*'

Part 6: 1919

The battalion saw in the New Year at the cavalry barracks – and to keep the men occupied, educational classes and sports tournaments were held. The battalion war diary recorded that its football XI was defeated in the third round of the Divisional Cup competition by the team from the RAMC. Towards the middle of the month, the French authorities requested the return of the cavalry barracks – and as a result, the battalion found itself being re-homed in the PoW Camp at St Omer.

Jack Smallshaw was rather luckier – and had been granted some home leave:

Mon Jan 13th/19: Left the Batt., to go on leave from St Omer. Was 'Zig-Zag' when I went up to see Wilton at the Mess. We entrained at 11 p.m. tonight and reached landings about 2-30. Went into the rest Camp and embarked at 1 p.m. and sailed at 2 p.m. A very rough passage we had coming over to Folkestone. Sent Archie a wire and stopped in London for the night. Had a reply from him this dinner-time Wed Jan 15th saying he was unable to meet me so I caught the 2-10 p.m. from Euston, arriving at Manchester at 7 a.m. was home by 9-30.

'The Returned Soldier'

The soldier, full of battles and renown,
And gaping wonder of each quiet lown,
And strange to every face he knew so well,
Comes once again in this old town to dwell.
But man alone is changed; the very tree
He sees again where once he used to swee;
And the old fields where once he tented sheep,
And the old mole-hills where he used to leap,
And the old bush where once he found a nest,
Are just the same, and pleasure fills his breast.
He sees the old path where he used to play
At chock and marbles many a summer day,
And loves to wonder where he went a boy,
And fills his heart with pleasure and joy.[1]

---

1 Poem by John Clare (1793-1864).

Now that the war was over, returning to Accrington should have been a happy time for Jack – a chance for him to catch up with old friends and family whom he hadn't seen for a year – but upon his return, he was shocked to find that his brother, Joe, was seriously ill:

'*Poor Joe he is ill! Knocking about Accrington and getting things for Joe*'.

'*Fri Jan 17th/19: Went to Preston for my Credits*'.[2]

'*Sat Jan 18th/19: Went to Wigan*'.

'*Sun Jan 19th/19: Arrived home again finding Joe much brighter*'.

'*Wed Jan 22nd/19: I got my 'guarantee papers' of employment from Waite today*'.

These 'guarantee papers' were provided by the soldiers' former employers (where they had worked prior to joining the army); they were a guarantee that the soldier would be able to take up his former employment upon his discharge from the army. In Jack's case, he had worked for the wholesale grocer, J. T. Waite.
    His guarantee paper said:

Dear Sirs,
I. J. T. Waite, Wholesale Grocer & Provision Merchant, of Bradshaw Street Mill, Accrington, hereby declare that 15148, Private Jack Smallshaw, 11th East Lancashire Reg., 'Z' Coy., B.E.F., France was in my employment before 4th August 1914 and that I am prepared to offer him employment immediately on his return to civil life.
    (Signed J. T. Waite)

'*Thurs Jan 23rd/19: Went along to Records Preston only to find out I've got to return back to France on account of sailing from there on the 14th [of] January. Men who left France previous to the 12th were demobilised. On my way back from Preston I went again to* [name erased]. *What a 'splendid' time this weekend*'.

'*Fri Jan 24th/19: Had a half day at Liverpool this afternoon, and went to the Royal Court Theatre this evening to see the Pantomime 'Cinderella' a fine show. We arrived back at* [name erased] *no time for respectable folk to be out*'.

'*Sat Jan 25th/19: Left by the 2 p.m. train. Called at Wigan and then went on to Accrington*'.

---

2   Payment from the army.

'*Sun Jan 26th/19: Stayed at Morris' at Church[3] all night. Young Harry is over on leave (looking well too) had dinner there and Jennie had tea with us at Cash's also. We had a most enjoyable evening singing and etc. after supper I went home, bid the folks at home 'Good Night' and went by the 9.30 p.m. from Accrington to Preston and Euston. (London)*'.

'*Mon Jan 27th/19: Landed in London at 5.15 this morning but missed Archie at the Station, however saw him at his 'digs' and had breakfast with him. We went to the 'Ambassadors' to the Yankee Show there. Lee White in 'U.S.' topping show! Went back to the digs with Archie to the Melton Hotel*'.

Back in Accrington – and unbeknown to Jack – his brother Joe had taken a turn for the worse. Jack was already on his way down to Folkestone to catch the ferry to return to his unit in France, but once again, fate was to intervene – and Jack found himself returning home:

'*Tue Jan 28th/19: Archie came with me to Vic Station at 8 this morning. He goes near New Market today. On reaching Folkestone we find there are no boats going across so with a lot of messing about we all get a single journey pass home again. (There are about 3000 of us) I eventually arrive home in Accrington again about 10-30 the following morning feeling quite pleased*'.

'*Wed Jan 29th/19: Landed home from Folkestone and found poor Joe much worse, almost unconscious of his surroundings*'.

'*Sat Feb 1st/19: Harry and Jennie came over to see Joseph today. (Brother and s.i.l.[4])*'

'*Sun Feb 2nd/19: They went back tonight Mrs Cash stayed all night with Auntie to look after Joe*'.

'*Mon Feb 3rd/19: At 4.20 this morning Joseph died. May God rest his soul. Auntie and Mrs Cash laid him out*'.

'*Thu Feb 6th/19: We buried our Joe at 12 o'clock today at the Accrington Cemetery and in the same grave as my dear Mother. May they both Rest in Peace*'.

'*Fri Feb 7th/19: Archie went back this evening*'.

---

3   The village of Church, which is situated one mile to the west of Accrington.
4   Sister-in-law.

Some two weeks after the funeral, Jack finally started his journey back to France and his eventual release from the army:

'*Tue Feb 18th/19: Went to Records at Preston this morning. At 9.30 p.m. I went back to France from Church after having supper there. I've had <u>five</u> weeks on leave at home this time*'.

'*Wed Feb19th/19: Landed at Victoria then on to the Camp at Shorncliffe. Embarked at 2 pm arriving at Calais at 4 p.m. Stayed in Rest Camp there the night*'.

'*Thu Feb 20th/19: Got a Motor from Calais up to the Battalion at St Omer. Nearly all the 1914 and 1915 have gone from here demobilised (Handed my guarantee in at the Demobilisation Office)*'.

'*Fri Feb 21st/19: Lt Walker asks me to be his Batman, have taken it on for the time being*'.

'*Fri Feb 28th/19: After being with the Batt. only one week (just back from leave), am being sent back Demobilised; 26 of us today leave the Unit at St Omer. Rickman shakes hands with us all at the Station. Left at dinner time and trained it to the Demob Camp at Hazebrouck. Had a feed of Pork and Chips and Coffee and returned back to Camp*'.

'*Sat March 1st/19: Left Hazebrouck and marched to Hondeghem to the train arriving there at 3 p.m. Tea there, and then I went to pass an hour away at the Cinema. The train didn't start for Boulogne until 11 p.m. tonight! (Had the old brazier going in the truck all the way)*'.

'*Sun March 2nd/19: Arrived in Boulogne at 5 a.m. Went to St Martins Camp landing there about 6 a.m., had breakfast and 'fell in' for a bath about 9 a.m. Jolly good bath too, all new under-clothing as well. After that we had tickets stamped and marched off to Ostrohove Camp a kilo distant, where we drew blankets for the night and had a kit inspection. Had dinner and tea here. An awfully wet evening so I retired early to bed*'.

'*Mon March 3rd/19: Ostrohove Camp (Boulogne). Went to the 'Bohemians' Concert tonight in Camp to pass the dreary time away*'.

'*Tue March 4th/19: Reveille at 6.0 'Fell In' for the Boat for Southampton at 8 a.m. Embarked at 10 a.m. and set sail about 11 a.m. arriving in Southampton at about 8 p.m. (The Prince George) and we were kept on board all night*' *without rations or anything (packed like herrings in a tin!) and didn't disembark until 8.30 a.m. this morning – Wed March 5th. Got a bit of breakfast in Southampton and entrained for Prees Heath Dispersal Camp at 1.0 p.m. and passed through Basingstoke, Oxford (coffee here), Stratford-on-Avon, Birmingham, Wolverhampton, Shrewsbury, arriving at Prees-Heath at 9.30 p.m. Here we were put in a hut for an hour, then we started with the 'Demob. Stunt' first we dump the old equipment, rifle and bayonet, Gas Respirator and etc. After that followed over an hour's touring different huts getting all sorts of papers signed, about a dozen altogether! Had a bit of supper chucked at us about 3 a.m. this morning, then Thurs 6th March/19: Entrained at the Camp siding at 9.30, after getting our 'tickets'. Passed thro' Crewe, Warrington, Wigan, Preston and changed there for Accrington, landing home by 2.30 this afternoon – now feeling absolutely tired out after seven days journeying getting Demobilised'.*

'Sun March 16th/19: Went to Church this morning'.

'April 7th/19: My month's Demobilisation furlough finished. I received a Gratuity of £25-10 but drew in all about £36-7-10d. Back again to civil-life once more'.

Jack's war was finally at an end. On May 14th 1919, he moved to Powell Street in Latchford, Warrington and started work at Bibby's Electricians, where he remained for about five months.

Shortly after leaving the army, Jack received a letter from The Reverend Meskel, for whom he had served as batman:

'Ballmamella'
Cappagh
Co Waterford
May 11th 1919

My Dear Smallshaw

I received your letter a few days ago. I am glad to see that you are back again in civie [sic] life & I suppose I am no less glad than you are yourself. It is certainly pleasant to throw off the formalities of soldiering to say nothing of its discomforts.

I have not heard a word about the Batt. since I left but from what you say I gather that it is demobilised.

I have been at the above now over three months and have by this become a perfect rustic. It is certainly a change and a pleasant one after France. I never want to see that country again.

Has any definite news been heard of Sgt Bentley? He was wounded in March last year and was afterwards reported as being a prisoner.

Remember me to Holden. I hope he has completely recovered from his wounds. Is Power home? I think he was from Accrington too. If you see him give him my best wishes. Also to that other boy whose name I can never remember. The boy who used to serve Mass for me and who was a friend of O'Donnell and poor Lyons.

Remember me also to Lewis. I can't remember all the boys but give my best wishes to all of them.

I am sorry that you find it so difficult to get a job. I hope you will like the Police Force.

I had a letter from Fr Millby a few days ago. He is still in France but attached to a Prisoner of War Camp. Fr. Scully is I understand at home.

I am curious to know if any of the boys who were missing on the 1st July 1916 were prisoners.

Give my best wishes to Capt Watson and Hayes and last but not least to yourself.

Sincerely yours

P Meskel

P.S. I enclose Testimonial

P.M.

TESTIMONIAL

J Smallshaw was my batman for twelve months and I have great pleasure in testifying to his excellent character. He was scrupulously honest, strictly truthful, assiduous in his work; intelligent beyond the ordinary. Kind & courteous. I found him to be a 'grand character'.

P Meskel

Late C.F. 11th East Lancs.

11-5-19

It is interesting to note that The Rev Meskel enquired about the fate of the men from the battalion who were reported as missing during the Battle of the Somme. It would appear that even after the end of the war, there were hopes that some may return.

On December 25th 1920, Jack married Mary Alice Spence – a widow with five children – at St James' Church in Latchford. Over the next three years, he moved from job to job, although it is not known if he ever applied to join the police force.

On December 31st 1923, Jack started work at Winwick Hospital as an attendant. He and Alice went on to have a child of their own, Jack Kenneth, but he died in tragic circumstances during the Second World War: on October 2nd 1942, young Jack was serving on the light cruiser HMS *Curacoa* when she was sunk in a collision with the liner *Queen Mary*, which at the time, was being

The letter to Jack from The Reverend Meskel.

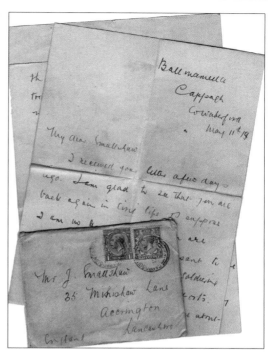

The dedication ceremony of the Garden of Remembrance at All Saints' Church, Thelwall in November 1954. Jack is in the immediate right of the picture – acting as an escort to the Standard bearer.

used as a troop carrier and was packed with American soldiers. Of the 439 crew members on board the *Curacoa*, only 101 were rescued. Jack and Alice's son was one of those who went down with the ship.

Jack continued to work at Winwick Hospital as a male nurse until his retirement in 1954. He was a founder member of the Grappenhall and Thelwall British Legion, where he tended the Garden of Remembrance at All Saints' Church, Thelwall. In later years, Jack was plagued by ill-health as a result of his two bouts of trench fever and his gassing in 1918, which left him with breathing difficulties. He died suddenly at home on April 26th 1957.

'Dirge for a Soldier'

Close his eyes; his work is done.
What to him is friend or foeman,
Rise of moon or set of sun,
Hand of man or kiss of woman?

Lay him low, lay him low,
In the clover or the snow.
What cares he? He cannot know.
Lay him low!

As man may, he fought his fight,
Proved his truth by his endeavour:
Let his sleep in solemn night,
Sleep for ever, and for ever.

Fold him in his country's stars,
Roll the drum and fire the volley!
What to him are all our wars?
What but death bemocking folly?

Leave him to God's bewatching eye:
Trust him to the hand that made him.
Mortal love weeps idly by:
God alone has power to aid him.

Lay him low, lay him low,
In the clover or the snow.
Who cares he? He cannot know.
Lay him low![5]

---

5   Poem by George Henry Boker (1823-1890).

Bibliography

Selected Books

Barton, Peter, *The Somme: A new panoramic perspective* (Constable, 2006).

Corrigan, Gordon, *Mud, Blood and Poppycock* (Cassell, 2003).

Gliddon, Gerald, *The Battle Of The Somme: A Topographical History* (Sutton Publishing, 1996).

Holmes, Richard, *Tommy: The British Soldier On The Western Front 1914 -1918* (HarperCollins 2004).

Horne, Alistair, *The Price Of Glory: Verdun 1916* (Penguin, 1981).

Jackson, Andrew, *Accrington's Pals: The Full Story: The 11th Battalion, East Lancashire Regiment (Accrington Pals) and the 158th (Accrington and Burnley) Brigade, Royal Field Artillery (Howitzers)* (Pen & Sword Books Ltd, 2013).

Macdonald, Lyn, *Somme* (PAPERMAC, 1986).

——— *1914: The Days of Hope* (Penguin Books, 1989).

Rogerson, Sidney, *Twelve Days on the Somme* (Greenhill Books, 2006).

Sheffield, Gary, *The Great War: 1914 – 1918: The Story Of The Western Front* (Sevenoaks, 2014).

Turner, William, *The Accrington Pals: A Tribute to the Men of Accrington and District, Blackburn, Burnley, Chorley and the Neighbouring Villages, who Volunteered, Fought and Died in the Great War 1914-1918* (The Lancashire Library, 1986).

Pals: The 11th (Service) Battalion (Accrington) East Lancashire Regiment – A History of the Battalion raised from Accrington, Blackburn, Burnley and Chorley in World War One (Wharncliffe Publishing Ltd, 1987).

——— *Accrington Pals* (Pen & Sword Books Ltd, 1993).

——— *Accrington Pals Trail: Home and Overseas (Battleground Europe)* (Pen & Swords Book Ltd, 1998).

Internet Sources

The Accrington Pals: <www.pals.org.uk>

Canadian Great War Project: <www.canadiangreatwarproject.com>

Lost Hospitals of London: <www.ezitis.myzen.co.uk>

<www.battlefields1418.com>

<www.bbc.co.uk/remembrance/wall/record/12158>

<www.chorleypalsmemorial.org.uk>
<www.epitaphsofthegreatwar.com>
<www.ramc-ww1.com>
<www.ssmaritime.com>
<www.uboat.net>

Museums and Libraries

Accrington Library: <accrington.library@lancashire.gov.uk>
The Lancashire Infantry Museum: <www.lancashireinfantrymuseum.org.uk>

The National Archives: WO 95 series of documents

TNA WO 95/2341/6: 31st Division war diaries, November–December 1916.

TNA WO 95/2341/6: 'Report of Raids Carried Out by Troops of the 94th Infantry Brigade on the Night of 6th/7th November, 1916'.

TNA WO 95/2342/3: 15th West Yorkshire Regiment report.

TNA WO 95/2342/3: 16th (S) Battalion, West Yorkshire Regiment document ('Report on Operations of 3rd May, 1917').

TNA WO 95/2342/3: 31st Division S.G. 104/178; Appendix 197.

TNA WO 95/2342/3: 31st Division war diaries, May 1917.

TNA WO 95/2342/3: 'Report by 2nd Lieut Hitchin? [sic] D.S.O. (18th D.L.I.) on Capture of Windmill Gavrelie [sic], 3rd May, 1917'.

TNA WO 95/2342/3: 'Report of Attack on Oppy Wood and Village on 3rd May, 1917', which was written by Lieutenant Colonel S.H. Ferrand, CO 11th Battalion, East Yorkshire Regiment.

TNA WO 95/2342/3: 'Report of Events in Connection with Operations on the 3rd Inst.'.

TNA WO 95/2342/3: 'Report of Events in Connection with Operations on the 3rd Inst.'; Appendix 'C'(1), Appendix 'C'(11), Appendix 'D'(1), Appendix 'F'(1) and Appendix 'F'(11).

TNA WO 95/2342/3: 'Report of Operations on the 10th (Service) Bn. East. Y. R. on the Night of 2nd/3rd May, 1917'.

TNA WO 95/2342/3: 'Report of the Action of May 3rd, 1917'.

TNA WO 95/2343/2: 31st Division war diaries, March 1918.

TNA WO 95/2343/2: 'Narrative of Operations of 31st Division between March 22nd and April 1st, 1918'.

TNA WO 95/2343/2: 'Narrative of Operations of 31st Division between March 22nd and April 1st, 1918'; Appendix 344.

TNA WO 95/2343/3: 31st Division war diaries, April–May 1918.

TNA WO 95/2343/3: 'Summary of Operations of 31st Division from 10th April to 14th April, 1918'.

TNA WO 95/2356/3: 92nd Infantry Brigade Order Nos.204, 207, 210, 214 and 215.

TNA WO 95/2356/3: 92nd Infantry Brigade war diaries, January–April 1918.

TNA WO 95/2356/3: 'Narrative of Operations around Ervillers & the Aerodrome, from March 23rd to 27th Inclusive'.

TNA WO 95/2356/3: 'Operations. 10th – 15th April'.

TNA WO 95/2356/4: 92nd Infantry Brigade war diaries, May–July 1918.

TNA WO 95/2356/4: 'Narrative of Operations Carried by the 31st Division on the 28th June, East of Foret de Nieppe'.

TNA WO 95/2356/5: 92nd Infantry Brigade Order No.295.

TNA WO 95/2356/5: 92nd Infantry Brigade war diaries, August 1918–January 1919.

TNA WO 95/2356/5: 'Operations around Vieux Berquin'.

TNA WO 95/2356/5: 'Report of Operations Carried Out by the 92nd Infantry Brigade'.

TNA WO 95/2356/5: 'REPORT ON OPERATION CARRIED OUT BY THE 11TH E. LAN. RGT. 5-9-18'.

TNA WO 95/2358/1: 11th East Lancashire Regiment war diaries, February 1918–July 1919.

TNA WO 95/2359/4: 93rd Infantry Brigade war diary, May 1917.

TNA WO 95/2362/2: 18th West Yorkshire Regiment war diary.

TNA WO 95/2362/2: 18th Battalion, West Yorkshire Regiment document ('Report of Operations of 3rd May, 1917').

TNA WO 95/2363/1: 94th Infantry Brigade document ('Instructions to Commanding Officers in relation to the forthcoming advance').

TNA WO 95/2363/1: 94th Infantry Brigade Operation Order No.45.

TNA WO 95/2363/1: 94th Infantry Brigade Operation Order No.46.

TNA WO 95/2363/1: 94th Infantry Brigade war diaries, March–June 1916.

TNA WO 95/2363/2: 94th Infantry Brigade document ('Operations of 94th Infantry Brigade, on July 1st, 1916').

TNA WO 95/2363/2: 94th Infantry Brigade war diaries, July–September 1916.

TNA WO 95/2363/3: 94th Infantry Brigade Operation Order No.90.

TNA WO 95/2363/3: 94th Infantry Brigade Situation Report (morning and evening, November 1916; Appendix A).

TNA WO 95/2363/3: 94th Infantry Brigade war diaries, October–December 1916.

TNA WO 95/2363/4: 94th Infantry Brigade war diaries, January–April 1917.

TNA WO 95/2363/5: 94th Infantry Brigade Operation Order No.140.

TNA WO 95/2363/5: 94th Infantry Brigade war diaries, May–July 1917.

TNA WO 95/2366/1: 11th East Lancashire Regiment war diaries, March 1916–January 1918.

And the diaries, papers, letters and photographs of 15148 Pte Jack Smallshaw, 'W' Company, 11th (Service) Battalion, East Lancashire Regiment.